THE COLD WAR AND BEYOND

SECOND EDITION

THE COLD WAR

AND BEYOND

*US Relations with Soviet
and Post-Soviet Russia*

JAMES FITZGERALD

Nelson

an International Thomson Publishing company I(T)P®

Melbourne • Albany, NY • Belmont, CA • Boston • Cincinnati • Johannesburg
London • Madrid • Mexico City • New York • Pacific Grove, CA
Scottsdale, AZ • Singapore • Tokyo • Toronto

Nelson I(T)P®
102 Dodds Street
South Melbourne 3205

Email nelsonitp@nelson.com.au
Website http://www.nelsonitp.com

Nelson I(T)P® *an International Thomson Publishing company*

First published in 1988 as *Soviet-American Relations in The Nuclear Age*
Reprinted 1989
Reprinted with revisions 1991, 1992
This second edition published in 1995
10 9 8 7 6 5 4
99

Copyright © James Fitzgerald 1988, 1991, 1995

National Library of Australia
Cataloguing-in-Publication data

Fitzgerald, James, 1941–
    The Cold War and Beyond.
    Rev. ed.
    Bibliography.
    Includes index.
    ISBN 017 008785 9.
    1. World politics – 1945 - . 2. Arms race. 3. Nuclear arms control. 4.
    Soviet Union – Foreign relations – United States 5. United States –
    Foreign relations – Soviet Union. I. Fitzgerald, James, 1941 - . Soviet-
    American relations in the nuclear age. II. Title. III. Title: Soviet-
    American relations in the nuclear age.
327.47073

Edited by Judy Brookes
Designed by R.T.J. Klinkhamer
Maps by Alan Laver
Cover by Erika Budiman from a design concept of Elspeth Lacey's
Cover photographs: Left, Imperial War Museum; Right, APL/Bettman.
Typeset in 10/13 pt Trump Mediaeval by Post Typesetters
Printed in Singapore by Kin Keong Printing Pte Ltd

Nelson Australia Pty Limited ACN 058 280 149 (incorporated in
Victoria) trading as Nelson ITP.

CONTENTS

66 Let us re-examine our attitude toward the Cold War, remembering we are not engaged in a debate, seeking to pile up debating points. We are not here distributing blame or pointing the finger. We must deal with the world as it is. **99**

President John F. Kennedy, 10 June 1963

66 How to avoid nuclear war without succumbing to nuclear blackmail, how to prevent the desire for peace from turning into appeasement, how to defend liberty and maintain peace — this is the overwhelming problem of our age... **99**

Former US Secretary of State Henry Kissinger, 24 February 1982

66 When one country sees another as evil incarnate, and itself as the embodiment of absolute good, relations between them have reached a stalemate. I am not thinking of anti-communist rhetoric here, however pernicious, but of the inability, or reluctance, to realize that we all represent one human race, that we share a common destiny and have to learn to be civilized neighbours on our planet. Today's generations inherited Soviet–American confrontation from the past. But are we doomed to carry enmity on? **99**

Mikhail Gorbachev, *Perestroika: New Thinking for Our Country and the World*, Collins, London, 1987, p.221

EXPLAINING THE COLD WAR

THE PERIOD from the end of World War II until 1989 was dominated by the great confrontation between the Union of Soviet Socialist Republics (USSR) and the United States of America (USA). For most of this time the confrontation was of a political/ideological nature. The Soviet Union regarded itself as the custodian of world communism; the United States saw itself as the bastion of capitalism. Each side viewed the other with deep mistrust and portrayed the other in damning terms. The Soviet Union painted the United States as an imperialist power, bent on dominating the world and thwarting the spread of communism. The United States painted the Soviet Union as the promoter of world revolution, set on destroying capitalism. Mutual suspicion meant that both sides made statements and took action that greatly reinforced the prejudice and mistrust.

From time to time the confrontation spilled over into regional military conflict. After 1945 both the United States and the Soviet Union moved to establish alliances to reinforce their military position. The two sides competed widely across the globe in their attempts to ensure that the other side did not gain any significant advantage. The tension between the two powers was heightened by the development of nuclear weapons. These frightening weapons have made the destruction of life on this planet as we know it a distinct possibility. Some would argue, however, that without these weapons there would almost certainly have been a war between the two superpowers. Although somewhat reduced by recent arms control measures, the threat of nuclear war remains.

Despite the recurring tension and regional conflict, the two superpowers themselves never had direct military conflict, and nuclear weapons were never used in anger. Hence the term 'Cold War' is appropriate to describe the relationship between the Soviet Union and the United States in the years following 1945. This book traces its origins, different phases, and recent ending. The narrative examines the history of Soviet–American relations in both political/ideological and nuclear/strategic dimensions.

THE ORIGINS OF THE CONFLICT

Historians differ in their explanations of the origins of the confrontation between the Soviet Union and the United States during the Cold War. Some see it as primarily an issue of power politics, while others see it as a conflict between opposing ideological systems.

Those historians who see the Cold War as a balance of power confrontation have taken as their starting point the remarkably prophetic observations of the Frenchman Alexis de Tocqueville, who wrote in 1835:

Alexis de Tocqueville, *Democracy in America*, Washington Square Press, New York, 1964, pp.124-5 [orig. French edn 1835]

> 66 There are at the present time two great nations in the world, which started from different points, but seem to tend towards the same end. I allude to the Russians and the Americans... Their starting point is different, and their courses are not the same; yet each of them seems marked out by the will of Heaven to sway the destinies of half the globe. 99

If the struggle for power and prestige between the United States and the Soviet Union is the logical outcome of modern history, then its significance far transcends what is known as the Cold War. This is precisely the position adopted by Walter LaFeber. Writing of the need for 'understanding the causes of this struggle between the United States and Russia', LaFeber says:

Walter LaFeber, *America, Russia and the Cold War 1945-84*, 5th edn, Knopf, New York, 1985, p.1

> 66 That conflict did not begin in 1945 or even with the communist victory in Russia during 1917. The two powers did not initially come into conflict because one was communist and the other capitalist. Rather, they first confronted one another on the plains of Asia in the late nineteenth century. That meeting climaxed a century in which Americans had expanded westward over half the globe and Russians had moved eastward across Asia. 99

A similar conclusion is reached by Louis J. Halle, who considers de Tocqueville's observations in some detail, especially why his prediction was so accurate. Halle emphasises that when de Tocqueville wrote, he knew nothing of Marx or Marxism, nor did he foresee the coming of communism to Russia.

> 66 He foresaw that what in fact came to pass would come to pass regardless of the ideological label attached to the authoritarian regime that governed Russia.
>
> The implications of this seem to me essential to an understanding of the Cold War. The behaviour of Russia under the Communists has been Russian behaviour rather than Communist behaviour. Under the Communists Russia has continued to behave essentially as it behaved under the czars. There has been the same centralisation and authoritarianism. There has been the same conspiratorial approach to international relations. There has been the same profound mistrust of the outside world. There has been the same obsession with secrecy and espionage. There has been the same cautiousness, the same capacity for retreat. There has been the same effort to achieve security by expanding the Russian space, by constantly pushing back the menacing presence of foreigners across the Russian borders.
>
> What the revolution of 1917 did was simply to reinvigorate the traditional principle of authoritarianism in Russia. It replaced a decadent and enfeebled

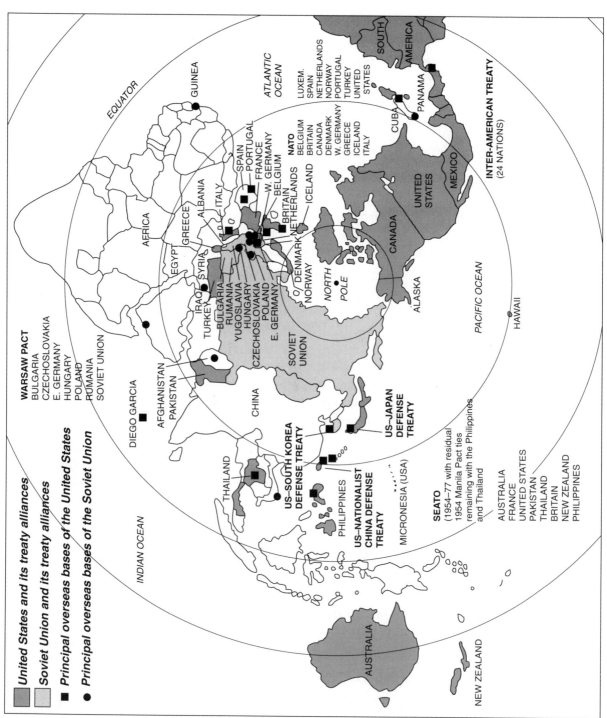

The United States and the Soviet Union: alliances and overseas bases at the height of the Cold War

authoritarian dynasty with a new vigorous, and ruthlessly determined authoritarian dynasty. All this is implicit in the fact that de Tocqueville was able to predict both the polarisation of the world and the ideological contest between the two superpowers without foreseeing Marxism–Leninism.

The Cold War, then, represents a historical necessity to which the Communist movement is incidental rather than essential...

99

Louis J. Halle, *The Cold War as History*, Harper, New York, 1971, pp.11–12

Those historians who see the Cold War in terms of ideological conflict — Leninist-inspired doctrines of communist revolution versus the anti-communist attitudes that such doctrines have produced — pinpoint the origins of the conflict in the Bolshevik revolution of 1917. One such writer is André Fontaine, author of an important two-volume history of the Cold War. Fontaine takes into account great power considerations but concludes that aggressive Russian foreign policy initiatives can largely be attributed to communist ideology.

66 There would have been no Cold War had there not been, at mid-century, two — and only two — sufficiently large and populous powers that were confident enough in the worth of their beliefs and weapons to contest which would assume world leadership, without either's being able to prove a decisive superiority.

Their rivalry exploded only after their common enemies, Germany and Japan, were crushed in 1945. But its roots go back to two events of 1917: America's entry into the war and the Russian Revolution. President Wilson's exhortation in his message to Congress on April 2 of a year of high hopes and black despair that 'peace must be planted upon the tested foundations of political liberty,' collided head on with the profession of faith that Leon Trotsky, People's Commissar for Foreign Affairs, proclaimed before the Congress of Soviets just after the victorious insurrection: 'Either the Russian Revolution will create a revolutionary movement in Europe, or the European powers will destroy the Russian Revolution.' Or, as Trotsky put it in a striking epigram, Lenin and Wilson were 'the apocalyptic antipodes of our time.'

99

André Fontaine, *History of the Cold War from the October Revolution to the Korean War 1917–1950*, trs. D.D. Paige, Secker & Warburg, London, 1968, pp.11–12

One of the most cogent arguments against explaining Soviet foreign policy in terms of traditional nation state balance of power considerations has been presented by Arthur M. Schlesinger, Jr.

66 The fundamental explanation of the speed with which the Cold War escalated... lies precisely in the fact that the Soviet Union was *not* a traditional national state. This is where the 'mirror image' invoked by some psychologists falls down. For the Soviet Union was a phenomenon very different from America or Britain: it was a totalitarian state, endowed with an all-explanatory, all-consuming ideology, committed to the infallibility of government and party, still in a somewhat messianic mood, equating dissent with treason, and ruled by a dictator who, for all his quite extraordinary abilities, had his paranoid moments.

Marxism–Leninism gave the Russian leaders a view of the world according to which all societies were inexorably destined to proceed along appointed roads by appointed stages until they achieved the classless nirvana. Moreover, given the resistance of the capitalists to this development, the

Soviet leaders Khrushchev and Bulganin lay a wreath at Karl Marx's tomb, Highgate cemetery, London, April 1956 (The Photo Library). Why was the memory of Karl Marx important to the Soviet leaders? What role has Marxism played in shaping Soviet foreign policy objectives and tactics?

existence of any non-communist state was *by definition* a threat to the Soviet Union. 'As long as capitalism and socialism exist,' Lenin wrote, 'we cannot live in peace: in the end, one or the other will triumph — a funeral dirge will be sung either over the Soviet Republic or over world capitalism'...

An analysis of the origins of the Cold War which leaves out these factors — the intransigence of Leninist ideology, the sinister dynamics of a totalitarian society and the madness of Stalin — is obviously incomplete. It was these factors which made it hard for the West to accept the thesis that Russia was moved only by a desire to protect its security and would be satisfied by the control of Eastern Europe; it was these factors which charged the debate between universalism and spheres of influence with apocalyptic potentiality.

"

Arthur M. Schlesinger, Jr., 'Origins of the Cold War', *Foreign Affairs*, October 1967, pp.46–7, 49–50

Schlesinger's account of the origins of the Cold War is representative of the historical position that has been called the traditional or orthodox view. According to apologists for the position, the Soviet Union was responsible for the Cold War. Stalin violated the Yalta Agreement (see p. 20), imposed Soviet control on Eastern Europe, and schemed to spread communism throughout the world (see p. 27). The United States, reacting defensively, tried to 'contain' Soviet expansion by means of the Truman Doctrine (see p. 34), the Marshall Plan (see p. 38) and the North Atlantic Treaty Organisation (NATO) (see p. 48). In the 1950s American historians with few exceptions agreed substantially with the orthodox view of the Cold War origins.

As time passed, and especially after the Vietnam War disillusioned many Americans about the containment policy, an increasing number of historians began to revise the orthodox interpretation of the Cold War. The pioneer was William Appleman Williams, who wrote a number of works including *The Tragedy of American Diplomacy* (1959). Williams explained the onset of the Cold War in terms of the 'dollar diplomacy' of the United States. Linking US foreign policy to the 'needs' of American capitalism, he viewed containment as the latest manifestation of a traditional American diplomacy of economic expansionism, dating at least from the days of the 'open door' policy at the turn of the century. For Williams, American diplomatic activities were designed not to contain communist aggression but to promote commercial penetration of Eastern Europe. Williams' approach has been taken further by some of his pupils, especially Gabriel Kolko, whose writings offer the most extreme indictment of US foreign policy available.

One other revisionist thesis needs to be mentioned. As early as 1948 British physicist P.M.S. Blackett wrote that the dropping of the atomic bombs on Hiroshima and Nagasaki was 'not so much the last military act of the second World War as the first major operation of the cold diplomatic war with Russia'. Taking up the idea, a Cambridge political economist, Gar Alperovitz, suggested in his *Atomic Diplomacy* (1965) that the United States dropped the bombs on an already defeated Japan in order to impress the Russians and make them more 'manageable'. Orthodox historians, among them Herbert Feis, a former official in the Roosevelt and Truman administrations, argued that the USA used the bombs simply to assure a quick and complete victory over Japan with a minimum loss of American lives.

The most recent development in the Cold War debate is the appearance of so-called post-revisionist histories. Post-revisionists do not exactly split the difference between the traditional and revisionist positions but rest somewhere in between. The foremost spokesperson of the post-revisionist position is John Lewis Gaddis. He concludes his major study of Cold War origins by stressing that 'neither side can bear sole responsibility for the onset of the Cold War'.

> ❝ Historians have debated at length the question of who caused the Cold War, but without shedding much light on the subject. Too often they view that event exclusively as a series of actions by one side and reactions by the other. In fact, policy-makers in both the United States and the Soviet Union were constantly weighing each other's intentions, as they perceived them, and modifying their own courses of action accordingly. In addition, officials in Washington and Moscow brought to the task of policy formulation a variety of preconceptions, shaped by personality, ideology, political pressures, even ignorance and irrationality, all of which influenced their behavior. Once this complex interaction of stimulus and response is taken into account, it becomes clear that neither side can bear sole responsibility for the onset of the Cold War.
>
> But neither should the conflict be seen as irrepressible... The power vacuum in central Europe caused by Germany's collapse made a Russian–American confrontation likely; it did not make it inevitable. Men as well as circumstances make foreign policy, and through such drastic expedients

as war, appeasement, or resignation, policy-makers can always alter difficult situations in which they find themselves... The Cold War is too complicated an event to be discussed in terms of either national guilt or the determinism of inevitability...

The Cold War grew out of a complicated interaction of external and internal developments inside both the United States and the Soviet Union. The external situation — circumstances beyond the control of either power — left Americans and Russians facing one another across prostrated Europe at the end of World War II. Internal influences in the Soviet Union — the search for security, the role of ideology, massive postwar reconstruction needs, the personality of Stalin — together with those in the United States — the ideal of self-determination, fear of communism, the illusion of omnipotence fostered by American economic strength and the atomic bomb — made the resulting confrontation a hostile one. Leaders of both superpowers sought peace, but in doing so yielded to considerations which, while they did not precipitate war, made a resolution of differences impossible. **99**

John Lewis Gaddis, *The United States and the Origins of the Cold War 1941–1947*, Columbia University Press, New York, 1972, pp.359–61

The writer of this book is sympathetic to the post-revisionist interpretation put forward by John Lewis Gaddis and Walter LaFeber. This interpretation stresses the unavoidable clash of interests between the two superpowers, their spiralling misperceptions in the unsettled conditions of the late 1940s and the dynamic interplay of action and reaction in the sequence of events. Rather than pointing the finger of blame exclusively at one or other side, the post-revisionist interpretation focuses on the complexities of the interrelationship.

This interpretation stresses the understandable Soviet desire for security and its traditional mistrust of the Western powers. Stalin, like any Soviet leader, wanted a weakened Germany and the creation of a defensive cordon of satellite states in Eastern Europe. The Soviet Union was naturally determined to retain the territory it had occupied in the course of defeating Nazi Germany. However, the actions that it took to enhance its security, together with exaggerated Western fears of Soviet military strength, led to inflated estimates of the Soviet threat to Western Europe. Stalinist ideological belligerence and general militancy — probably more an expression of weakness rather than confidence or ambition — magnified Western fears.

Meanwhile, on the other side of what Churchill called the Iron Curtain, Stalin greatly exaggerated the active military challenge posed to the Soviet Union by the Western powers. This was helped by the fact that, compared with the Roosevelt years, under President Truman US policy towards Russia did become appreciably tougher.

Both superpowers jockeyed for position in the late 1940s, with each trying to gain advantages in the unsettled years of post-war reconstruction. Soviet power increasingly dominated Eastern Europe and culminated in the coup in Czechoslovakia in 1948. Meanwhile US economic and military power poured into Western Europe, with the Marshall Plan and NATO. Eastern Europe was saved from nazism and for the Soviet Union. Western Europe was saved from both nazism and communism, and within a remarkably short space of time grew into a community of prosperous, liberal democratic states.

The interesting thing about the history of Soviet–American relations since 1945 is that there is a parallel between the evolution of the Cold War itself and the evolution of the explanations for the Cold War. What is true of the political understanding of the Cold War, i.e. the evolution from an ideological to a great power perspective, is also true of the historical understanding of the Cold War, which exhibits a similar evolution from an ideological perspective (orthodox and then revisionist) to a great power perspective (post-revisionist).

PART ONE

The Cold War Begins

THE ROOTS OF
HOSTILITY

RUSSIAN-AMERICAN relations, which had been harmonious for most of the nineteenth century, were subject to increasing tension from the 1890s. The major area of conflict was northern China, particularly the rich province of Manchuria. The United States believed its economic prosperity required an open door policy, i.e. that all powers should have equal access to China. Russia was determined to close off and colonise the areas of China adjoining her own territory.

From the 1890s America tried to contain Russian expansion, often by supporting Japan, which favoured the open door policy for its own purposes. There was also increasing American antagonism towards the tsarist autocracy and particularly its treatment of Jews. President Theodore Roosevelt, a forceful advocate of US interests, expressed American sentiments in strong terms: '[The Russians] are utterly insincere and treacherous; they have no conception of the truth ... and no regard for others.'

THE RUSSIAN REVOLUTION

These views did not change in 1914 when tsarist Russia was allied with England and France against Germany. In March 1917 — one month before America entered World War I — the Tsar was overthrown by a group of moderates seeking to establish a constitutional government. President Woodrow Wilson, who firmly put idealism ('ideology') before self-interest in the field of international relations, waxed lyrical about the change of government in Russia. In his message to Congress on 2 April 1917 he proclaimed that:

> 66 Russia was known by those who knew it best to have always been in fact democratic at heart, in all the vital habits of her people that spoke their natural instinct, their habitual attitude towards life. The autocracy that crowned the summit of her political structure ... was not in fact Russian in origin, character or purpose. 99

Quoted in Fontaine,
History of the Cold War,
p.17

The provisional government was shortlived. Any chance for improved understanding between Russia and the West was shattered in November 1917 when the Bolsheviks led by Lenin overthrew the provisional regime. When the Soviet Union emerged from the Bolshevik revolution, its relations with the West were to be guided by two sets of considerations: first, the tenets of Marxist–Leninist ideology; second, an awareness of the reality of balance of power matters.

Initially the power of ideology was strong. Lenin and Trotsky pulled Russia out of World War I (the Treaty of Brest–Litovsk gave vast territories to Germany as the price for peace), executed the Tsar and his family, exposed the secret treaties the Tsar had made with his allies, and repudiated tsarist and provisional government debts. Lenin believed that the Russian revolution could be consolidated only if revolution spread to the centres of advanced capitalism in Western Europe. Russia would provide the 'spark' to ignite the revolution in Western Europe.

The new Soviet government declared that within a short time the revolutionary tide of communism would spread to the Western nations. To speed up the process, Lenin instructed the Comintern (the Communist International) — which had become a formidable revolutionary instrument — to concentrate its activity on Germany and England.

Reporting to the Party Congress in March 1919, Lenin declared that the struggle between communism and the West was 'inevitable'.

> **66** We are living not merely in a state but in a system of states and the existence of the Soviet Republic side by side with imperialist states for a long time is unthinkable. One or the other must triumph in the end. And before that end supervenes a series of frightful collisions between the Soviet Republic and the bourgeois states will be inevitable. **99**

V.I. Lenin, *Works*, vol.24, 3rd Russian edn, Beekman Publishers, New York, 1975, p.122

The West's reaction was a mixture of awe and terror. Many Western intellectuals were sincerely attracted by the bold new Soviet experiment. But the vast majority of the people of Western Europe and America recoiled from the Red Terror. Diplomatic recognition was withheld and communist sympathisers were persecuted. US Secretary of State Bainbridge Colby used strong words to describe his government's view of Russia in 1920:

> **66** ... the existing regime in Russia is based upon the negation of every principle of honour and good faith, and every usage and convention, underlying the whole structure of international law, the negation, in short, of every principle upon which it is possible to base harmonious and trustful relations, whether of nations or of individuals...
>
> In the view of this Government, there cannot be any common ground upon which it can stand with a Power whose conceptions of international relations are so entirely alien to its own, so utterly repugnant to its moral sense. **99**

Arthur M. Schlesinger Jr. (ed.), *The Dynamics of World Power*, vol.2, McGraw-Hill, New York, 1973

It soon became clear that widespread revolution was not going to occur in Western Europe. Not only had the Comintern failed in its international revolutionary efforts, the Soviet Union itself was in dire straits domestically.

Lenin, always a shrewd pragmatist, decided that compromise — in both domestic and foreign affairs — was the only option. In the domestic sphere he launched the New Economic Policy; almost all industry was denationalised and foreign investors were reinvited to the Soviet Union. A similar approach was adopted in the international arena. Co-operation with capitalist powers was now possible, where this could be shown to be of mutual benefit.

The Western world greeted the New Economic Policy with relief, many observers concluding that the period of storm and stress in Soviet politics was over. The view that the Red Terror had been only a passing phase was strengthened when Lenin died in 1924 and a bitter struggle for the succession resulted in the triumph of Stalin over Trotsky.

THE EMERGENCE OF STALIN

Differences over ideology were at the forefront of the leadership struggle between Stalin and Trotsky. Stalin emphasised the national power and security of the Soviet state. His major contribution to Marxism–Leninism was the notion of 'socialism in one country'. His rival, Trotsky, proposed a theory of 'permanent revolution'. Trotsky argued that, given the absence of a strong proletarian base in the USSR, Soviet communism would be distorted unless revolution occurred in the centres of advanced capitalism; Russia would have to await the spread of revolution to industrialised Europe before it could successfully build its own socialist society. Stalin's position proved to be more politically effective. It offered hope that a new society, independent of what happened in the West, could be built in Russia. It also promised the Russian people some respite from further revolution and war.

Stalin did not see any inconsistency between 'socialism in one country' and the future goal of world revolution. In his view, the more powerful the Soviet Union was as a national state, the better equipped it would be to export its revolutionary ideology later. Stalin did not completely abandon the notion of an inevitable conflict between the Soviet Union and the capitalist West. In fact, during the 1920s and 1930s he developed the notion of the 'two camps'. According to this notion, the world had become polarised into two hostile camps with neither camp in a position to destroy the other. In 1925 he reported to the Party Congress:

> 66 The basic and new feature, the decisive feature that has affected all the events in the sphere of foreign relations during this period, is the fact that a certain temporary equilibrium of forces has been established between our country... and the countries of the capitalist world, an equilibrium which has determined the present period of 'peaceful co-existence' between the land of the Soviets and the capitalist countries. What we at one time regarded as a brief respite after the war has become a whole period of respite. 99

Joseph Stalin, Report to 14th Party Congress, 18 December 1925, quoted in Myron Rush (ed.), *The International Situation and Soviet Policy*. Charles E. Merrill, Columbus, Ohio, 1970, p.38

Stalin did not regard this co-existence as permanent, however. In the relative security of 1936, he is reported as saying in an interview with a Western journalist:

Joseph Stalin, Interview with Roy Howard, in A.E. Senn (ed.), *Readings in Russian Political and Diplomatic History*, vol.2, Dorsey, Homewood, Ill., 1966, p.198

" …we Marxists believe that revolution will occur in other countries, as well. But it will occur at a time when it will be considered possible or necessary by revolutionaries of those countries. Exported revolution is non-sense. Each country, if it so desires, will make its own revolution. And if no such desire exists, no revolution will occur. **"**

In responding to the rise of fascism during the 1930s, Stalin confirmed that security interests rather than communist revolutionary orthodoxy would be the basis of Soviet actions. Initially Stalin underestimated the nazi menace. German Communists were ordered to ignore the nazi threat and concentrate their attacks on the Social Democrats — their traditional rivals in the struggle to gain working class support. In fact, this division among the left wing made it easier for Hitler to come to power (1933). Very quickly the nazis outlawed the Communist Party and arrested most of its leaders. Stalin now took the nazi menace far more seriously.

DIPLOMATIC RECOGNITION

America gave formal diplomatic recognition to Soviet Russia in November 1933. Franklin D. Roosevelt was now President and the world economic scene had changed. The Depression caused business leaders to urge diplomatic recognition as a way of further opening trade. There were strategic reasons as well. China experts in the US State Department had been worried for some time about the rise of Japanese power at the expense of China. For a brief period in the 1920s the Soviet Union had been allied with the Chinese, but relations had broken down in 1927. State Department officials now wanted to use Russia as a counter to Japan. This, however, required some kind of official relations between the Americans and the Soviets. The government in Moscow was also keen to end its long period of diplomatic isolation. In 1934 the Soviet Union joined the League of Nations, in which its representative, Maxim Litvinov, became the foremost spokesperson for collective security against Germany's military revival.

The first American ambassador to the Soviet Union soon lost his initial enthusiasm for the task. William C. Bullitt had left America in 1933 as a friend of Russia. Within two years he was preaching the 'hard line' and had resigned his post. Stalin's purges played a significant role in the hardening. George F. Kennan, a member of the embassy staff and himself later ambassador to Russia, found those days 'a sort of liberal education in the horrors of Stalinism'. Kennan attended many of the purge trials in person. He was among the first of the US Foreign Service experts on the Soviet Union to alert politicians to the danger of Soviet communism.

By 1938 Stalin felt increasingly insecure in his temporary alliance with the West. There are reasonable grounds for concluding that Stalin suspected that the West was prepared to tacitly encourage Hitler to strike to the East to promote a life and death struggle between the Soviet Union and Germany. The lesson was not lost on Stalin. He was not invited to attend the Munich conference; nor did he intervene when Hitler occupied the Sudetenland (October 1938) or the rest of Czechoslovakia (March 1939).

THE NAZI–SOVIET PACT

The Munich fiasco led to a major revision in Stalin's thinking about maintaining Russia's security interests. In the light of Western inaction and nazi ambition, an alliance with Hitler seemed to be of greater advantage. Stalin calculated that a pact with Russia would appeal to Hitler: it would safeguard the nazi dictator's eastern flank and thus give him the go-ahead to launch an offensive against the West. A mutually exhausting war between Germany and the West would give the Soviet Union an opportunity to grow stronger while peace in the East prevailed. Such a pact would buy time. In light of the effect of Stalin's purges on the Soviet military machine, time was most necessary.

In August 1939 the Russian and German foreign ministers (Vyacheslav Molotov and Joachim von Ribbentrop) had talks in Moscow, which resulted in the Nazi–Soviet Non-Aggression Pact. The published part of the pact said that Germany and Russia would remain neutral towards each other, but there were secret clauses as well. In these clauses Russia and Germany agreed to divide Poland between themselves. The Germans gave the Russians a free hand to determine the future of Bessarabia, Latvia, Lithuania, Estonia and part of Finland — all territories that had been lost as a result of the Treaty of Brest-Litovsk. The significance of this agreement is summed up by historian A.J.P. Taylor:

> 66 The [agreement] was a milestone in world history; it marked the moment when Soviet Russia returned to Europe as a Great Power. No European statesman had ever addressed Stalin before. Western leaders had treated him as though he were... remote and ineffectual... Now Hitler recognised him as the ruler of a great state... 99

Taylor goes on to make some interesting observations about Western reactions to the pact.

> 66 It was no doubt disgraceful that Soviet Russia should make any agreement with the leading Fascist state; but this reproach came ill from the statesmen who went to Munich and who were then sustained in their own countries by great majorities. The Russians, in fact, did only what the Western statesmen had hoped to do; and Western bitterness was the bitterness of disappointment, mixed with anger that professions of communism were no more sincere than their own professions of democracy. 99

A.J.P. Taylor, *The Origins of the Second World War*, Penguin, Harmondsworth, 1965, pp.316–18

Germany invaded Poland in September 1939 without any fear of Soviet reaction. Russia occupied eastern Poland in the same month. By the end of 1939 the Russians had forced Latvia, Lithuania and Estonia to accept Soviet garrisons in their territory and these countries were formally incorporated into the USSR in August 1940. In November 1939 Russia invaded Finland to secure territory regarded by the Soviets as strategically necessary for the defence of Leningrad and Murmansk. These Russian gains were acknowledged by the Treaty of Moscow (March 1940). Russia's attack on Finland led to her expulsion from the League of Nations. The Russians completed the secret arrangements of the Nazi–Soviet Non-Aggression Pact by occupying Bessarabia in June 1940.

As it turned out Stalin's hopes for a quiet life in Eastern Europe had been based on a great miscalculation: it took Hitler not years but weeks to conquer most of Western Europe. On 22 June 1941 nazi troops crossed the Soviet border, taking the Russians by surprise. By late 1941 the Germans had advanced almost to Moscow. Their advance was halted as much by the severity of the Russian winter, for which they were ill-prepared, as by Russian resistance. Stalin reacted by unleashing a torrent of patriotic and nationalist propaganda, urging his people to fight out of loyalty to Mother Russia. (He was shrewd to doubt that they would fight for him or for communism.)

As Hitler's forces advanced deep into Russian territory, Soviet foreign policy became one desperate cry to the Western powers for help. There were those in the West who initially viewed the conflict with some relish. A little-known US senator from Missouri, Harry S. Truman, was quoted as saying:

> 66 If we see that Germany is winning [the war] we ought to help Russia, and if Russia is winning we ought to help Germany and that way let them kill as many as possible... although I don't want to see Hitler victorious under any circumstances. Neither of them think anything of breaking their pledged word. 99

New York Times, 24 June 1941

In June 1941 neither the American nor British governments followed this advice. Although the Americans were not yet at war, President Roosevelt regarded the defeat of Hitler as the absolute priority. The British Prime Minister, Winston Churchill, also immediately offered support to Moscow and is said to have confided to his private secretary that 'if Hitler invaded Hell I would make at least a favourable reference to the Devil in the House of Commons'.

THE ATLANTIC CHARTER

In August 1941 Roosevelt and Churchill met for the first time at Placentia Bay, off the coast of Newfoundland, Canada, where they hammered out a set of principles to be used in the war against the Germans. Roosevelt declined to declare publicly that the USA would enter the war, believing that American public opinion would not support him. He did, however, endorse Churchill's suggestion of a joint communiqué, called the Atlantic Charter, which outlined the two leaders' vision of the post-war world. Especially significant were points 3 and 4, which pledged the two leaders of the English-speaking world to the restoration of sovereign rights and self-government to those nations that had been deprived of them and to the establishment of conditions that would allow all states access to the trade and raw materials of the world.

The Atlantic Charter became a moral and ideological propaganda tool for the war against the Axis powers. In September 1941 at an Inter-Allied meeting in London, representatives of the nations battling Hitler (the United Nations) formally adhered to the 'common principles' set forth in the Atlantic Charter. The Soviet Union gave qualified approval. In signing the charter the Soviet ambassador entered a caveat about the 'historic peculiarities of particular countries' — presumably a reference to Russian interests in Eastern Europe. Churchill himself, speaking in the House of Commons on 9 September, insisted that the charter applied only to 'nations of Europe now under the Nazi yoke'.

The decision to send military supplies to Russia under the Lend–Lease Act (Britain was already receiving supplies under Lend–Lease) was also confirmed at the Placentia Bay meeting. American aid to Russia began in mid-1941. Between June 1941 and April 1944 nearly 17 million tonnes of supplies were shipped to Russia by the USA and Britain. US Congress support for continued Lend–Lease supplies was confirmed in the aftermath of the Japanese attack on Pearl Harbor (December 1941) and Hitler's consequent declaration of war on the USA.

PLANNING TO WIN THE WAR

Immediately after the bombing of Pearl Harbor, Roosevelt and Churchill met in Washington to produce a strategy for waging war and producing a peace settlement. One outcome of the talks was the creation of a combined British–American Chiefs of Staff. Anglo–American military agreement was easier to reach than East–West military co-operation. Despite the shock of Pearl Harbor, Roosevelt never wavered from the view that the war in Europe must have first priority. His view was strengthened by the nearly unanimous view that the German army was a more formidable opponent than Japan. If Germany lost, Japan too would fall, but if the Allies knocked Japan out of the war, Germany would still remain a fighting force.

When Soviet Foreign Minister Molotov visited London and Washington in May 1942, further allied co-operation and assistance were very much on the Soviet agenda. From Moscow's point of view, the most urgent requirement was the launching of a second front — a British–American invasion of north-western Europe — to absorb a sizeable percentage of the 200 German divisions tearing away at the Soviet Union. However, Molotov did not get a promise

'Under the Broomstick': a Russian cartoon of 1942 (source unknown). The words on the signpost say: 'To the German front' and the strip of water separating the man in the armchair from the man with the broomstick is labelled 'The Channel'. Who is the man in the armchair? Who is the man with the broomstick? What is he doing? The man in the armchair has trampled on a promise dated 1942. What was the promise? Why did the Soviets feel let down?

of a rapid invasion of the continent: hard military realities led to the post-ponement of the second front. The Soviets were bitter at the delay, highlighting the fact that although the war against fascism made Britain and the United States allies of the USSR, the relationship was strained from the start. Stalin's distrust of Churchill dated back to the latter's support for British intervention in the Russian civil war. Suspicion and ideological hostility were never far from the surface. Roosevelt and Churchill feared that a victorious Russia would dominate Eastern Europe, but they had to depend on the Russians to bear the brunt of the land war against Germany. Both the Russians and their Western allies at times were concerned that the other might negotiate a separate peace with Hitler.

The policy-makers themselves, while emphasising co-operation in the sentiments expressed for public audiences, were clear in their own minds that the alliance was one of mutual necessity and not one of mutual admiration. And yet the politics of coalition warfare meant that public opinion, especially in the USA, had to be carefully cultivated. The image of Soviet Russia, now an ally of America and Britain, received careful attention in the West.

Bernard A. Weisberger,
Cold War, Cold Peace,
American Heritage
Magazine © Forbes, Inc.,
New York, 1985, p.24

❝ It was, in the words of General John R. Davies, who headed the U.S. military mission to Moscow, a 'strange alliance.' The mills of wartime 'public information' promptly ground out new images of the Russians, tailored to the American habit of seeing all international confrontations in terms of shootouts between the rustlers and the posse. Now the Soviet leaders were wearing the white hats. Suddenly it appeared that they were not only brave anti-Fascists, but virtually undistinguishable from next-door neighbours. *Life*, in 1943, labeled the Russians 'one hell of a people' who 'to a remarkable degree... look like Americans, dress like Americans, and think like Americans.' A movie version of Ambassador Davies's book almost made Stalin a cuddly bear of a man. The *New York Times* informed its readers in April 1944 that 'Marxian thinking in Soviet Russia is out. The... competitive system is back...' Not all Americans were totally convinced of Soviet benevolence, but the propaganda war, which inflated a few small truths with a great deal of hot air, created expectations that were cruelly disappointed afterwards, leading to overreaction in the opposite direction. ❞

Review and Discuss

- What images of the Russian people were emphasised in American wartime propaganda? Why?

- What effect did the propaganda have on later American perceptions of the Russian people?

In January 1943 Roosevelt met Churchill at Casablanca in recently liberated North Africa. They decided that the United Nations would insist upon an unconditional surrender from Germany, Italy and Japan and that none of the Allies would sign a separate peace with the Axis powers. Churchill was unhappy with the idea of unconditional surrender, believing that the plan took away a potential bargaining tool with the Germans. He accepted it, however, as a way of buying Soviet friendship without opening a second front in Europe.

THE TEHERAN CONFERENCE

The first occasion on which the Big Three policy-makers — Stalin, Churchill and Roosevelt — all met was at the Teheran Conference (Iran) in November 1943. It was now inevitable that discussion would focus on questions related to the post-war settlement. The Teheran Conference confirmed the unconditional surrender of Germany as the Allied objective. There was also political manoeuvering over the future conduct of the war against Germany. Roosevelt supported Stalin in his insistence that Operation Overlord (the Allied codename for the invasion of northern France) should be given the highest priority.

At Teheran there was also discussion over the boundaries of post-war Poland. In effect, Poland was moved westward. Churchill suggested that the Russians should be allowed to keep the areas of eastern Poland they had seized in 1939, with Poland being compensated by receiving territory on her western border from Germany. By agreeing to the Molotov–Ribbentrop Polish boundary in the east, the Western Allies created a situation which no independent Polish government could accept and ensured that a puppet government would have to be installed. Further, by compensating Poland with a large amount of German territory in the west, German–Polish enmity was assured. On both counts the 'new' Poland would have to look towards the Soviet Union for its security.

The Teheran Conference also had its positive aspects. Sentiment in favour of a peace dictated by the big powers, an international organisation and a weakened post-war Germany were important points of agreement. Roosevelt was also impressed when Stalin paid tribute to Lend–Lease. On his return to Washington the American President optimistically told a national radio audience: 'I got along fine with Marshall Stalin… I believe that we are going to get along very well with him and the Russian people — very well indeed.'

SOVIET ADVANCES IN EASTERN EUROPE

The second half of 1944, with Operation Overlord finally launched and the Red Army marching westward, produced some clear examples of the way in which Stalin's military strategy was designed to harmonise with his political aspirations. Stalin later explained the rationale:

Milovan Djilas,
Conversations with Stalin,
Penguin, Harmondsworth,
1963, p.90

> 66 This war is not as in the past; whoever occupies a territory also imposes on it his own social system. Everyone imposes his own system as far as his own army has the power to do so. It cannot be otherwise. 99

Rumania, for example, was occupied by the Red Army, despite that country's break from the Axis alliance. The Soviets declared war on Bulgaria just as the government was in the process of suing for peace in talks with the British and Americans. The most dramatic example of all came in Poland in August 1944. As the Red Army neared Warsaw, Polish underground forces, commanded by the Polish government in exile in London, rose up against the Germans. But the Red Army stopped, less than twenty kilometres from Warsaw. For two months the Germans hammered the Polish fighters, eventually killing almost 200 000 and levelling half the city. Late in 1944 the Soviets liberated Poland, installed a provisional government of their own choosing in the city of Lublin and began to deal with it in matters relating to Poland's future. A major row broke out between the Western Allies and Stalin when the Kremlin formally recognised the Lublin Committee as the legal government of Poland, thereby ignoring the claims of the London Poles.

The Soviet handling of the Warsaw uprising convinced many Western observers that Soviet callousness had few limits. British Air Marshal John

Slessor later wrote: 'How, after the fall of Warsaw, any responsible statesman could trust any Russian Communist further than he could kick him, passes the comprehension of ordinary men.'

As the Soviet armies penetrated more deeply into Eastern Europe, Winston Churchill travelled to Moscow for the last time in October 1944. He concluded with Stalin the so-called Balkan Bargain:

Winston S. Churchill, 'The Second World War', vol.6, *Triumph and Tragedy*, Cassell, London, 1954, p.198

66 Let us settle about our affairs in the Balkans. Your armies are in Roumania and Bulgaria. We have interests, missions, and agents there. Don't let us get at cross-purposes in small ways. So far as Britain and Russia are concerned, how would it do for you to have ninety per cent predominance in Roumania, for us to have ninety per cent of the say in Greece and go fifty-fifty about Yugoslavia. 99

Churchill later summarised the conversation by cable for Roosevelt, who promptly indicated that the arrangements were not valid without American participation, and that there would be an appropriate time for such arrangements to be discussed. In any case, the percentage bargain did not last, but the agreement probably reinforced Stalin's view that his developing sphere of influence did have tacit Western approval.

At the time of the Churchill–Stalin agreement on spheres of influence (which of course was not public knowledge), the *Times* of London went out of its way to explain to its readers the nature of Russian security concerns about Eastern Europe (E.H. Carr was assistant editor at the time).

66 Russia, like Great Britain, has no aggressive or expansive designs in Europe. What she wants on her Western frontier is security. What she asks from her Western neighbours is a guarantee, the extent and form of which will be determined mainly by the experience of the last twenty-five years, that her security shall not be exposed to any threat from across their territories. Admittedly she is unlikely to regard with favour intervention by other Great Powers in these countries.

But Great Britain has traditionally resisted such intervention in the Low Countries or in the vicinity of the Suez Canal, and the United States in Central America — regions which these two powers have properly adjudged vital to their security. It would be incongruous to ask Russia to renounce a similar right of reassurance; and it would be foolish, as well as somewhat hypocritical, to construe insistence on this right as the symptom of an aggressive policy. Essentially British and Russian interests in this respect not only do not clash, but are precisely the same. 99

© The *Times* (London), 6 November 1944

THE YALTA CONFERENCE

The fate of Poland had been decided by the Red Army's occupation well before the last conference between Roosevelt, Churchill and Stalin at the Black Sea resort of Yalta in February 1945. For Churchill, Poland was 'the most urgent reason for the Yalta Conference'. Stalin made his position very clear:

The Big Three at Yalta, February 1945 (Popperfoto). The photo on the front cover of this book also shows these three leaders (with their foreign ministers). Who were they? What was the purpose of the Yalta meeting? What agreements were reached? How justified was criticism of the Western leaders' handling of Stalin?

Stephen E. Ambrose, *Rise to Globalism*, 4th edn, Penguin, Harmondsworth, 1985, p.58

“ For the Russian people, the question of Poland is not only a question of honour but also a question of security. Throughout history, Poland has been the corridor through which the enemy has passed into Russia. Twice in the last thirty years our enemies, the Germans, have passed through this corridor... Poland is not only a question of honour but of life and death for the Soviet Union. ”

Seven of the eight plenary sessions at Yalta grappled with the Polish issue. After endless hours of discussion Stalin agreed to take a few London Poles into the newly established Lublin government. Much controversy would later surround the wording of the Yalta Agreement. At the time the American Chief of Staff, Admiral William Leahy said: 'Mr President, this is so elastic that the Russians can stretch it all the way from Yalta to Washington without technically breaking it', to which Roosevelt responded: 'I know, Bill — I know it. But it's the best I can do for Poland at this time.' He did try to lessen the elasticity by proposing a Declaration on Liberated Europe — a restatement of the principles of the Atlantic Charter. The declaration provided that each of the three powers would pledge co-operation in applying the self-determination principle to newly liberated nations. Roosevelt could do nothing to prevent Soviet amendments to the declaration which rendered it virtually meaningless.

At Yalta Roosevelt was anxious to confirm agreement on the establishment of the United Nations Organisation to replace the League of Nations. Stalin promised the Soviet Union would participate in the forthcoming San Francisco conference to draft the United Nations Charter. All three leaders agreed on the big power veto in the proposed UN Security Council. After much discussion it was finally agreed that the USSR would have three votes in the General Assembly — one for itself and one each for its constituent republics Ukraine and Byelorussia.

Further compromises were struck at Yalta over the Far East. The Americans wanted Soviet participation in the war against Japan, and Stalin agreed to enter the war against Japan three months after the German surrender — enough time to permit the transfer of his troops to Asia. He agreed to sign a pact of friendship with Jiang Jie-shi's (Chiang Kai-Shek) regime, rather than with Mao Zedong's rival communist group. In return, Russia regained territories and privileges it had lost in 1905: the Kuriles and southern Sakhalin from Japan; from China, Darien as a free port, Port Arthur as a naval base, and joint operation of the principal Manchurian railways. China was not consulted about these arrangements.

On the vital issue of Germany's future, Stalin tried his hardest to prevent a post-war revival of the German threat to Soviet security. The three leaders at Yalta agreed that Germany would be divided into four zones of occupation. The Russians also insisted on reparations from Germany for the tremendous damage done by her invading forces. Although there were reservations, especially British, remembering the consequences of post-World War I reparations, the principle was accepted and a tentative sum of US$20 billion (half to go to Russia) was suggested as a basis for future discussion.

Few international agreements have aroused as much controversy as those reached at the Yalta Conference. Its critics contend that the Western leaders made genuine concessions in return for worthless promises. In particular, they condemn the territorial arrangements that Roosevelt and Churchill made at Poland's and China's expense. In the highly charged Cold War climate of the 1950s, the view was widespread that Roosevelt simply handed over Eastern and Central Europe to Stalin at Yalta.

A more sober examination shows that the major lines of post-war influence in Europe had already been drawn by the respective positions of the Allied armies. Historian Forrest C. Pogue points out: 'all in all, the military backdrop for the Yalta negotiations... did not yet afford Roosevelt or Churchill the luxury of renouncing or forgoing Soviet military co-operation in Europe and Asia'. The situation was conspicuously clear: as close as victory was, Britain and the USA still needed the Russians to win the war.

The later critics ignored the advantages the West carried away from the Yalta Conference: broadening of the Polish government, the Russian promise to fight Japan, Russian recognition of Jiang Jie-shi's government, an agreed voting formula in the United Nations, postponement of the reparations question. The critics charged that Roosevelt had given away too much — the truth is that he had little to give away.

It is sobering to reflect on the mood of the Allied delegations as they returned from the Yalta conclave. President Roosevelt's closest adviser, Harry Hopkins, described his and his colleagues' feelings:

> We really believed in our hearts that this was the dawn of a new day we had all been praying for and talking about for so many years. We were absolutely certain that we had won the first great victory of the peace — and by 'we' I mean *all* of us, the whole civilized human race. The Russians had proved that they could be reasonable and farseeing and there wasn't

Quoted in Robert E.
Sherwood, *Roosevelt and
Hopkins*, Harper, New
York, 1948, p.97

any doubt in the minds of the President or any of us that we could live
with them peacefully as far into the future as any of us could imagine. **99**

No sooner had the ink dried on the Yalta Agreement than Stalin began
to consolidate the Soviet hold over Eastern Europe. The participation of democratic elements in Poland was seriously restricted, with the arrest of sixteen
leaders of the Polish underground movement. A communist government was
forced on Rumania, and communists and their allies moved into leading positions in the new regimes in Bulgaria, Hungary and Czechoslovakia. In Yugoslavia, Tito's communist faction broke off its coalition arrangement with non-
communist elements and moved to consolidate its hold on the reins of power.
Diplomatic protests from the West went unheeded.

The methods Stalin used in subjugating Eastern Europe were later described
by a Hungarian communist as 'salami tactics'. Beginning with a broad alliance
of anti-fascist parties, Stalin and his subordinates gradually sliced away from
governmental power one party after another, until all that remained was the
communist core. This accomplished, Stalin then got rid of those communists
who had strong local roots and replaced them with those who had made their
careers in Moscow.

TRUMAN'S 'GET TOUGH' POLICY

Roosevelt died on 12 April 1945. Harry S. Truman assumed the US Presidency
and immediately informed the Secretary of State that '[w]e must stand up to
the Russians'. Vyacheslav Molotov (on his way to the foundation UN conference
in San Francisco) had two meetings with Truman in late April. The new President
berated the Soviets for breaking the Yalta Agreement on Poland and demanded
a 'new' Polish government. Molotov was astonished at the tone of Truman's
demands and is reported to have said: 'I have never been talked to like that
in my life', to which Truman replied: 'Carry out your agreements and you
won't get talked to like that.'

The Russians were puzzled and upset as is indicated in a prompt letter from
Stalin to Truman and Churchill on 24 April 1945.

66 Poland borders on the Soviet Union which cannot be said about Great Britain
or the USA ... I do not know whether a genuinely representative Government
has been established in Greece, or whether the Belgian Government is a
genuinely democratic one. The Soviet Union was not consulted when those
Governments were being formed, nor did it claim the right to interfere
in those matters, because it realizes how important Belgium and Greece
are to the security of Great Britain. **99**

Ambrose, *Rise to
Globalism*, p.63

Truman's 'get tough' policy can clearly be traced to the advice coming from
the State Department. In May 1945 Joseph C. Grew, Under Secretary of State,
put on paper his reflections on Soviet behaviour. In Grew's judgement the
war's result

> 66 will be merely the transfer of totalitarian dictatorship from Germany and Japan to Soviet Russia which will constitute in future as grave a danger as did the Axis... With her certain strangle hold on these countries, Russia's power will steadily increase and she will in the not too distant future be in a favourable position to expand her control, step by step, through Europe... A future war with Soviet Russia is as certain as anything in the world can be certain... The most fatal thing we can do is to place any confidence whatever in Russia's sincerity, knowing without question that she will take every opportunity to profit by our clinging to our own ethical international standards. She regards and will continue to regard our ethical behaviour as a weakness to us and an asset to her. 99

Joseph C. Grew, *Turbulent Era*, vol.2, Houghton Mifflin, Boston, 1952, p.1446

Review and Discuss

- What view did Grew take of Russian intentions in Eastern Europe?

- What were the implications for US policy?

THE POTSDAM CONFERENCE

The last wartime gathering of the Big Three convened in the Berlin suburb of Potsdam in July and August 1945. There were changes in personnel. Russia was represented by Stalin and Foreign Minister Molotov, the United States by President Truman and Secretary of State James Byrnes, and Britain by Prime Minister Churchill and Foreign Secretary Anthony Eden, then (after Labour won a general election) Clement Attlee and Ernest Bevin.

The most important issues discussed at Potsdam once again focused on Germany and Poland. Germany was divided into four zones of occupation (at Yalta Stalin had agreed to a French occupation zone). In addition, they split Berlin into four zones. The administration of Germany was vested in an Allied Control Council composed of the top four Allied military commanders in Europe.

There was also agreement on reparations. The Russians would have twenty-five per cent of the industrial plant confiscated from western Germany, as well as anything confiscated from the Soviet zone. In return, the Russians were to send food, coal and raw materials from their zone to the West to the value of sixty per cent of the industrial plant they received from the Western zones.

The conferees tangled over Poland. Whenever Churchill complained about the absence of free elections in Poland, Stalin mentioned the British domination of Greece. They did agree, however, to set the line of the Oder–Neisse rivers as Poland's temporary western boundary, pending a final peace conference.

In fact the Russians had already turned over to Polish administration the German lands east of the Oder–Neisse line, thereby forcing several million refugees to move to the Western zones.

The Big Three also established the Council of Foreign Ministers (CFM) to continue discussions on issues not resolved at Potsdam: peace treaties with Italy and the former Axis satellites (Hungary, Rumania, Bulgaria, Finland).

Although few people realised it at the time, the Potsdam Conference coincided with the birth of the nuclear age. On 18 July 1945, one day after his arrival at Potsdam, Truman received word that two days earlier American scientists had successfully detonated the world's first atomic bomb at Alamogordo in the New Mexico desert. The news, cryptic though it was — 'Diagnosis not yet complete but results seem satisfactory and already exceed expectations' — had an uplifting effect on Truman. A memo from the British Chief of Staff, which was read directly to Truman and Churchill on 18 July, clearly stated the implications: 'It was no longer necessary for the Russians to come into the Japanese war... Furthermore we now had something in our hands which would redress the balance with the Russians.' Truman certainly recognised that he now had a weapon which could offset the offensive power of the Red Army. Moreover, he believed himself to be in a stronger position to insist more firmly than before that the Soviets live up to the principles of the Atlantic Charter and the Declaration on Liberated Europe, especially as these principles might be applied to Eastern Europe. Churchill shared Truman's sentiments:

> We seemed suddenly to have become possessed of a merciful abridgement of the slaughter in the East and of a far happier prospect in Europe. I have no doubt that these thoughts were present in the minds of my American friends.

Churchill, *The Second World War*, vol.6, p.639

On 24 July Truman 'casually' told Stalin 'that we had a new weapon of unusual destructive force'. Truman records in his *Memoirs* that 'Stalin showed no special interest. All he said was that he was glad to hear it and hoped we would make "good use of it against the Japanese".' Stalin's aplomb left the Americans guessing as to how much he knew about the bomb. In retrospect it would appear that Stalin was aware of Russia's own atomic research programme and the reports of Soviet intelligence monitoring American progress.

THE COLD WAR BEGINS IN EUROPE

CHAPTER TWO

THE COLLAPSE OF THE WARTIME ALLIANCE

B Y MID-1945 the wartime alliance of America, Britain and Russia had all but disintegrated and in its place there arose a stalemate. Put bluntly, it was the presence of the Soviet Red Army and the American atomic bomb that held the scales in balance. By 1946 Europe was clearly divided into opposing blocs: one (the West) led by the United States, the other (the East) led by the Soviet Union. The hostile relationship between these two groups of states formed the substance of what historians and other commentators have called the Cold War.*

The collapse of the wartime alliance and the immediate origins of the Cold War are bound together. As we have already seen, much of the growing animosity stemmed from Stalin's policy of using the Red Army to consolidate Soviet political influence in Eastern Europe. In Stalin's view, Russia had to arm herself against the relentless, hostile nations of the capitalist West, especially the USA, whose industrial might and nuclear weapons made her a formidable opponent.

As a consequence Stalin's post-war foreign policy included the periodic testing of Western defences — no doubt to assess the West's will to resist as well as keeping the 'imperialists' off guard and confused about Russian intentions. Meanwhile, Stalin concentrated Soviet resources on heavy industry and on intensive research and development programmes aimed at producing nuclear bombs and missiles before American superiority in these areas became unchallengeable. Further, to bolster morale, Stalin embarked on a programme of

*The term appears to have been coined by American politician/businessman Bernard Baruch late in 1946 and popularised by journalist Walter Lippmann in 1947.

ideological strengthening to prepare the Russian people for the struggle with the West.

American and other Western observers tended to see the above picture in a very different light. To them, Soviet acquisitions in Central and Eastern Europe represented cynical betrayals of Soviet commitments. Few in the West saw Stalin's actions in terms of his need to protect what he regarded as the legitimate security interests of the Soviet Union. Instead, Western observers tended to view developments in Eastern Europe as involving the fate of peoples who wanted political freedom through democratic elections, but who were prevented from going to the polls by brute force.

Reflection on Soviet actions crystallised a number of questions in the minds of Western policy-makers. Was not Stalin's seizure of Eastern Europe but the first step of a communist leader dedicated to world revolution? Had not the Allies just defeated in battle a European dictator who, were it not for policies of appeasement, would not have been as successful as he was? Why was Soviet Russia so mistrustful of its wartime allies and so pugnacious towards them if not for purposes dangerous to the West? The posing of questions such as these by Western policy-makers after 1945 further eroded wartime cohesion. They led to the gradual implementation by the USA of a far-reaching programme for the defence of the West.

SOVIET ATTEMPTS AT CONSOLIDATION

Although the presence of the Red Army was a strong factor in the rise of communism in Eastern Europe, it was not the only reason. In Poland, Hungary and Czechoslovakia the pace of consolidation of communist control over the government was relatively slower than in Yugoslavia or Albania, where communist guerrilla forces had proved effective against their opponents. In Poland, American and British pressure led to a temporary broadening of the governing coalition, though key positions were retained by the communists. In Hungary and Czechoslovakia, relatively free elections produced governments containing, but not controlled by, the communists. Nevertheless, communist control of important ministries and the presence of Soviet troops in the background ensured the success of the salami tactics through which genuine coalitions became sham coalitions. The gradual tightening of political control was accompanied by a process of tying the economies of the Eastern European countries to that of the USSR. A new term 'people's democracy' was created to describe the diverse regimes now under the jealous tutelage of the Soviet Union. Stalin's comment to Djilas (p. 19) was fulfilled: 'Whoever occupies a territory also imposes on it his own social system.'

Stalin's ambitions were not limited to those territories under Red Army occupation. In June 1945 Moscow suggested joint control of the Dardanelles to the Turkish government. Such a proposal would have led to the establishment

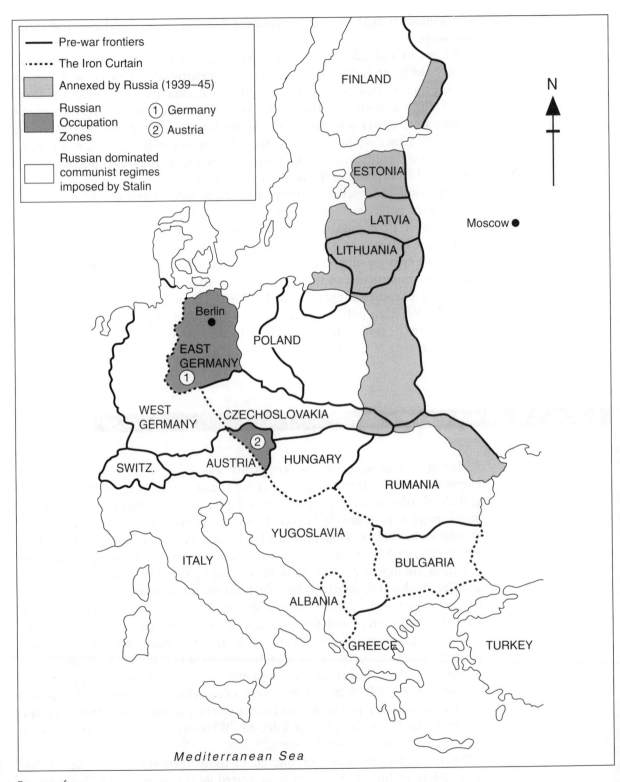

Legend:
— Pre-war frontiers
····· The Iron Curtain
Annexed by Russia (1939–45)
Russian Occupation Zones
① Germany
② Austria
Russian dominated communist regimes imposed by Stalin

N

FINLAND

ESTONIA

LATVIA

LITHUANIA

Moscow ●

Berlin ●
EAST GERMANY ①
POLAND

WEST GERMANY
CZECHOSLOVAKIA
SWITZ.
AUSTRIA ②
HUNGARY
RUMANIA

YUGOSLAVIA

ITALY
BULGARIA

ALBANIA
GREECE
TURKEY

Mediterranean Sea

Europe after World War II

of a Soviet garrison on the Dardanelles. At the same time Turkey was asked to return to Russia three frontier districts ceded to Turkey in 1921.

The most serious of the immediate post-war crises occurred in Iran, a strategic border state that has proved of continuing interest to the rulers in Moscow. Iran had been jointly occupied by British and Soviet troops in August 1941 in an effort to secure supply lines to the USSR. At the Teheran Conference Stalin had agreed to terminate the occupation shortly after the end of the war. However, when the appointed time came and British troops began to leave southern Iran, the Soviets found excuses to keep their 30 000-strong force in the northern provinces.

In November 1945 the Iranian government reported that Russian troops were interfering with its efforts to suppress rebellion in the northern part of the country, especially in the province of Azerbaijan. Requests from Iran that foreign troops be withdrawn by 1 January 1946 were flatly rejected by Moscow. The Russians, in fact, announced the establishment of a revolutionary government in Azerbaijan.

On 5 January 1946 Truman wrote to Secretary of State Byrnes:

> 66 Iran was our ally in the war. Iran was Russia's ally in the war... Yet now Russia stirs up rebellion and keeps troops on the soil of her friend and ally — Iran. There isn't a doubt in my mind that Russia intends an invasion of Turkey and the Black Sea Straits to the Mediterranean. Unless Russia is faced with an iron fist and strong language war is in the making. Only one language do they understand — 'How many divisions have you?' I do not think we should play compromise anymore... We should let our position on Iran be known in no uncertain terms... I'm tired of babying the Soviets. 99

Letter from President Harry Truman to Secretary of State James Byrnes, 5 January 1946, quoted in W. Hillman, *Mr President*, Farrar, Strauss & Young, New York, 1952, p.28

Early in March both Britain and the USA lodged formal protests with the Soviets over their failure to honour the troop withdrawal agreement. Towards the end of the month the Iranian government raised the dispute in the UN Security Council, the first major crisis brought before it. Under strong Anglo-American pressure Moscow announced the withdrawal of its troops.

CHURCHILL'S IRON CURTAIN SPEECH

On 5 March 1946 Winston Churchill gave an address at Westminster College in Fulton, Missouri, with Truman sitting next to him on the platform. His speech is considered one of the most important documents of the Cold War.

> 66 A shadow has fallen upon the scenes so lately lighted by the allied victory. Nobody knows what Soviet Russia and its Communist international organization intends to do in the immediate future, or what are the limits, if any, to their expansive proselytizing tendencies. I have a strong admiration and regard for the valiant Russian people and for my war-time comrade, Marshal Stalin. There is sympathy and goodwill... toward the peoples of all the Russias... We understand the Russian need to be secure on her western frontiers from all renewal of German aggression. We welcome her

to her rightful place among the leading nations of the world... It is my duty, however, to place before you certain facts about the present position in Europe.

From Stettin in the Baltic to Trieste in the Adriatic, an iron curtain has descended across the Continent. Behind the line lie all the capitals of the ancient states of central and eastern Europe — Warsaw, Berlin, Prague, Vienna, Budapest, Belgrade, Bucharest and Sofia. All these famous cities and the populations around them lie in the Soviet sphere and all are subject in one form or another, not only to Soviet influence but to a very high and increasing measure of control from Moscow... The Russian-dominated Polish government has been encouraged to make enormous and wrongful inroads upon Germany, and mass expulsions of millions of Germans on a scale grievous and undreamed of are now taking place. The Communist Parties, which were very small in all these eastern states of Europe, have been raised to pre-eminence and power far beyond their numbers and are seeking everywhere to obtain totalitarian control. Police governments are prevailing in nearly every case... Whatever conclusions may be drawn from these facts... this is certainly not the liberated Europe we fought to build up. Nor is it one which contains the essentials of a permanent peace...

On the other hand I repulse the idea that a new war is inevitable; still more that it is imminent... I do not believe that Soviet Russia desires war. What they desire is the fruits of war and the indefinite expansion of their power and doctrines... Our difficulties and dangers will not be removed

'Peep under the Iron Curtain': a British cartoon of 1946 (source unknown). Identify 'Joe', referred to in the cartoon. Who is the cigar-smoking figure peeping under the Iron Curtain? What was the background to his use of the phrase 'the Iron Curtain'? What steps did 'Joe' take to ensure his 'No Admittance' sign would be observed? How did this cartoon foreshadow later events?

by closing our eyes to them. They will not be removed by mere waiting to see what happens; nor will they be relieved by a policy of appeasement... From what I have seen of our Russian friends and allies during the war, I am convinced that there is nothing they admire so much as strength, and there is nothing for which they have less respect than for military weakness... If the western democracies stand together in strict adherence to the principles of the United Nations Charter, their influence for furthering these principles will be immense... If, however, they become divided or falter in their duty... then indeed catastrophe may overwhelm us all. **"**

W.S. Churchill, Address at Westminster College, Fulton, Missouri, 5 March 1946, in *Vital Speeches of the Day*, vol.12, 15 March 1946, pp.331–2

Review and Discuss

- What did Churchill mean by the term 'Iron Curtain'?
- How did he view the political situation in the Eastern European states?
- What kind of Western policy did he advocate to meet the Soviet challenge?

SOVIET REACTION

Churchill's Fulton speech provoked a swift Soviet reaction. Towards the end of the speech Churchill had suggested that a fraternal association of English-speaking peoples should lift the Iron Curtain and resist Soviet expansion everywhere. Within a week Stalin attacked Churchill and his 'friends' in America, comparing them to Hitler in that they held to a 'racial theory' that the English-speaking peoples should rule over the remaining nations of the world. Stalin interpreted the speech as 'a set-up for war, a call to war with the Soviet Union'.

Within three weeks of Churchill's Iron Curtain speech Stalin launched a series of policies which, in retrospect, mark the middle months of 1946 as a significant milestone in the history of the Cold War. The Soviets rejected membership of the recently established World Bank and International Monetary Fund (IMF), announced the start of a new five-year plan designed to make Russia self-sufficient in the event of another war, stepped up pressure on Turkey and Greece, and mounted an intense ideological effort to eliminate Western influence and propagate Stalinist dogma. (The ideological campaign was directed by Andrei Zhdanov.)

In August 1946 Stalin sent a formal note to Turkey, which US Under Secretary of State Dean Acheson interpreted as a Soviet attempt to dominate Turkey, threaten Greece and intimidate the remainder of the Middle East. He advised a showdown. Truman agreed: 'We might as well find out whether the Russians were bent on world conquest now as in five or ten years.' Turkey was instructed to stand firm. America sent a powerful naval force, including its most modern aircraft carrier, to the eastern Mediterranean. Soviet pressure on Turkey eased.

Stalin, no doubt, believed that because of its geographic location and wartime sacrifices, Russia had as much right to Iranian oil and control of the Dardanelles as anyone else. Indeed, in February 1946 Stalin had raised in the UN Security Council the matter of British repression of the Greek rebellion. Molotov presented the Soviet view in stinging words at the Council of Foreign Ministers (CFM) in Paris three months later:

> **❝** Nineteenth century imperialism may be dead in England, but there are new twentieth century tendencies. When Mr. Churchill calls for a new war and makes brilliant speeches on two continents, he represents the worst of twentieth century imperialism... Britain has troops in Greece, Palestine, Iraq, Indo-China and elsewhere. Russia has no troops outside the security zones and their lines of communication. This is different. We have troops only where provided by treaties. Thus we are in Poland, for example, as our Allies are in Belgium, France and Holland. I also recall that Egypt is a member of UNO [the United Nations]. She demands that British troops be withdrawn. Britain declines... What shall we say of UNO when one member imposes its authority upon another? How long can such things go on? **❞**

LaFeber, *America, Russia and the Cold War*, pp.37–8

Review and Discuss

- How genuine were the grounds for Molotov's complaint?

AMERICAN VIEWS OF SOVIET POLICY

By the middle of 1946 Truman was running out of patience with Russia and with the sole remaining voice sympathetic to Russia in his administration, that of Secretary of Commerce Henry Wallace. In July 1946 Wallace addressed a long private letter to the President, putting the case for a softening of tone. He then went public with his views in a speech at New York's Madison Square Garden on 12 September 1946. The speech focused on the need for a political understanding with Russia.

> **❝** ...we are reckoning with a force which cannot be handled successfully by a 'get tough with Russia' policy. Getting tough never brought anything real and lasting — whether for schoolyard bullies or businessmen or world powers. The tougher we get, the tougher the Russians will get... The real peace treaty we now need is between the United States and Russia. On our part, we should recognize that we have no more business in the *political* affairs

of Eastern Europe than Russia has in the *political* affairs of Latin America, Western Europe and the United States. We may not like what Russia does in Eastern Europe. Her type of land reform, industrial expropriation, and suppression of basic liberties offends the great majority of the people of the United States. But whether we like it or not the Russians will try to socialize their sphere of influence just as we try to democratize our sphere of influence... Under friendly peaceful competition the Russian world and the American world will gradually become more alike. The Russians will be forced to grant more and more of the personal freedoms; and we shall become more and more absorbed with the problems of socio-economic justice... There will always be an ideological conflict — but this is no reason why diplomats cannot work out a basis for both systems to live safely in the world side by side.

Henry A. Wallace, Address at Madison Square Garden, 12 September 1946, in *Vital Speeches of the Day*, vol. 12, 1 October 1946, pp.738-41

"

Review and Discuss

- How did Wallace view Truman's 'get tough' policy?
- What was Wallace's attitude to the establishment of a Soviet sphere of influence in Eastern Europe?
- What kind of advice did Wallace offer for the conduct of 'peaceful competition'?

At the same time as Wallace's speech in New York, Secretary of State James Byrnes and Senator Arthur Vandenburg were at a CFM meeting in Paris, painfully and unsuccessfully negotiating with Molotov. They immediately cabled Washington, demanding Wallace's resignation. Truman complied. The vigour of their reaction to Wallace's speech was a measure of the distance American policy had moved since the end of World War II. In fact, in the second half of 1946 a growing conviction in the inner circle of the Truman administration had developed that negotiation with the Russians was a waste of time and possibly dangerous.

This conviction was explored in July and August by Clark Clifford, a young and trusted Truman aide whom the President had asked to prepare a comprehensive report on prospects for future Soviet–American relations. Clifford sounded out senior officials in the War, Navy and State Departments. The Russian experts in the State Department were particularly grateful for the consultation after what they saw as years of being bypassed. In his final report Clifford testified to a 'remarkable agreement' among them all that Soviet leaders cling to 'the Marxian theory of the ultimate destruction of capitalist states by Communist states'. All international questions in the long run revolved around the basic threat. 'So long as these men [the Kremlin hierarchy] adhere to these beliefs,' said the Clifford memorandum, 'it is highly dangerous to conclude that hope of international peace lies only in "accord", "mutual under-standing" or "solidarity" with the Soviet Union.' Concessions only raised their hopes and increased their demands. 'The language of military power is the only language which disciples of power politics understand.'

The language and argument of Clifford's memorandum conveyed a similar message about the nature of Soviet conduct to one sent from Moscow in February 1946, by US diplomat George F. Kennan in the famous Long Telegram. 'At bottom of Kremlin's view of world affairs is traditional and instinctive Russian sense of insecurity,' wired Kennan. In post-1917 Russia this became highly explosive when 'oriental secretiveness and conspiracy' mixed with communist ideology. In Kennan's view, the desire to advance communism was a factor in Moscow's aspirations, but the danger was fundamentally Muscovite, not Marxist. Further, Soviet foreign policy 'is not based on any objective analysis of situation beyond Russia's border... it arises mainly from basic inner-Russian necessities which existed before recent war and exist today.' The Kremlin's leaders, stated Kennan, did not know how to govern by any means other than repression; they needed excuses 'for the dictatorship without which they did not know how to rule, for cruelties they did not dare not to inflict, for sacrifices they felt bound to demand'. Picturing the outside world as 'evil, hostile and menacing' provided such an excuse. 'A hostile international environment is the breath of life for prevailing internal system in this country.' The Soviets were fanatically and implacably hostile to the West, in Kennan's view. But they were not suicidal. 'Impervious to logic of reason Moscow [was] highly sensitive to the logic of force. For this reason it can easily withdraw — and usually does — when strong resistance is encountered at any point.'

The Long Telegram brought Kennan to the attention of the Secretary of the Navy, James Forrestal, who had it reproduced and made required reading for thousands of senior officers. Kennan was brought back to Washington to head up the State Department's Policy Planning Staff. In the latter part of 1946 the Clifford memorandum and Kennan's 'logic of force' argument led to a hardening of the American stance in diplomatic dealings with the Russians.

THE TRUMAN DOCTRINE

In January 1947 Truman's Secretary of State Byrnes resigned and was replaced by General George Marshall. On 21 February 1947, as Britain faced economic disintegration after a crippling series of blizzards, the British government informed the State Department that London's role as patron and protector of the Greek and Turkish regimes would have to be surrendered by the end of March. To Marshall, this 'was tantamount to British abdication from the Middle East with obvious implications as to their successor'. State Department experts had been closely monitoring the situation and the British note came as no surprise.

Within a week of the British note Truman and his chief advisers met to formulate policy and confer with Congressional leaders. A low-key presentation by Secretary of State Marshall, focusing on the strategic importance of the eastern Mediterranean and the need for economic aid, evoked little response. Under Secretary of State Dean Acheson then made a forceful presentation. He recalls the occasion in his memoirs:

> " This was my crisis. For a week I had nurtured it. These congressmen had no conception of what challenged them; it was my task to bring it home... Never have I spoken under such a pressing sense that the issue was up to me alone. No time was left for measured appraisal. In the past eighteen months, I said, Soviet pressure on the Straits, on Iran, and on northern Greece had brought the Balkans to a point where a highly possible Soviet break through might open three continents to Soviet penetration. Like apples in a barrel infected by one rotten one, the corruption of Greece would infect Iran and all to the east. It would also carry infection to Africa through Asia Minor and Egypt and to Europe through Italy and France, already threatened by the strongest domestic Communist parties in Western Europe. The Soviet Union was playing one of the greatest gambles of history at minimal cost. We and we alone were in a position to break up the play. "

Dean Acheson, *Present at the Creation*, Hamish Hamilton, London, 1970, p.219

Review and Discuss

- Why did Acheson view the crisis in such a personal way?
- What was the message conveyed by the 'apples in a barrel' analogy?
- In what ways were Acheson's 'apples in a barrel' (in the eastern Mediterranean) similar to Eisenhower's later reference to 'dominoes' (in South-East Asia) (see p. 74)?

(see p. 74)?

Arthur Vandenberg (now Chairman of the Senate Foreign Relations Committee) told Truman that his presidential message to Congress requesting aid for Greece and Turkey must include Acheson's explanation. Indeed, the Senator advised Truman to 'scare hell' out of the American people.

The message that was delivered to Congress on 12 March 1947, requesting $400 million for military aid for Greece and Turkey, was both broad in character and militant in language. The new policy soon became known as the Truman Doctrine.

> " One of the primary objectives of the foreign policy of the United States is the creation of conditions in which we and other nations will be able to work out a way of life free from coercion... We shall not realize our objectives... unless we are willing to help free peoples to maintain their free institutions and their national integrity against aggressive movements that seek to impose upon them totalitarian regimes. This is no more than a frank recognition that totalitarian regimes imposed upon free peoples,

by direct or indirect aggression, undermine the foundations of international peace and hence the security of the United States...

At the present moment in world history nearly every nation must choose between alternative ways of life. The choice is too often not a free one.

One way of life is based upon the will of the majority, and is distinguished by free institutions, representative government, free elections, guarantees of individual liberty, freedom of speech and religion and freedom from political oppression.

The second way of life is based upon the will of a minority forcibly imposed upon the majority. It relies upon terror and oppression, a controlled press and radio, fixed elections, and the suppression of personal freedoms.

I believe that it must be the policy of the United States to support free peoples who are resisting attempted subjugation by armed minorities or by outside pressures.

I believe that we must assist free peoples to work out their own destinies in their own way.

I believe that our help should be primarily through economic and financial aid which is essential to economic stability and orderly political processes...

It is necessary only to glance at a map to realise that the survival and integrity of the Greek nation are of grave importance in a much wider situation. If Greece should fall under the control of an armed minority, the effect upon its neighbour, Turkey, would be immediate and serious. Confusion and disorder might well spread through the entire Middle East...

Should we fail to aid Greece and Turkey in this fateful hour, the effect will be far reaching to the West as well as the East...

The seeds of totalitarian regimes are nurtured by misery and want. They spread and grow in the evil soil of poverty and strife. They reach their full growth when the hope of a people for a better life has died. We must keep that hope alive.

The free people of the world look to us for support in maintaining their freedoms. If we falter in our leadership, we may endanger the peace of the world — and we shall surely endanger the welfare of our own Nation. **99**

Harry S. Truman, Special Message to Congress, 12 March 1947, Public Papers of the Presidents... Harry S. Truman... 1947, Government Printing Office, Washington, 1963, pp.178–80

Review and Discuss

- What contrast was Truman highlighting in his reference to 'alternative ways of life'?
- Why did Truman choose to present the issue of economic aid to Greece and Turkey in such strongly ideological terms?
- Why did Truman view the economic dimension as important in its own right?

The announcement of the Truman Doctrine marked the formal abandonment of the historic US policy of avoiding entanglements in European politics. It also marked the first clearly public step toward active American resistance to 'Communist expansion'. The nature of the policy recommendations and

The US President and his key foreign policy advisers in 1950 (Wide World). Identify the men in the photograph. In what ways were these two advisers to the President the main architects and managers of US foreign policy in the late 1940s and early 1950s?

ideological rationale with which they were presented contained the seeds of future problems. Historian Walter LaFeber presents a longer term assessment of the significance of the Truman Doctrine.

> 66 The Truman Doctrine was a milestone in American history ... First, it marked the point at which Truman used the American fear of Communism both at home and abroad to convince Americans they must embark upon a Cold War foreign policy ... Second ... Congress was giving the President great powers to wage this Cold War as he saw fit. Truman's personal popularity began spiraling upward after his speech. Third, for the first time in the post-war era, Americans massively intervened in another nation's civil war. Intervention was justified on the basis of anti-Communism. In the future, Americans would intervene in similar wars for supposedly the same reason and with less happy results ... Finally, and perhaps most important, Truman used the doctrine to justify a gigantic aid program to prevent a collapse of the European and American economies. Later such programs were expanded globally ... Thus, as Truman and Acheson intended, the doctrine became an ideological shield behind which the United States marched to rebuild the Western political and economic system and counter the radical left. From 1947 on, therefore, any threats to that Western system could be easily explained as communist inspired, not as problems which arose from difficulties within the system itself. That was the most lasting and tragic result of the Truman Doctrine. 99

LaFeber, *America, Russia and the Cold War*, pp.57–8

THE MARSHALL PLAN

Truman's programme developed naturally into the Marshall Plan. Upon his return from Moscow and another fruitless CFM meeting, Secretary of State Marshall declared in a nationwide broadcast that the economy of Western Europe required immediate help: 'The patient is sinking while the doctors deliberate.' Believing that the United States must give the lead in restoring Europe, Marshall set up a planning team under the direction of George F. Kennan.

Weeks of feverish activity were put in by Kennan's team. Before Marshall delivered the formal announcement of the plan, the stickiest point of all needed to be resolved. Would the Soviet Union and Eastern Europe be invited to participate? Marshall asked Kennan what he would say if reporters asked if the Soviets were to be included. After careful reflection Kennan determined that the answer should be yes. He believed, however, that the Russians were certain to turn down the invitation. For one thing they would not like the idea of their Eastern European satellites looking towards the United States for help. For another, they would almost certainly not be prepared to open their economic records to the kind of scrutiny proposed in the plan.

On 5 June 1947, speaking at Harvard University, Marshall announced the plan.

> 66 It is logical that the United States should do whatever it is able to do to assist in the return of normal economic health in the world, without which there can be no political stability and no assured peace. Our policy is not directed against any country or doctrine but against hunger, poverty, desperation and chaos. Its purpose should be the revival of a working economy in the world so as to permit the emergence of political and social conditions in which free institutions can exist... Any government that is willing to assist in the task of recovery will find full cooperation... on the part of the United States Government.
>
> Before the United States Government can proceed much further in its efforts to alleviate the situation and help start the European world on its way to recovery, there must be some agreement among the countries of Europe as to the requirements of the situation and the part those countries themselves will take in order to give proper effect to whatever action might be undertaken by this Government. It would be neither fitting nor efficacious for this Government to undertake to draw up unilaterally a program designed to place Europe on its feet economically. This is the business of the Europeans. The initiative, I think, must come from Europe. 99

George C. Marshall, Address at Harvard University, 5 June 1947, in *Department of State Bulletin*, XVII, 15 June 1947, pp.1159–60

Review and Discuss

- Speaking about Marshall aid to Europe, Acheson stated: 'Relief and reconstruction are chiefly matters of American self interest.' Was this a reasonable judgement on the value of the Marshall Plan from an American perspective?

The reaction to Marshall's speech in Western Europe was enthusiastic. In the middle of June 1947 British Foreign Secretary Ernest Bevin travelled to Paris for talks with his French counterpart Georges Bidault. After initial hesitation it was decided to invite the Russians. Molotov arrived in Paris on 26 June with a team of eighty-nine economic advisers. The Russians were taking the Marshall Plan seriously. Molotov proposed that each nation establish its own recovery programme. The British and French insisted that the conference draw up a European-wide programme as the United States had requested. Molotov angrily walked out, warning of the dangers of a revived Germany and of growing American control of Europe. He declared the plan would 'divide Europe into two groups of states... creating new difficulties in the relations between them'. Within a week of his return to Moscow the Soviets had announced a Molotov Plan for their satellites. Poland and Czechoslovakia, both of whom had expressed initial interest in Marshall's proposals, now informed the Paris Conference that they would not be participating as 'it might be construed as an action against the Soviet Union'.

The remaining sixteen Western European nations put together a request for a four-year aid programme of $17 billion, which still had to be accepted by the American Congress. There was opposition to the Bill and it was not until March 1948 that the Senate, influenced by the communist coup in Czechoslovakia in February 1948, finally endorsed the plan.

Historian LaFeber offers a retrospective judgement.

> 66 The Marshall Plan now appears not the beginning but the end of an era. It marked the last phase in the administration's use of economic tactics as the primary means of tying together the Western world. The plan's approach... soon evolved into military alliances. Truman proved to be correct in saying that the Truman Doctrine and the Marshall Plan 'are two halves of the same walnut.' Americans willingly acquiesced as the military aspects of the doctrine developed into quite the larger part. 99

LaFeber, *America, Russia and the Cold War*, pp.62–3

Review and Discuss

- Why was the United States economic commitment to Western Europe soon translated into a military commitment?

'CONTAINMENT' — PUBLICISED AND CRITICISED

The Truman administration increasingly came to accept the doctrine of containment as a major foreign policy goal. The architect of containment was George F. Kennan, of Long Telegram fame, who published an article in the July 1947 issue of *Foreign Affairs* titled 'The Sources of Soviet Conduct', signed

'Caucasian Dance': a French cartoon of 1950 (source unknown; sighted in History of the 20th Century, Octopus, London, 1976). Identify the dancer in the cartoon. What do the daggers represent? What countries have already received the dagger? What country is the next target? (The communist leaders of that country are accompanying the dancer.)

Mr X. The author's identity was soon widely known and its reception was spectacular. It was excerpted in *Life* and in the *Reader's Digest*. It quickly came to be regarded as a quasi-official statement of American foreign policy.

Kennan's central message and recommendations were presented largely in metaphorical terms:

> The Kremlin is under no ideological compulsion to accomplish its purposes in a hurry... The Kremlin has no compunction about retreating in the face of superior force. And being under the compulsion of no timetable, it does not get panicky under the necessity for such retreat. Its political action is a fluid stream which moves constantly, wherever it is permitted to move, toward a given goal. Its main concern is to make sure that it has filled every nook and cranny available to it in the basin of world power. But if it finds unassailable barriers in its path, it accepts these philosophically and accommodates itself to them. The main thing is that there should always be pressure, increasing constant pressure, towards the desired goal...
>
> These considerations make Soviet diplomacy at once easier and more difficult to deal with than the diplomacy of individual aggressive leaders like Napoleon and Hitler. On the one hand it is more sensitive to contrary force, more ready to yield on individual sectors of the diplomatic front when that force is felt to be too strong, and thus more rational in the logic and rhetoric of power. On the other hand it cannot be easily defeated or discouraged by a single victory on the part of its opponents. And the

patient persistence by which it is animated means that it can be effectively countered not by sporadic acts which represent the momentary whims of democratic opinion but only by intelligent long range policies on the part of Russia's adversaries — policies no less steady in their purpose, and no less variegated and resourceful in their application, than those of the Soviet Union itself.

In these circumstances it is clear that the main element of any United States policy toward the Soviet Union must be that of a long-term, patient but firm and vigilant containment of Russian expansive tendencies...

The Soviet pressure against the free institutions of the Western World is something that can be contained by the adroit and vigilant application of counter-force at a series of constantly shifting geographical and political points, corresponding to the shifts and manoeuvres of Soviet policy, but which cannot be charmed out of existence.

Mr X (George F. Kennan), 'The Sources of Soviet Conduct', *Foreign Affairs*, vol. 25, July 1947, pp.566–82

Review and Discuss

- What did Kennan see as the main characteristics of Soviet foreign policy?

- What were the implications for United States foreign policy?

Although Kennan's article contained many qualifications, he would later complain that he had not qualified sufficiently, and that therefore in 1947 his article was misread. In particular he did not believe that the Russians posed any serious military threat, nor did he think they wanted war. The challenge he saw was political and economic. Nevertheless the widely quoted sentence that the United States policy needed the 'adroit and vigilant application of counter-force' did lead to misunderstanding. Most readers took Kennan to mean that crisis would follow crisis around the world as Soviet agents conspired to accelerate the flow of communist power into every 'nook and cranny'. Containment was certainly interpreted to mean building up America's military strength and that of her allies and being prepared to stand up to the Russians wherever they applied the pressure.

Kennan's article triggered one of the more interesting debates of the Cold War. In a series of newspaper articles later published in book form, Walter Lippmann, dean of American journalists, replied to Mr X. Lippmann argued forcefully that Soviet policy was moulded more by traditional Russian expansionism than by communist ideology.

Walter Lippmann, *The Cold War: A Study in United States Foreign Policy*, Harper, New York, 1947, pp.23, 26

Mr X has neglected even to mention the fact that the Soviet Union is the successor of the Russian Empire and that Stalin is not only the heir of Marx and Lenin but of Peter the Great, and the Czars of all the Russians... It was the mighty power of the Red Army, not the ideology of Karl Marx, which enabled the Russian government to expand its frontiers.

By interpreting the Soviet advance in terms of the traditional Russian quest for security, it followed in Lippmann's argument that the Soviets would be agreeable to an offer of withdrawal of both Russian and American power from Central Europe. This would defuse the potentially explosive situation there.

Lippmann rejected Truman's 'two halves of the same walnut' argument. He condemned the military aspects of the Truman Doctrine, while applauding the Marshall Plan. He stressed that there was a fundamental difference between them.

> The Marshall proposal was not, as Mr Molotov and many Americans who do not understand it have tried to make out, an extension to Europe as a whole of the experiment in Greece. Quite the contrary. In Greece we made an American plan, appropriated the money, entered Greece and are now trying to induce the Greek government to carry out our plan. In the Harvard speech Secretary Marshall reversed the procedure. He told the European governments to plan their own rehabilitation, and that then he would go to Congress for funds, and that then the European governments would have to carry out their plans as best they could with the funds he could persuade Congress to appropriate.
>
> The difference is fundamental. The Truman Doctrine treats those who are supposed to benefit by it as dependencies of the United States, as instruments of the American policy for 'containing' Russia. The Marshall speech at Harvard treats the European governments as independent powers, whom we must help but cannot presume to govern, or to use as instruments of an American policy...

Lippmann, *The Cold War: A Study in United States Foreign Policy*, p.45

Review and Discuss

- What was the fundamental difference between the Marshall Plan and the Truman Doctrine, according to Lippmann?

- Why did Lippmann have such high regard for the Marshall Plan?

RUSSIAN REACTIONS AND RESPONSES

The Soviet Union had played a relatively quiet role in international affairs since the Iranian and Turkish crises of 1946. However, Molotov's departure from the Paris Conference discussing the Marshall proposals in July 1947 signalled a turning point. Rebuilding Europe through a plan closely tied to the interests of American capital clearly threatened Stalin's hopes of influencing developments in Western Europe. Far worse, from Stalin's perspective, was the linking of that Europe to a revived West Germany.

The Soviet view of the purpose of the Truman Doctrine and Marshall Plan as instruments of American foreign policy was presented to the Russian people in August 1947 in an article in *Pionerskaya Pravda*, a newspaper for young people:

> President Truman has announced the following principles of American foreign policy: the United States will everywhere support with weapons and money reactionaries, Fascists who are hateful to their own people but who on the other hand are ready to place their country under American control. Two countries suitable for this were found at once: Greece and Turkey. Now they both have in fact come under American domination. Americans are building their military bases there, American capitalists are opening businesses and buying up all that seems to them profitable. For this the Greek and Turkish reactionaries, who are in power, are receiving from the Americans money and weapons for the struggle against their own people. But Greece and Turkey are too small, and American appetites are great. American expansionists are dreaming of all Europe, or at least Western Europe. Directly to propose that the European countries become American colonies such as Greece and Turkey is somewhat inconvenient. And so the 'Marshall Plan' emerges in America. It was announced that the United States wanted 'to help' the European countries to reconstruct their war-destroyed economies. Many believed this. But it was soon evident that the 'Marshall Plan' was simply a cunning way of subjecting all Europe to American capital.

Quoted in Walter Beddel Smith, *Moscow Mission 1946-1949*, Heinemann, London, 1950, pp.165-6

Review and Discuss

- According to the Soviet view, why did the United States become involved in the internal affairs of Greece and Turkey?
- Why was Stalin anxious to persuade the public in the Soviet Union and Eastern Europe that the Marshall Plan was 'a cunning way of subjecting all Europe to American capital'?

On his return from Paris, Molotov moved quickly to tighten Soviet control of the Eastern bloc. The so-called Molotov Plan, a programme of bilateral trade agreements, began to link the bloc countries with the Soviet Union. The final step in this programme was the establishment in January 1949 of the Council for Mutual Economic Assistance (Comecon), which created a centralised agency for stimulating and controlling economic development in the Eastern bloc.

Of greater significance was Molotov's announcement of the establishment of the Communist Information Bureau (Cominform). Comprising communists from Russia, Yugoslavia, France, Italy, Poland, Bulgaria, Hungary and Rumania, the Cominform was designed as another instrument for increasing Stalin's control. At the inaugural meeting in Warsaw in September 1947 Stalin's chief ideological lieutenant, Andrei Zhdanov, delivered a major speech on Soviet foreign policy. A recent writer, Myron Rush, has called the speech 'the classic

Soviet statement on the origin and significance of the cold war'. The master image used by Zhdanov (as Stalin had before him) in his address — a massive struggle between 'two camps' — acknowledged the essentially bipolar nature of post-war politics.

Zhdanov's speech began with an analysis of the 'nature of the present epoch'. The decisive role played by the Soviet Union in the victory over fascism 'sharply altered the alignment of forces between the two systems — the socialist and the capitalist — in favour of socialism'. As a result of the war, only two great imperialist powers remained, Britain and the United States. The former had been seriously weakened, in part by the 'crisis of the colonial system'. The latter was attempting to consolidate its monopoly position and reduce its capitalist partners to a state of dependency and 'proclaimed a new frankly predatory and expansionist course'.

Zhdanov's analysis climaxed with the announcement that American economic power, fattened by the war, was organising Western Europe and 'countries politically dependent on the United States, such as the Near Eastern and South American countries and China' into an anti-communist bloc. Its purpose was 'to strengthen imperialism, to hatch a new imperialist war, to combat socialism and democracy, and support reactionary and anti-democratic, pro-fascist regimes and movements everywhere'.

The second camp was based on but not limited to the Soviet Union and the new 'democracies' in Eastern Europe; 'Indonesia and Vietnam are associated with it; it has the sympathy of India, Egypt and Syria.' Backed by the 'fraternal communist parties in all countries', its purpose was to 'resist the threat of new wars and imperialist expansion, to strengthen democracy and to extirpate the vestiges of fascism'.

The two camps view of the world bore a striking resemblance to Truman's two worlds scenario. The mirror image was even more striking in Zhdanov's urging of the socialist camp not to lower its guard.

Andrei Zhdanov, Report on the International Situation to the Cominform, 22 September 1947, in Rush (ed.), *The International Situation and Soviet Foreign Policy*, p.138

66 The chief danger to the working class at this present juncture lies in underrating its own strength and overrating the strength of the enemy. Just as in the past the Munich policy untied the hands of the Nazi aggressors, so today concessions to the new course of the United States and the imperialist camp may encourage its inspirers to be even more insolent and aggressive. 99

Review and Discuss

● What similarities or differences are there in the views of the world held by Zhdanov and Truman?

In the latter part of 1947 and early 1948 there was a significant tightening of Soviet control in the Eastern bloc. By the end of 1947 the Soviet Union and her client communist parties were in firm control of all Eastern Europe, except Czechoslovakia.

Then came the fall of Czechoslovakia. The Western world had a strong emotional interest in Czechoslovakia — no doubt partly the result of guilt feelings over the Munich agreement. By late 1947 the lure of Western aid and internal political changes began to pull Czechoslovakia away from Soviet influence. In February 1948 Stalin moved. The resignation of twelve non-communist ministers from the coalition government led to the demand by the leader of the Czech Communist Party for the formation of a new government under communist control. The demand was backed up by intense Soviet diplomatic pressure and the veiled threat of armed interference. Sensing his country's isolation, President Eduard Beneš complied with the demands. Two weeks later Foreign Minister Jan Masaryk died in mysterious circumstances. The coup in Czechoslovakia, in the words of Truman, 'sent a shock wave throughout the civilized world'.

Ironically, this extension of Soviet control to Czechoslovakia occurred just as the solidarity of relations between the Soviet Union and Yugoslavia was being questioned. Although there was little doubt about Marshal Tito's communist orthodoxy and loyalty to the Soviet Union, his ability to operate in Yugoslavia from an army and party base under his own and not Stalin's control was annoying the Soviet dictator. Despite a sustained campaign of diplomatic,

'The two blocs': an American cartoon of 1949 (courtesy Walt Kelly; sighted in Robert O. Paxton, Europe in the Twentieth Century, HBJ, New York, 1975). Who are the two leaders and their unruly children? What message is conveyed by the quotation from Keats?

economic and military pressures, and Yugoslavia's expulsion from the Cominform, the solidarity of the Yugoslavs' internal support for Tito, together with timely assistance from the West, enabled Tito to stand firm.

Apparently unwilling to risk war to remove Tito, Stalin launched a series of bloody purges in Eastern Europe. As the whole region underwent purges and forced Sovietisation, the main functions of the Cominform came to be the enforcement of uniformity and the conduct of the struggle against Titoism.

THE BERLIN BLOCKADE

With Tito thus excluded from the fold, the one remaining chink in the Iron Curtain from Stalin's viewpoint was Germany and particularly Berlin. In June 1948 Berlin became the scene of the most dramatic confrontation between East and West in this phase of the Cold War.

The Yalta image of occupied Germany as a single administrative and economic unit had been consistently eroded, but the Soviets did not seem ready to opt finally for a divided Germany. They were still both attracted by the possibility of a unified and demilitarised Germany under pro-communist rule, and haunted by fears of the threat that might emanate from a rebuilt and rearmed Western Germany tied into the American sphere of influence. This concern was evident from the stance adopted by the Soviets at the CFM Moscow meeting in March–April 1947, which again failed to reach agreement on the German question.

In February 1948 the Western allies began to carry out much-needed currency reform in their zones. Moscow apparently interpreted these moves as a prelude to the remilitarisation of West Germany and its transformation into the armed instrument of America's anti-Soviet coalition.

On 5 March 1948 the American General in Berlin, Lucius D. Clay, sent a telegram to Washington which had a powerful effect. '[Although] I have felt and held that war was unlikely for at least ten years, within the last few weeks, I have felt a subtle change in the Soviet attitude which... gives me a feeling that it may come with dramatic suddenness.' The Soviet officials in Germany had adopted a new attitude, 'faintly contemptuous, slightly arrogant, and certainly assured'.

In Washington, London and Paris there was a real war scare. In Brussels a series of meetings was held between France, Britain and the Benelux countries and on 16 March 1948 they signed the Brussels Union, pledging mutual defence arrangements. Truman applauded the treaty and the United States Joint Chiefs of Staff proposed a military alliance with the Brussels powers.

Stalin's foreign policy, based on an occupied and divided Germany, a weakened Western Europe and tight control in Eastern Europe, faced a major challenge. The Soviet Union was being hemmed in by the West with plans for West Germany to play a key role in the new coalition. Worst of all, deep in the heart of the Soviet security belt, the Western sector of Berlin remained a symbolic outpost. Stalin now reasoned that since the West had abandoned the idea of German reunification there was no longer any point in retaining Berlin as the future capital of a united Germany. The logic of their own policies dictated that the Western powers should retire to their own zones. On 24 June 1948 the Soviets placed a total blockade on all land and water traffic between Berlin and the Western zones. The Western allies imposed a counter-blockade on the movement of goods from the East into West Germany.

In the West there was some sentiment to abandon Berlin. After all, there was force in Stalin's argument that if the West was going to create a West German state it had no business remaining in East Germany. Clay and Truman soon put an end to such talk. In a telephone conference with the War Department, General Clay was adamant:

> We have lost Czechoslovakia, Norway is threatened. We retreat from Berlin. When Berlin falls Western Germany will be next. If we mean... to hold Europe against Communism we must not budge. We can take humiliation and pressure short of war in Berlin without losing face. If we withdraw, our position in Europe is threatened. If America does not understand this now, does not know that the issue is cast, then it never will and Communism will run rampant. I believe the future of democracy requires us to stay... This is not heroic pose because there will be nothing heroic in having to take humiliation without retaliation.

Lucius D. Clay, *Decision in Germany*, Doubleday, New York, 1950, pp.361–2

Review and Discuss

- Why were the Russians trying to force the West out of Berlin?

- Why did General Clay oppose withdrawal from Berlin?

General Clay was prepared to shoot his way through to run the Soviet blockade. In his view the United States might just as well find out immediately if the Russians wanted war or not. The Army Chief of Staff, Omar Bradley, conscious of the ten-to-one disparity in ground strength in Europe, convinced Truman that there had to be a better way. It was found with air transport. For nearly eleven months West Berlin was supplied by air and vast quantities of supplies were flown in at immense cost.

The war scare continued for some time. On 15 July Truman's National Security Council decided to send two groups of B–29 bombers to Britain. The B–29s were known around the world as the bombers that carried atomic weapons. Secretary of Defense James Forrestal clearly noted the rationale in his diary: (1) it would show the American public 'how seriously the government... views the current sequence of events'; (2) it would provide experience for the Air Force and 'would accustom the British' to the presence of the US Air Force; and (3) 'we have the opportunity *now* of sending these planes, and once sent they would become somewhat of an accepted fixture', whereas if America waited, the British might change their minds about the wisdom of having American planes on their soil.

Truman assured Forrestal and Marshall that, although he prayed that the A-bomb would not have to be used, he was prepared to use it if it became necessary. He denied, however, a Pentagon request to have control of the bomb transferred from the President to the military. Truman did not intend, as Forrestal noted in his diary, 'to have some dashing lieutenant colonel decide when would be the proper time to drop one'.

The United States military obviously made giant strides out of the Berlin crisis. It is true they were denied control of the A-bomb, but the principle of American forward bases in Europe had been established. It was obvious to the military that if they were to be effective there would need to be more of them and they would need to be scattered. Meanwhile the recent events had emphasised the need for closer military connection with Western Europe. The draft was reintroduced and there was a move to build up the United States Army.

THE FORMATION OF THE NORTH ATLANTIC TREATY ORGANISATION

Having been re-elected at the end of 1948, Truman pledged in his inaugural address to aid those European nations willing to defend themselves, while the new Secretary of State, Dean Acheson, moved to cement an alliance with the Western Europeans. On 4 April 1949 in Washington the North Atlantic Treaty was signed by twelve nations: the United States, Canada, Britain, France, Italy, Portugal, the Benelux countries, Denmark, Norway and Iceland. They pledged to use force only in self-defence, and to develop 'free institutions', particularly through the encouragement of 'economic collaboration between any or all' of the parties. The heart of the matter was Article 5:

> ❝ The Parties agree that an armed attack on one or more of them in Europe or North America shall be considered an attack against them all; and consequently they agree that, if such an armed attack occurs, each of them… will assist the Party or Parties so attacked by taking forthwith, individually and in concert with the other Parties, such action as it deems necessary, including the use of armed force, to restore and maintain the security of the North Atlantic area. ❞

North Atlantic Treaty, 4 April 1949, in E. May (ed.), *Anxiety and Affluence*, McGraw Hill, New York, 1966, p.87

The formation of the North Atlantic Treaty Organisation (NATO) was followed by victory by the West in Berlin. On 12 May 1949 the Russians lifted the blockade. On 23 May 1949 the Federal Republic of Germany, with its capital in Bonn, came into being. A constitution was drawn up and elections were held in September 1949. Konrad Adenauer became the new republic's first Chancellor. The Soviets responded by establishing the German Democratic Republic (GDR) in their zone of occupation. The Soviet Union refused to recognise the existence of the Federal Republic and the West refused to recognise East Germany.

The NATO alliance came into effect on 24 August 1949. By this time the economic recovery of Western Europe was well under way. West Berlin had been successfully defended, while in Greece the communist partisans had been crushed. Yugoslavia was still independent of the Soviet orbit. B–29 bombers of the US Air Force were stationed in East Anglia in the United Kingdom and were the ultimate guarantee of Western collective security. A new balance of power had been achieved in Europe thanks to the resolution of the Western allies.

THE SHIFT
TO ASIA

I N ITS EARLY STAGES the Cold War was centred in the eastern Mediterranean and Europe, and the American policy of containment, while worldwide in its implications, was largely confined to Europe in its application. If Stalin were to resort to military force to expand his communist empire, it was expected that the blow would come in the West. Barely a year after NATO was formed, Stalin did attempt to extend his empire by military means, but the blow came not in the West but the Far East in remote Korea.

THE SOVIET UNION AND CHINA

At first glance it is somewhat surprising that the Soviet Union paid so little attention to Asian affairs in the years immediately following World War II. Not only was a communist army challenging the ruling elite of the world's largest country, but the old British, French and Dutch colonial empires in South-East Asia were collapsing, leaving considerable anti-Western feeling and political instability in their wake. Stalin obviously gave priority to protecting Soviet security in Europe. There was also the memory of his unsuccessful involvement in China in 1927, making him wary of co-operating with communist forces that he could not directly control.

Thus Mao Zedong's rise to leadership of the Chinese Communist Party (CCP) in 1935 had taken place without Soviet involvement. Further, Mao's peasant-based struggle with the nationalist regime of Jiang Jie-shi had grown and endured without Soviet support or endorsement. The Soviets did turn over to Mao in March 1946 the portion of Manchuria under their occupation and the arms captured from the Japanese. This forced Jiang to dissipate enormous resources in trying to recapture it from the communists. Even as late as 1947, following the failure of Marshall's effort at mediation and the turning of the tide of battle in Mao's favour, the Soviets continued to play down the CCP's successes.

CCP efforts were virtually ignored in the Soviet media. The Chinese communists were not invited to the founding conference of the Cominform.

By 1947 the nationalists and communists were locked in an all-out military struggle. The initial advantages appeared to be with the nationalists, but by early 1949 Jiang had lost half his troops and eighty per cent of the equipment given to him by the United States. Before the end of 1949 he fled with the remnants of his army to the island of Formosa (Taiwan). Meanwhile in September 1949 Mao Zedong had announced the formation of the People's Republic of China with its capital at Beijing (Peking). Not until then did the Soviets formally recognise the changed situation in China.

The Soviets had adopted a similar ambivalent stance towards revolutionary movements elsewhere in Asia. Only in 1949, with the success of the Chinese communists, did the Soviets publicly support the armed struggle already being carried out by communists in Indo-China, Indonesia, India, Burma, Malaya and the Philippines. By the end of 1949 the Soviet press was explicitly commending to its Asian comrades the 'Chinese path' to revolution and was unambiguously endorsing armed struggle as the primary tactic in this process. In February 1950 a Sino–Soviet Treaty of Alliance, Friendship and Mutual Assistance was concluded.

AMERICA AND CHINA

Meanwhile the Truman administration in America, confronted with the impending nationalist collapse in China, undertook the task of explaining to the nation the failure of its China policy. In August 1949 the United States State Department issued a lengthy White Paper that sought to silence opponents of its China policy. The two volumes contained the diplomatic correspondence between the United States and China over the previous generation. The United States had extended over $2 billion in grants and credits to Jiang's nationalists, but the nationalist failure was the result of a great internal change within China, a genuine revolution that was beyond the control of the United States.

In the introduction to the White Paper, Secretary of State Dean Acheson said:

> 66 It has been argued that relatively small amounts of additional aid — military and economic — to the National Government would have enabled it to destroy communism in China. The most trustworthy military, economic, and political information available to our Government does not bear out this view.
>
> A realistic appraisal of conditions in China, past and present, leads to the conclusion that the only alternative open to the United States was full-scale intervention on behalf of a Government which had lost the confidence of its own troops and its own people. Such intervention would have required the expenditure of even greater sums than have been fruitlessly

Dean Acheson, Extract
from State Department
White Paper on China,
1949, in May (ed.), *Anxiety
and Affluence*, p.105

spent thus far, the command of Nationalist armies by American officers, and the probable participation of American armed forces — land, sea and air — in the resulting war. Intervention of such scope and magnitude would have been resented by the mass of the Chinese people, would have diametrically reversed our historic policy, and would have been condemned by the American people. **99**

Review and Discuss

- What kind of American intervention would have been required to prevent the Nationalist collapse of China?

- How far were the consequences of such intervention later realised as a result of United States involvement in Vietnam?

During the last months of 1949 the foreign policy of the Truman administration received a series of blows: the loss of China to the communists, a divisive debate over NATO and the news that the Soviets had exploded a nuclear device. There was also the matter of the relationship with Japan. Having occupied Japan since the end of the war, the United States had begun to negotiate a peace treaty to normalise relations. However, there was mounting uneasiness and to a certain extent open hostility among the Japanese because of the American desire to retain military bases on the islands.

In January 1950 Truman ordered 'an overall review and reassessment of American foreign and defence policy'. Officials of the Departments of State and Defense and the National Security Council prepared a report that was ready by April 1950. National Security Council Memorandum 68 (NSC–68) has been described by historian Walter LaFeber as 'one of the key historical documents of the Cold War'.

NSC–68 forecast 'an indefinite period of tension and danger' and advocated 'an immediate and large scale build-up in our military and general strength and that of our allies with the intention of righting the power balance and in the hope that through means other than all-out war we could induce a change in the nature of the Soviet system'. The paper called for a build up of conventional United States forces and the annual expenditure of $50 billion on defence, a rise of 300 per cent.

How real was the Soviet threat? Later revisionist historians have rightly criticised the perceptions of Soviet behaviour and intentions presented in NSC–68 and other security assessments. But it is necessary to remember the political context.

William S. Taubman,
Stalin's American Policy,
Norton, New York, 1983,
p.199

66 Revisionists may contend that NSC–68, like the Truman Doctrine before it, presented a false rationale for expansion having little to do with any real Soviet threat. In fact, Acheson and others were deliberately overstating a case in which they genuinely believed — the better to rouse those in government whom they considered dangerously complacent or unwilling to put their money where their anti-communist mouths were. **99**

Would Americans be prepared to 'put their money where their anti-communist mouths were'? Would they be prepared to foot the bill for the 'bold and massive program' recommended by NSC-68 to meet the Soviet challenge? Events in Korea would answer these questions.

WAR IN KOREA

Russian troops moved into the northern part of Korea shortly before the Japanese surrender in August 1945 and a short time later American troops occupied the south. The occupation zones were divided arbitrarily at the 38th parallel, and it was assumed that an independent Korean government would eventually take over.

In late 1947 the United States took the Korean question to the United Nations General Assembly. Elections were held under United Nations auspices in South Korea, but UN representatives were denied entry to North Korea. The Russians proceeded to establish a People's Republic, led by Kim Il Sung, and to train and equip a strong army in North Korea. The United Nations-sponsored election established the Republic of Korea led by Syngman Rhee in the south. There were frequent border clashes between the two Koreas, neither of which recognised the legitimacy of the other government.

The United States substantially reduced its military forces in South Korea in June 1949. General Douglas Macarthur wanted troops in Japan and military planners believed that Korean forces could resist an attack. These American moves created a certain ambiguity about the degree of United States commitment in Korea. Moscow in all probability calculated that Washington would decide not to come to South Korea's defence. On 25 June 1950 seven North Korean infantry divisions and an armoured division launched an all-out attack across the 38th parallel. They were equipped with Soviet weapons, while Soviet instructors advised the higher ranks of the North Korean army. It is inconceivable that the attack could have been launched without Moscow's sanction.

Truman's response was immediate and decisive. Within hours of the news of the invasion, he instructed Macarthur to send arms and supplies to the South Koreans. He also sent the United States Seventh Fleet to the Formosan Straits to counter any Chinese moves over Formosa. In an emergency session on the afternoon of 25 June the UN Security Council adopted a resolution branding the North Koreans as aggressors, and demanding a withdrawal beyond the 38th parallel. The absence of the Soviet delegate, protesting over the failure of the United Nations to admit communist China, meant the Soviet veto was not used.

Within three days the invaders had captured the capital Seoul and Truman began to commit American air and naval forces into the fighting. On 27 June the UN Security Council, with the Soviet delegate still absent, adopted an American-sponsored resolution calling on member nations to provide all necessary assistance to the Republic of Korea. Three days later Truman made

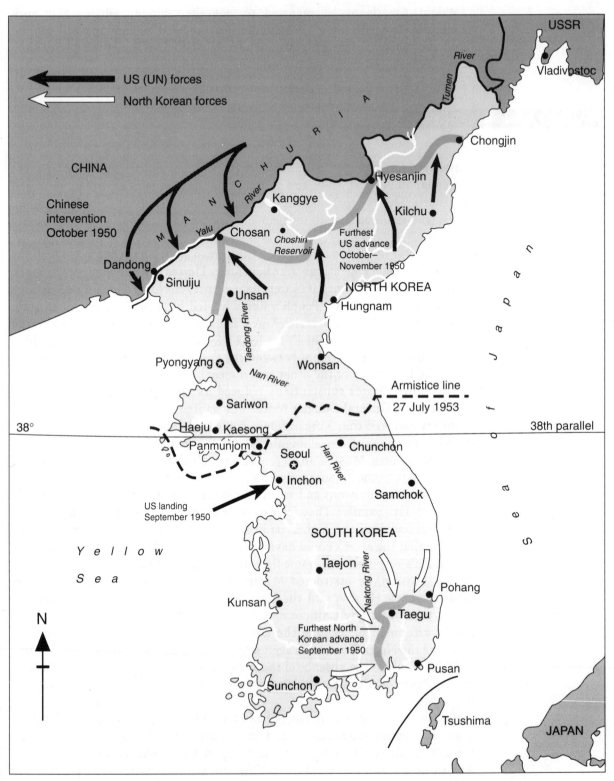

US (UN) forces

North Korean forces

CHINA

Chinese
intervention
October 1950

M A N C H U R I A

Kanggye

Yalu River

Dandong

Chosan

Choshin
Reservoir

Furthest
US advance
October–
November 1950

Kilchu

Hyesanjin

Chongjin

Tumen River

USSR

Vladivostoc

Sinuiju

Unsan

Taedong River

NORTH KOREA

Hungnam

S e a   o f   J a p a n

Pyongyang

Nan River

Wonsan

Armistice line
27 July 1953

Sariwon

38°

Haeju   Kaesong

Panmunjom

Seoul

Han River

Chunchon

38th parallel

Inchon

Samchok

US landing
September 1950

Y e l l o w

S e a

N

SOUTH KOREA

Taejon

Naktong River

Pohang

Kunsan

Taegu

Furthest North
Korean advance
September 1950

Pusan

Sunchon

Tsushima

JAPAN

The Korean War
1950–53

the difficult decision to send two divisions of American ground troops from Japan to Korea. America was now at war on the mainland of Asia.

Truman gave his own account of the reasoning behind the decision to resist North Korean aggression in his *Memoirs*:

> In my generation this was not the first occasion when the strong had attacked the weak. I recalled some earlier instances: Manchuria, Ethiopia, Austria. I remember how each time the democracies failed to act it had encouraged the aggressors to keep going ahead. Communism was acting in Korea just as Hitler, Mussolini, and the Japanese had acted ten, fifteen, and twenty years earlier. I felt certain that if South Korea was allowed to fall communist leaders would be emboldened to override nations closer to our own shores. If the Communists were permitted to force their way into the Republic of South Korea without opposition from the free world, no small nation would have the courage to resist threats and aggression by stronger Communist neighbours. If this was allowed to go unchallenged it would mean a third world war, just as similar incidents had brought on the second world war. It was clear to me that the foundations and the principles of the United Nations were at stake unless the unprovoked attack on Korea could be stopped.

Harry S. Truman, *Memoirs*, vol.2, Doubleday, New York, 1955, p.333

Review and Discuss

- Why did Truman conclude that resistance to North Korean aggression was necessary?

- How did Truman make use of a 'lessons of history' approach to foreign policy?

It is interesting to compare Truman's account of the rationale for US involvement in Korea with the official statement on the outbreak of war issued by Andrei Gromyko, Soviet Deputy Minister of Foreign Affairs, on 4 July 1950.

> The events now taking place in Korea broke out on June 25 as the result of a provocative attack by the troops of the South Korean authorities on the frontier areas of the Korean People's Democratic Republic. This attack was the outcome of a premeditated plan.
>
> From time to time Syngman Rhee himself and other representatives of the South Korean authorities had blurted out the fact that the South Korean Syngman Rhee clique had such a plan.
>
> As long ago as October 7, 1949, Syngman Rhee, boasting of success in training his army, stated outright, in an interview given to an American *United Press* correspondent, that the South Korean Army could capture Pyongyang in the course of three days...
>
> Only one week before the provocative attack of the South Korean troops on the frontier areas of the Korean People's Democratic Republic, Syngman Rhee said, in a speech of June 19 in the so-called 'National Assembly' where Mr. Dulles, adviser to the U.S. State Department, was present: 'If we cannot protect democracy in the cold war, we shall win in a hot war.'

It is not difficult to understand that representatives of the South Korean authorities could only make such statements because they felt that they had American support behind them...

Only one week before the events... Mr. Dulles, adviser to the State Department, declared in the above-mentioned 'National Assembly' of South Korea that the United States was ready to give all necessary moral and material support to South Korea which was fighting against Communism.   **"**

A.A. Gromyko, Statement on American Intervention in Korea, *Soviet News*, no.2393, 5 July 1950, pp.1–2

Review and Discuss

- What is the major weakness in Gromyko's explanation for the outbreak of hostilities in Korea?

- How did Gromyko perceive America's role? Was this perception justified?

THE CHANCE OF 'ROLLBACK'

By mid-September 1950 the American and South Korean forces had turned back the North Korean invasion, thanks largely to Macarthur's brilliant amphibious landing at Inchon near the western end of the 38th parallel. Within days Seoul was recaptured and Macarthur's men had driven the North Koreans back to the 38th parallel. The Truman administration then made the crucial decision to advance into North Korea to the Yalu River (the border with China), in an attempt to reunify Korea. The United Nations General Assembly voted for a 'united, independent and democratic Korea'. The decision was taken despite the administration's assertions in June and July that the US effort aimed only at clearing South Korea north to the 38th parallel. Stephen Ambrose comments:

" In Washington there was a surge of optimism. Perhaps it was possible to do more than contain the communists. Macarthur wanted to reunify Korea, an idea that found great favour in the White House. It would mean rollback not containment, and thus represented a major policy change, but the opportunity was too tempting to pass up. On September 1 Truman announced that the Koreans had a right to be 'free, independent and united.' Pyongyang, the Americans boasted, would be 'the first Iron Curtain capital' to be liberated. This seemed to imply that others would follow...

Macarthur's broad authority to invade North Korea... came after full discussion and consideration at the highest levels of the American government. Truman later implied, and millions believed, that Macarthur had gone ahead on his own, that it was the general in the field, not the government at home, that had changed the political objective of the war in the middle of the conflict. Such was never the case. Truman, with the full concurrence of the State and Defense Departments and the Joint Chiefs, made the decision to liberate North Korea and accept the risks involved.   **"**

Ambrose, *Rise to Globalism*, pp.121–3

Macarthur's forces crossed the 38th parallel on 7 October 1950 and began a rapid advance up the peninsula. By the end of October they were within eighty kilometres of the Yalu River. Although the Truman administration did not believe the Chinese would intervene in the war in Korea, it wanted to ensure that air strikes were confined to the Korean peninsula. This concern was the major reason for Truman's famous conference with Macarthur on Wake Island in mid-October. Macarthur assured Truman repeatedly that 'the Korean conflict is over and that there was little possibility of the Chinese coming in'.

On 11 November 1950 the Chinese Foreign Ministry issued a public statement delivered to the United Nations via India, indicating its support for North Korea and willingness to 'repel United States aggression in Korea'.

> **“** Righteously indignant, many Chinese citizens are expressing a desire to help the Korean people and resist American aggression. Facts have shown that the aim of United States aggression in Korea is not only Korea itself but also the extension of aggression to China. The question of the independent existence or the downfall of Korea has always been closely linked with the security of China. To help Korea and repel United States aggression means to protect our own homes and our own country. It is, therefore, completely natural for the Chinese people to be ready to help Korea and offer resistance to United States aggression...
>
> The American aggressors have gone too far. After making a five-thousand mile journey across the Pacific they invaded the territories of China and Korea. In the language of the American imperialists that is not aggression on their part, whereas the just struggle of the Chinese in defence of their land and their people is aggression. The world knows who is right and who is wrong...
>
> The Korean question can be solved only by the people of North and South Korea themselves; this is the only way in which the Korean problem can be solved peacefully. The Chinese people ardently loves peace but it will not be afraid to take action against aggressors and no aggressors can intimidate it. **”**

United Nations Document S/1902, 15 November 1950, pp.2–4

This Chinese account of the nature of American involvement in Korea should be considered alongside the following account by a British historian:

> **“** [The Chinese] could not tolerate the loss of the North, anymore than the United States had been able to tolerate the original invasion. It was not simply that they would lose face if they allowed an ally to be defeated, or that communism might lose an adherent state. The Chinese also had too much reason to fear that if they allowed the United States to appropriate North Korea they would shortly have to face another Yankee initiative elsewhere. Chiang Kai-shek might be launched on an attempted reconquest of China itself with full American assistance. There was a lot of loose talk going around to that effect... The Chinese looked at the Americans through the same sort of telescope as that which the Americans were pointing at them. They too seemed to see a self-confident aggressor power making the first moves in a campaign that, unless checked, might lead on to world conquest. They too felt that the moment to avert a Third World War was now, the place here. **”**

Hugh Brogan, *The Pelican History of the United States of America*, Penguin, Harmondsworth, 1986, pp.625–6

Review and Discuss

- How do these two sources explain Chinese intervention to save North Korea?
- What similarities and differences are there between the two accounts?

- How useful is the 'telescope' metaphor in explaining Chinese and American actions in Korea?

In late November 1950, thirty-three Chinese divisions hit the middle of the United Nations line. The communists forced the United Nations troops to retreat, within weeks had quickly cleared the northern peninsula and Seoul changed hands for the third time. The speed of the Chinese victory caused Truman to contemplate whether to use the atomic bomb on China. This offhand remark at a press conference sent a perturbed British Prime Minister rushing to Washington, counselling against the use of the 'winning weapon' for the third time in five years against an Asian people. Truman withdrew the threat.

The Korean War now changed its character. It was realised by the Truman administration that the war could only be brought to a successful conclusion if the original objective, of saving South Korea, was accepted as all that was attainable.

Macarthur was informed by Washington on 20 March 1951 that Truman was about to seek a settlement of the war through diplomatic means. At this point the General openly challenged the President. On 24 March Macarthur defiantly threatened mainland China with an attack. In Truman's judgement this threat effectively killed any hope of an early truce. But Macarthur went further. In early April a letter from Macarthur to a United States Congressman was read out in the House of Representatives. It called for a new direction in American foreign policy. The General wanted to reunify Korea, unleash Jiang for an attack on the mainland and fight communism in Asia rather than in Europe. In Macarthur's words: 'Here in Asia is where the communist conspirators have elected to make their play for global conquest. Here we fight Europe's war with arms while the diplomats there still fight it with words.'

Truman exploded. 'If what Macarthur had proposed had happened ... we would have wound up being at war not only with Red China but with Russia too and ... it might have meant the destruction of a good part of the world.' On 11 April the President, with the approval of the Joint Chiefs of Staff, relieved Macarthur of his command.

Macarthur's sacking created a public furore in America. The White House received a flood of complaining letters and telegrams. Flags were flown at half mast in Massachusetts and Ohio and Truman was burned in effigy in towns across the country. Republican leaders in Washington urged a Congressional investigation and talked of impeaching the President.

"We've Been Using More Of A Roundish One"

US strategic
objectives in Korea:
an American cartoon
of 1951 (Washington
Post). Identify the
two figures in the
cartoon. What is
meant by the
reference to using a
'roundish one'? What
is the danger of the
'squarish one'?

THE MACARTHUR HEARINGS

Within a few days Macarthur flew into San Francisco and began a triumphal
tour of the United States. Millions crowded downtown Manhattan for the largest
New York ticker-tape parade since Charles Lindbergh's triumphal procession
in 1927. Macarthur was given an opportunity to explain how the President
had forbidden him to win when he addressed a joint session of Congress on
19 April:

> Our victory [in Korea] was complete and our objectives within reach when
> Red China intervened with numerically superior ground forces... While
> no man in his right mind would advocate sending our ground forces into
> continental China... the new situation did urgently demand a drastic revi-
> sion of strategic planning if our political aim was to defeat this enemy
> as we had defeated the old...

It has been said in effect that I was a war-monger. Nothing could be further from the truth. I know war as few other men living know it, and nothing, to me, is more revolting... But once war is forced upon us, there is no other alternative than to apply every available means to bring it to a swift end... War's very object is victory, not prolonged indecision. In war there is no substitute for victory. There are some who, for varying reasons, would appease Red China. They are blind to history's clear lesson, for history teaches, with unmistakeable emphasis, that appeasement but begets new and bloodier war. It points to no single instance where this end has justified that means... Like blackmail it lays the basis for new and successively greater demands until, as in blackmail, violence becomes the only other alternative. Why, my soldiers asked of me, surrender military advantage to an enemy in the field? I could not answer. **99**

United States Senate, Committee on Armed Services and Committee on Foreign Relations, *Military Situation in the Far East [Macarthur Hearings]*, Government Printing Office, Washington, 1951, pp.353–8

Macarthur's attack on the Truman administration's limitation of the war in Korea was followed by an historic Congressional investigation into the General's dismissal, the conduct of the Korean War, and indeed Macarthur's claim that the Truman administration had 'no policy... nothing... no plan or anything'. Secretary of Defense George Marshall summed up the essence of America's containment policy:

66 There can be, I think, no quick and decisive solution to the global struggle short of resorting to another world war. The cost of such a conflict is beyond calculation. It is therefore our policy to contain Communist aggression in different fashions in different areas without resorting to total war... The application of this policy has not always been easy or popular. **99**

United States Senate, *Macarthur Hearings*, p.366

Possibly the strongest testimony against Macarthur's strategy in Korea was presented to the Congressional committee hearings by General Omar Bradley, Chairman of the Joint Chiefs of Staff, who reminded his listeners of the classical principles of strategy in relation to one's most dangerous enemy.

66 The Joint Chiefs of Staff, in view of their global responsibilities and their perspective with respect to the worldwide strategic situation, are in a better position than is any single theatre commander to assess the risk of general war. Moreover, the Joint Chiefs of Staff are best able to judge our own military resources, the raw materials, and the industrial capacity essential to world domination. If Soviet Russia ever controls the entire Eurasian land mass, then the Soviet-satellite imperialism may have the broad base upon which to build the military power to rule the world...

Korea, in spite of the importance of the engagement, must be looked upon with proper perspective. It is just one engagement, just one phase of this battle that we are having with the other power centre in the world which opposes us and all that we stand for...

As long as we keep the conflict within its present scope we are holding to a minimum the forces we must commit and tie down.

The strategic alternative, enlargement of the war in Korea to include Red China, would probably delight the Kremlin more than anything else we could do. It would necessarily tie down additional forces, especially our sea power and our air power, while the Soviet Union would not be obliged to put a single man in the conflict.

Under present circumstances, we have recommended against enlarging the war...

Red China is not the powerful nation seeking to dominate the world. Frankly, in the opinion of the Joint Chiefs of Staff, this strategy would involve us in the wrong war, at the wrong place, at the wrong time, and with the wrong enemy.

United States Senate,
Macarthur Hearings,
pp.730–2

"

Review and Discuss

- What strategy did Macarthur advocate in the Far East? Why?
- What was the reasoning behind the Joint Chiefs recommending against Macarthur's strategy?

- How did the debate over Macarthur's strategy illustrate the central role accorded to 'containment' in United States foreign policy?

The Korean drama was not ended with the uproar associated with Macarthur's recall. In April and May 1951 American forces and their United Nations allies repulsed two major Chinese communist offensives, trials of strength that in retrospect marked the end of Stalin's major offensive against the West. Military action had bogged down in the general vicinity of the 38th parallel. When the Soviet delegate to the United Nations suggested in June 1951 that an armistice be arranged with mutual withdrawal of the two sides behind the 38th parallel, Washington welcomed the move. Leaders of the opposing forces began discussions with a view to an armistice in July 1951. Talks broke down and continued in an 'on-again, off-again' fashion for the next two years.

STRENGTHENING THE WESTERN ALLIANCE: THE AMERICAN DIPLOMATIC OFFENSIVE

From the very beginning of the Korean conflict the Truman administration used the threat of communist expansion as an instrument to strengthen the Western alliance. Historian Walter LaFeber summarises the American initiatives:

" Although the war was limited to Korea, Truman and Acheson used the war as an opportunity to develop new American policies around the globe. Because of these American initiatives, the six months between June and December 1950 rank among the most important of the Cold War era.

Truman and Acheson moved to the offensive globally for two particular reasons: the Korean War gave them an opportunity to shut up their critics at home and to take advantage of new openings abroad...

> The offensive would... allow the administration to put plans into motion that had been on drawing boards up to a year or more. These included the NSC–68 blueprint and the revitalization of American military alliances around the world. So began the spectacular summer of 1950 in which Truman and Acheson transformed the United Nations, committed the United States to Formosa and IndoChina, began rearming Germany, nearly tripled American defence spending and invaded North Korea in order to show opponents at home and abroad that the United States was no longer content with mere 'containment' but now aimed for liberation. **99**

LaFeber, *America, Russia and the Cold War*, pp.105–6

Acheson's first step was to push through the UN General Assembly during the latter part of 1950 a Uniting for Peace proposal. This gave the assembly the right to recommend collective security measures to United Nations members, including the use of force, thus effectively nullifying the power of the Soviet veto in the Security Council. United Nations action in Korea had only been possible because of the absence of the Soviet delegate in the critical debates. This weakening of the Russian veto also weakened that of the United States. Henceforth power was passed to the General Assembly where all nations had equal voting power.

Acheson's diplomatic offensive also involved Formosa and Indo-China. On Macarthur's recommendation American advisers and assistance were sent to Jiang. This move signalled the United States decision to side with Jiang in the intra-Chinese dispute over Formosa.

Events in Korea also accelerated United States involvement in Indo-China. After World War II the United States had helped the French to return to power in Indo-China. For the first two years of the insurrection against the French the United States had not taken an active interest. Then with the collapse of Jiang's nationalists, American policy shifted as Washington saw the French standing in the way of a communist sweep of South-East Asia. In February 1950 the Truman administration agreed to send $18 million in military aid to the French to fight the war against Ho Chi Minh's Vietminh nationalists in Indo-China.

These Asian commitments were regarded as necessary, but Truman and Acheson continued to regard Europe as the area of most importance. A number of moves were implemented in order to tighten not only the military but political and economic aspects of the Western alliance. In September 1950 Acheson met with the British and French Foreign Ministers at the Waldorf Astoria Hotel in New York. There he dropped the 'bomb at the Waldorf'. The United States proposed to create ten divisions of German troops to be part of the Western alliance. The British and French were horrified. Acheson's insistence was accompanied by an offer of further United States financial aid, plus the sending of four divisions of United States troops to Europe, plus the establishment of an integrated NATO military command. Shortly after, General Eisenhower, popular and trusted in Europe, was appointed Supreme Commander of NATO forces. Reluctantly the British and French agreed.

Truman was clearly putting the United States on a cold war footing. At the end of 1950 the President was granted emergency powers by Congress to expedite war mobilisation. He submitted a $50 billion defence budget that followed NSC–68 guidelines — a significant contrast to the $13.5 billion budget of six months before. At the same time it was agreed that two more divisions be sent to Europe, making a total of six; that the size of the army be increased by fifty per cent to 3.5 million men, and that the number of air groups be doubled to ninety-five. New airfields were established in Morocco, in Libya and in Saudi Arabia; moves were set in train to admit Greece and Turkey to membership of NATO. Discussions were also begun with Franco's fascist administration in Spain, leading to the establishment of military bases there.

The Truman administration also stepped up the pace of negotiations on the peace treaty with Japan. The treaty, signed in September 1951, excluded the Russians, provided for American military bases and allowed for conditional Japanese rearmament and unlimited industrialisation. At the same time the United States signed the ANZUS Treaty with Australia and New Zealand, pledging the security of those two nations.

Historian Stephen Ambrose sums up the achievements and legacy of the Truman administration in the field of foreign affairs:

> Truman's accomplishments were breathtaking. He had given the United States a thermonuclear bomb… and rearmed Germany. He pushed through a peace treaty with Japan, extended American bases around the world, hemming in both Russia and China…
>
> There had to be a price… The Truman administration [wrote Walter Millis] left behind it 'an enormously expanded military establishment, beyond anything we had ever contemplated in time of peace… It evoked a huge and apparently permanent armament industry, now wholly dependent on government contracts. The Department of Defense had become the biggest industrial management operation in the world; the great private corporations, like General Motors, du Pont, the leading airplane manufacturers had assumed positions of monopoly power'… The administration produced thermonuclear super giant weapons, families of lesser atomic bombs, guided missiles, the B–52 jet bomber, new super carriers and tanks and other heavy weapons. It has increased the risk of war while making war immeasurably more dangerous.
>
> One other thing bothered Millis. For all that the Truman administration accomplished 'what it failed to do was to combine these men and weapons into a practicable structure of military policy competent to meet the new political and military problems that now stood grimly before us. We were to face them in a large measure of bewilderment as to where the true paths of military policy might lead.'

Ambrose, *Rise to Globalism*, pp. 126–7

Review and Discuss

- How would Truman's 'accomplishments' have appeared from the Soviet point of view?

- What 'price' did America have to pay for Truman's accomplishments?

SOVIET COUNTERMOVES

From the Soviet perspective the Korean War, like the Berlin blockade, had backfired. Each had failed to achieve its immediate objectives and both confrontations had helped to stimulate the military mobilisation of the West.

The rise of Georgi Malenkov to the position of Stalin's second in command had important implications for Soviet relations with the West. It appeared to coincide with a new effort on Moscow's part to break its isolation and broaden Soviet and communist appeal, while at the same time weakening Western solidarity. The most obvious example of the new Soviet approach was the so-called peace movement of 1948–52. Moscow's use of the peace movement to further its objectives is discussed in Chapter 14.

The Soviets did not rely only on arousing public opinion in their efforts to weaken the Western alliance. Formal diplomatic contacts were employed in the Soviet campaign to oppose the rearmament of West Germany and its incorporation into the NATO alliance.

As these efforts seemed to be making some progress, the Soviet Union proposed a meeting of foreign ministers in November 1950 to resume negotiations on a German peace treaty that would be accompanied by a united and demilitarised German state. Western diplomats did not take up the offer.

On 10 March 1952 Moscow made its most intriguing proposal on the status of Germany. The Soviet note proposed that discussions be held on a peace treaty that would declare Germany united and independent. The note further suggested that Germany be allowed to have its own army with ties neither to East nor West, and that all foreign troops be withdrawn from Germany. It was a breathtaking proposal, but one the Western powers refused to follow up.

Expert opinion has remained divided over the genuineness of the Soviet proposal of 10 March 1952. Some argue that Stalin was making a serious and last-ditch effort to reach a compromise on the persistent problem of Germany and that he was actually prepared to sacrifice communist East Germany for the larger purpose of preventing West Germany's rearmament and incorporation into the Western defence network. Others argue that the United States and the Adenauer government in Bonn were correct to reject the proposal as a flagrant attempt to derail the Western defence plans.

There is in fact some evidence to suggest that toward the end of his life Stalin moved towards a more accommodating position with the capitalist West. This he did in his last theoretical writing, *Economic Problems of Socialism in the U.S.S.R.*, written for the 19th Party Congress in October 1952. The main thrust of Stalin's argument was a restatement of the classic Leninist thesis that wars between capitalist states continued to be inevitable. Those comrades who believed that war was no longer inevitable were mistaken: 'To eliminate the inevitability of war, it is necessary to abolish imperialism.' The kind of war to be expected was unambiguously stated: 'wars between capitalist countries'.

But what about war between the Soviet Union and the United States? Stalin played down this possibility. He admitted that theoretically the contradictions between capitalism and socialism were greater than those between capitalist nations, but they were not so in reality, because 'the struggle of the capitalist countries for markets and their desire to crush their competitors proved in practice to be stronger than the contradictions between the capitalist camp and the socialist camp'. Although Stalin's theoretical analysis was poor, the political import of his message was clear: the Soviet Union was prepared to take steps to avoid a general war with the United States.

The message — that a lessening of tensions between the Soviet Union and the United States was possible — was confirmed in Malenkov's Report to the 19th Party Congress.

> The Soviet policy of peace and security of the peoples proceeds from the fact that the peaceful co-existence and co-operation of capitalism and Communism are quite possible provided there is a mutual desire to co-operate, readiness to adhere to commitments entered into, and observance of the principle of equality and non-interference in the internal affairs of other states...
>
> We are confident that in peaceful competition with capitalism, the socialist system of economy will prove its superiority over the capitalist system more and more vividly year by year. We have no intention, however, of forcing our ideology or our economic system on anybody. 'Export of revolution is nonsense,' says Comrade Stalin. 'Every country will make its own revolution if it wants to, and if it does not want to there will be no revolution.'

Georgi Malenkov, Report to 19th Party Congress, 5 October 1952, in Rush (ed.), *International Situation and Soviet Foreign Policy*, pp.152–3

There is therefore evidence to suggest that in Stalin's last years the militant tactics of class struggle and confrontation were giving way to an approach that sought to use political pressure against the West in an attempt to weaken its unity and alter its policies. Such tactical changes did not constitute a major reorientation of the Soviet approach to world affairs and it was only after Stalin's death in March 1953 that a more venturesome strategy to break the Cold War stalemate was attempted. By that time the American nation itself was under new leadership.

PART TWO

New Leaders, New Strategies

OPPORTUNITY FOR PEACE OR 'IRRECONCILABLE CONFLICT'?

CHAPTER FOUR

B Y THE TIME of Stalin's death many commentators on international affairs had come to the conclusion that a stalemate had been reached between Western and communist camps. In May 1953 the London *Observer* offered the following editorial comment:

> In every conflict there comes a moment when the true balance of forces is fully tested and established, and nothing can be gained by further hostilities. That is the moment which must be seized if a durable peace is to be made...
>
> In the present world conflict this moment is now upon us. For a year or so now, the balance and limit of the opposed forces have been clearly established both in Europe and in Asia...
>
> Both in Europe and Asia the methods of cold war — propaganda, subversion, boycott, blockade, armed demonstrations, local insurrections — have reached the end of their tether. Since nobody can want a war which would threaten to destroy the world without promising to unite it, the only chance today is between a prolonged military stalemate and a negotiated peace 'based on facts.'
>
> The Russians have given clear indications that they are prepared to try for the latter alternative... The most difficult part of the art of peacemaking, however, is the transition from the mentality of conflict to the mentality of conciliation, without which negotiations lead nowhere...
>
> No imaginable peace settlement can remove the deep ideological differences between Communism and western liberalism... All that a peace settlement can remove is the foreseeable causes of war, and the fear of war, between States. Further, no peace settlement based on the existing balance of power can have as its condition the liberation of the Communist countries in Eastern Europe. It might have as its result some liberalization both in their external relations and in their internal regimes.

The *Observer* (London),
17 May 1953

On Stalin's death, Georgi Malenkov assumed the role of Soviet Premier and Nikita Khrushchev became First Party Secretary. Vyacheslav Molotov reassumed his old position of Foreign Minister. Malenkov soon departed from

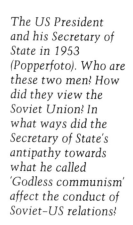

The US President and his Secretary of State in 1953 (Popperfoto). Who are these two men? How did they view the Soviet Union? In what ways did the Secretary of State's antipathy towards what he called 'Godless communism' affect the conduct of Soviet-US relations?

Stalin's foreign policy. In April 1953 he called for the opening of talks between East and West aimed at reducing forces in Europe and negotiating a settlement in Korea.

EISENHOWER, DULLES AND THE 'NEW LOOK'

The American reaction was hesitant and confused. Only six weeks before Stalin's death a new administration had taken office in Washington. The new president was former General Dwight Eisenhower, of whom a Republican adviser had remarked in early 1952: 'Let's face it. The only excuse for Ike's candidacy is that he's the man best qualified to deal with Stalin.' However, the personality of the new Secretary of State was to be more significant for East–West relations. John Foster Dulles was to dominate not only American foreign policy, but the whole of Western strategy until his death in 1959. In a famous article in the magazine *Life* in May 1952 Dulles put forward his view that in international relations 'dynamic' spiritual values prevailed over 'static' forces.

> 66 The dynamic prevails over the static; the active over the passive. We were from the beginning a vigorous, confident people, born with a sense of destiny

and mission. That is why we have grown from a small and feeble nation to our present stature in the world... Our dynamism has always been moral and intellectual rather than military or material...

There is a moral or natural law not made by man which determines right and wrong and in the long run only those who conform to that law will escape disaster. This law has been trampled by the Soviet rulers, and for that violation they can and should be made to pay...

We should let these truths work in and through us. We should be *dynamic*, we should use *ideas* as weapons; and these ideas should conform to *moral* principles. That we do this is right, for it is the inevitable expression of a faith — and I am confident that we still do have a faith... **99**

John Foster Dulles, 'A Policy of Boldness', *Life*, 19 May 1952

The intensely ideological nature of Dulles' view of Soviet Russia was confirmed by his testimony at his nomination hearing before the Senate Foreign Relations Committee.

66 Soviet Communism believes that human beings are nothing more than somewhat superior animals... and that the best kind of a world is that world which is organized as a well-managed farm is organized, where certain animals are taken out to pasture, and they are fed and brought back and milked, and they are given a barn as shelter over their heads... I do not see how, as long as Soviet communism holds those views... there can be any permanent reconciliation... This is an irreconcilable conflict. **99**

US Senate, 83rd Congress, 1st Session, on the Nomination of Dulles, 15 January 1953, pp.10–11

Review and Discuss

- Why is it appropriate to describe Dulles' view of Soviet communism as 'ideological'?

- What effects would the holding of such a view be likely to have on America's relationship with the Soviet Union?

At the time of Eisenhower's presidency it was widely believed that Dulles had a free hand and wide responsibility in conducting foreign policy. Later observers are not so sure. Historian Robert Divine has recently argued, in *Eisenhower and the Cold War* (1981), that Eisenhower used Dulles. The President gave Congress a Secretary of State so militant in his rhetoric that it would be appeased. Dulles did go a long way toward satisfying the most vulgar of Congressional critics, Senator Joseph McCarthy, who had called for a purge of 'comsymps' (communist sympathisers) in the State Department.

This was the background to the hesitant and confused American reaction to Malenkov's peace initiative. In part it can be explained in terms of the usual problems found in changing governments. Far more significant was the fear aroused by McCarthyism. No one in the State Department wanted to incur the wrath of Senator McCarthy by suggesting a positive response to the Soviet initiative. In any event, Secretary of State Dulles, with his ideological view of 'Godless communism' was loath to respond favourably to Malenkov's overture.

Senator Joe McCarthy during the Army–McCarthy hearings, June 1954 (UPI). What was McCarthy demonstrating with the aid of the map? Describe the appearance of the chief counsel for the Army, Joseph Welch. How justified was Welch's reference to McCarthy (9 July 1954) as a 'cruelly reckless character assassin'?

Eisenhower made the first formal response to the new Soviet Premier's tactics on 16 April 1953. Détente could come, the President admitted, if the Soviets agreed to 'free elections in a United Korea', the end of communist revolts in Malaya and Indo-China, 'a free and united Germany with a government based on free and secret elections', the 'free choice' of governments in Eastern Europe, and a treaty restoring Austria's independence. The following day Dulles appeared before the Senate Foreign Relations Committee. The *New York Times* headlined his remarks: 'DULLES BIDS SOVIETS CO-OPERATE OR FACE VAST WEST ARMING'.

This belligerent American approach was questioned by the foremost states-person in the Atlantic alliance, the arch anti-communist and opponent of appeasement, British Prime Minister Winston Churchill. On 11 May he called for a summit conference of world leaders to see which problems might be solved. Churchill recommended a piecemeal approach, tackling solvable problems but recognising the need to assure Soviet security concerns. Churchill's call unnerved officials in Washington, fearful of a 'Far Eastern Munich'. Despite Churchill's urging, no meeting with the Soviet leaders took place before 1955.

The Eisenhower administration proclaimed a New Look (Eisenhower's phrase) in the area of defence. The new Defense Secretary, Charles E. Wilson, summed up the administration's defence policy in terms of getting a 'bigger bang for the buck'. The New Look required the Defense Department to reduce the size of conventional forces and rely upon nuclear weapons to intimidate the Russians into acquiescence. The Air Force, with its nuclear-armed bombers, would win the race for more defence dollars, while the Army, especially the infantry, was cut by half a million men. Naturally enough, these changes upset the

Army — the Army Chiefs wanted enough flexibility to be able to meet the communist threat at the appropriate level. The problem with Eisenhower's New Look, they argued, was that it locked the United States into an all-or-nothing response.

BRINKMANSHIP AND ITS APPLICATION

Dulles confirmed, before the Council on Foreign Relations on 12 January 1954, that in future the United States would no longer be bound to use conventional arms to fight the Soviet Union. Instead he proclaimed a policy of 'massive retaliatory power' to halt aggression. The issues in the strategic debate on the doctrine of 'massive retaliation' are examined in Chapter 12. Dulles' speech ignited a firestorm of protest. Editorialists in the *New York Times* and Walter Lippmann in the *New York Herald Tribune* accused Dulles of going to the 'brink of war' to threaten the Soviets.

University of Chicago professor, Hans Morgenthau, was also sceptical of Dulles' position:

> The shift from the traditional weapons of local defense to atomic weapons... on the one hand, limits our ability to meet local aggression by local means, as we did in Korea, and, on the other, increases the temptation to use the atomic bomb against local aggression where under the old strategy we might have used traditional weapons... For the immediate threat to the security of the West arises not from local aggression, Soviet inspired or otherwise, nor from atomic war deliberately embarked upon by the Soviet Union, but from the revolutionary fire which is sweeping through much of Asia, Africa, Western Europe and Latin America. Atomic retaliation can only be an answer to open military aggression. It stands to reason that to drop atomic bombs on Moscow or Peking is no answer to the threat of Communist revolution in Italy or Indo-China. The crucial problem of national and social revolutions, that Moscow did not create but which it exploits, Mr Dulles fails to see.

Hans J. Morgenthau, 'Instant Retaliation', *The New Republic*, 29 March 1954

Review and Discuss

- What did Morgenthau regard as the major weakness of 'massive retaliation' as a defence strategy?

- What did Morgenthau see as the 'immediate threat' to Western security and how did he think it should be handled?

Eisenhower himself refused to join the debate. He told reporters that Dulles was 'merely stating what, to my mind, is a fundamental truth'. He informed a 17 March 1954 press conference that the beauty of the policy of massive retaliation was its purposeful vagueness. No one 'would undertake to say exactly what we would do under all that variety of circumstances'.

Dulles used the threat of massive retaliation as the chief instrument of containment. He called his overall method 'brinkmanship', which he explained in an interview published in *Life* magazine early in 1956.

> 66 You have to take chances for peace, just as you must take chances in war. Some say that we were brought to the verge of war. Of course we were brought to the verge of war. The ability to get to the verge without getting into the war is the necessary art. If you cannot master it, you inevitably get into wars. If you try to run away from it, if you are scared to go to the brink, you are lost. We've had to look it square in the face — on the question of enlarging the Korean war, on the question of getting into the Indo-China War, on the question of Formosa. We walked to the brink and we looked it in the face. We took strong action. 99

Interview with John Foster Dulles, *Life*, 16 January 1956

The three instances of going to the brink cited by Dulles in the *Life* interview were all in Asia. The first came in Korea. Eisenhower, determined to cut his losses and get out, warned that unless the war could be brought to an end quickly, the United States might retaliate 'under circumstances of our own choosing'. Dulles informed Beijing (through India) that if peace did not come, the United States would bring in atomic weapons. The communists indicated their willingness to resume the Korean truce talks and an armistice was signed in July 1953. The Korean War was finally over, but a permanent settlement failed to emerge in the aftermath of the armistice. Instead, Korea was divided like Germany, into communist and non-communist states.

THE WAR IN INDO-CHINA

The second application of Dulles' method of brinkmanship came in 1954, in Indo-China, where the French colonial rulers had encountered increasing resistance in the years after World War II. In 1949 France had broken up Indo-China and granted Laos, Cambodia and Vietnam 'independence within the French Union', but the French retained total control over foreign and military affairs and matters of internal security. They also still dominated the economic life of the area. A strong nationalist movement had developed in Vietnam, led by Ho Chi Minh.

War in Vietnam dragged on for years with Ho's resistance forces employing Mao Zedong's doctrines of peasant guerrilla warfare. Both the Truman and Eisenhower administrations regarded Ho Chi Minh as a communist agent of Beijing and Moscow and the war in Vietnam as another example of communist aggression. In August 1953 the National Security Council warned that 'the loss of Indochina would be critical to the security of the United States' and urged full support for the French war effort.

The war went badly for the French, however, and by early 1954 they were on the verge of military collapse at Dien Bien Phu. In March a panicky French government sent its Chief of Staff to Washington to request American intervention.

Eisenhower and his advisers were fully aware of the implications of a French defeat in the Indo-China War. Early in April the President warned:

Public Papers of the Presidents... Dwight D. Eisenhower, 1954, Government Printing Office, Washington, 1960, pp.382–3

> 66 You have a row of dominoes set up. You knock over the first one, and what will happen to the last one is that it will go over very quickly. So you have the beginning of a disintegration that would have the most profound significance. 99

Dulles felt strongly that the United States could not permit the loss of Vietnam to the communists and Vice-President Richard Nixon enthusiastically backed the suggestion for possible use of atomic weapons to lift the siege at Dien Bien Phu.

In the end, however, Eisenhower decided against intervention, feeling that the French had badly mishandled their affairs in Indo-China by clinging to an imperial role. More significant, Eisenhower would not act without support from the British government and the United States Congress, neither of which was forthcoming. Democrat Senator John F. Kennedy proclaimed that an American war in Indo-China would be 'dangerous, futile, and self-destructive'.

Dien Bien Phu fell to the Vietminh on 7 May 1954. A new French socialist government under Pierre Mendés-France came to power in June vowing to end the war in one month. France agreed to open negotiations at Geneva with the Vietminh and the British, Soviets and Chinese. American participation was ambiguous. Dulles had walked out of the Geneva Conference prior to the change of government in France, leaving behind an American observer.

The Soviets and the Chinese applied pressure to the Vietminh to accept a division of Vietnam at the 7th parallel, reasoning that it was only a matter of time before Ho Chi Minh's forces completed their unification of the country. Ho agreed to withdraw. Elections were to be held within two years and Western observers agreed with Ho's prediction that the polls would give him complete control of the whole of Vietnam.

The United States never signed the Geneva Accords (July 1954), nor did any South Vietnamese government. Dulles, however, did openly announce that the Americans would support 'free elections supervised by the United Nations' and would not use force to upset the agreements. Shortly after this the United States began a programme of direct aid to the government of South Vietnam. The United States also brought Ngo Dinh Diem (the aristocratic former leader of South Vietnam) from exile in New York to take over the government of South Vietnam over the strenuous objections of the French. The French withdrew from South Vietnam, and President Diem announced that he would not be holding the elections called for in the Geneva Accords. The United States supported the decision, arguing that Diem's government had not signed the Geneva agreement. The United States continued to arm and supply the government of South Vietnam.

Dulles moved to strengthen the US position in South-East Asia. On 8 September 1954 in Manila, the South East Asian Treaty Organisation (SEATO) was created by representatives of the United States, Britain, France, Australia, New Zealand, Pakistan, Thailand and the Philippines. Dulles welcomed SEATO as a vital part of the American security system in East Asia — an Asian counterpart to NATO — but it is important to note the differences between the two alliances. Unlike NATO, SEATO had no armed forces of its own and no permanent command structure or standing military organisation. India, Burma and Indonesia did not join. This was no NATO for South-East Asia but rather a Western — especially American — effort to regulate the affairs of Asia from the outside.

In its second application, in Indo-China, brinkmanship had failed. Dulles faced his third major challenge in the Formosa Straits, this time achieving his objective.

THE FORMOSA STRAITS

During the 1952 presidential campaign the Republicans complained that the Truman administration had hamstrung Jiang Jie-shi in his attempt to win back control of China, by sending the Seventh Fleet to the Formosa Strait to restrain him from invading China while the Korean War was going on. Vowing to 'unleash' Jiang, the Eisenhower administration had removed the fleet in 1953. In August 1954 Chinese communist Foreign Minister Zhou Enlai renewed the pledge to liberate Taiwan from the nationalists. Eisenhower responded by remarking that 'any invasion of Taiwan would have to run over the Seventh Fleet', which now returned to protect the nationalists. In September 1954 communist artillery on the mainland began shelling the nationalist positions on the islands of Quemoy and Matsu, possibly as a prelude to assaulting them.

Eisenhower resisted calls from the Joint Chiefs of Staff to bomb the mainland. He sent Dulles to Taiwan to restrain Jiang. The Secretary of State worked out a defence treaty with the nationalists under which the United States pledged itself to defend Taiwan and to station American military forces 'in and about' the area. In return Jiang agreed not to use force against the mainland without first consulting the USA.

Early in March 1955 Dulles returned from a further trip to Asia and announced that the situation in Asia was worse than he had realised. He told a news conference that he feared a communist attack on Quemoy and Matsu as a prelude to an invasion of Taiwan. A major war scare was touched off when the Secretary of State declared 'if we defend Quemoy and Matsu we'll have to use atomic weapons'. With war fever running high, Eisenhower began to backtrack. Asked about the use of atomic bombs to defend Quemoy at his 23 March press conference, the President replied that he could not make any predictions: 'Every war is going to astonish you in the way it occurred, and in the way it is carried out.' Eisenhower thereby managed to warn the Chinese without saying what he would actually do.

At a press conference on 28 April Eisenhower said he had a 'sixth sense' that the outlook for peace had brightened. He revealed that he had been in correspondence with his old wartime friend Marshal Zhukov, who was now one of the Soviet leaders. Chinese pressure on Quemoy and Matsu lessened and the crisis receded. (The two islands were the scene of a similar crisis late in 1958 when the communists resumed shelling.) Brinkmanship had held the line.

THE PATH TO THE GENEVA SUMMIT

On 8 August 1953, before the Supreme Soviet, Malenkov saluted the ending of the Korean conflict as a 'great victory for the camp of peace and democracy' in Korea. He listed the cases in which the Soviet Union had recently acted to reduce tensions or was actively seeking normalisation of diplomatic and trade relations, and saluted the 'friendly ties and brotherly co-operation between the countries of the democratic camp', including the 'strong and unbreakable ties of friendship' in Sino–Soviet relations. He went on to observe:

G. Malenkov, Report to the Supreme Soviet, 8 August 1953, in Rush (ed.), *International Situation and Soviet Foreign Policy*, p.160

> The active struggle for peace conducted with fixity of purpose by the Soviet Union and the entire democratic camp has yielded definite results. A change in the international atmosphere is to be observed. After a long period of mounting tension, one feels for the first time since the war a certain easing of the international situation.

The Soviet Premier commented on the American atomic programme and included the specific statement: 'The Government considers it necessary to inform the Supreme Soviet that the United States has no monopoly of the hydrogen bomb either.' In a concluding summary Malenkov declared:

> Soviet foreign policy is clear. The Soviet Union will consistently and firmly pursue a policy of preserving and consolidating peace, will promote co-operation and business relations with all states which have a like desire, and strengthen the ties of brotherly friendship and solidarity with the great Chinese people, with all the People's Democracies.
>
> We firmly stand by the belief that there are no disputed or outstanding issues today which cannot be settled peacefully by mutual agreement between the parties concerned.
>
> This also relates to disputed issues between the United States of America and the Soviet Union. We stand, as we have stood in the past, for the peaceful co-existence of the two systems. We hold that there are no objective reasons for clashes between the United States of America and the Soviet Union.

G. Malenkov, Report to the Supreme Soviet, 8 August 1953, in Rush (ed.), *International Situation and Soviet Foreign Policy*, p.162

Review and Discuss

- How did Malenkov's view of the current state of Soviet-American relations differ from that of Dulles? (See pp. 69–70).

- How did the political context of each statement help explain the difference in perception?

Mention has already been made of the fact that as early as April 1953 British Prime Minister Winston Churchill had expressed a desire to meet with the new Soviet leaders at a Big Four Summit. American reservations have been discussed. It seems that Malenkov, too, wished to proceed cautiously. Certainly the Soviets proceeded to a top level meeting only by a series of stages.

The first stage was a Conference of Foreign Ministers (CFM) in Berlin early in 1954 on the perennial issue of Germany. Molotov, the Soviet Foreign Minister, suggested that a provisional German government be set up by the West and East German regimes, to hold all German elections under conditions of 'genuine freedom'. The Western powers were sceptical that the Russians would allow genuinely free elections.

Molotov had a further proposal. He called for the abandonment of NATO and the conclusion of a treaty on European security between the West and Eastern European states. The proposal, which offered a security pact that excluded the United States and left the European continent open to Soviet hegemony, appeared 'so preposterous that when Molotov read it, laughter rippled around the Western sides of the table to the dismay of the Communist delegation' (according to Dulles' account). The first Big Four conference in five years broke up without agreement.

Following the ratification in October 1954 of the Paris Agreements (which created the Western European Union [WEU] and provided for West Germany's admission to NATO), the Soviet bloc states convened in Warsaw in May 1955 to adopt a Pact of Mutual Assistance and Unified Command. Article 5 of the Warsaw Pact established a joint command of the armed forces committed to the alliance, and Article 6 established a Political Consultative Committee to co-ordinate the foreign policies of the allies. In this way the Warsaw Pact (no doubt intentionally) mirrored the NATO alliance and provided a symbolic symmetry to the European defence systems. It provided a new basis for the stationing of Soviet troops in Eastern Europe, which was to be used by the Soviets in Hungary in 1956 and again in Czechoslovakia in 1968.

There was one further important step along the path to a Big Four Summit. Quite suddenly in February 1955, Molotov announced that the Soviets were prepared to drop their previous demand that the Austrian and German problems be treated together. In May 1955 a CFM in Vienna signed the Austrian State Treaty, which ended the four-power occupation and created an independent, neutral Austria. The Soviet change of policy was perhaps meant as an indication to the West Germans that the Soviet Union was prepared to make concessions if West Germany broke or loosened its close links with the Western powers, whose security arrangement had been much strengthened by the events of the previous six months.

THE SPIRIT OF GENEVA

Thus the scene was set for the Geneva Summit of July 1955 — the first meeting of the heads of government of the major powers since the Potsdam Conference of 1945. Khrushchev provides an interesting insight into Soviet expectations of the Geneva Summit in his memoirs:

> 66 Ever since Churchill gave his speech at Fulton calling for the capitalist countries of the world to encircle the Soviet Union, our relations with the West had been strained. I think it was actually Churchill's idea for the Western powers to open lines of communication with the new Soviet Government after Stalin's death and to do so quickly. Churchill believed that the West could take advantage of the fact that the new Soviet Government wasn't yet fully formed and would therefore be more vulnerable to pressure. The Western press was suddenly filled with articles urging a meeting of the four great powers. We, too, were in favour of such a meeting. It was our feeling in the Soviet Leadership that after such a bloody war, we and the West could come to terms and agree among ourselves on rational principles of peaceful co-existence and non-interference in the internal affairs of other states...
>
> The Geneva meeting was a crucial test for us: Would we be able to represent our country competently? Would we approach the meeting soberly, without unrealistic hopes, and would we be able to keep the other side from intimidating us? All things considered, I would say we passed the test. 99

Edward Crankshaw (ed.),
Khrushchev Remembers,
trs. Strobe Talbott,
Deutsch, London, 1971,
p.393 [order of paragraphs
reversed]

Review and Discuss

- How did Khrushchev regard the motives of the Western powers in approaching the Geneva Summit?

- How did the Soviet leaders approach the meeting?

Khrushchev's retrospective comment — 'the Geneva meeting was probably doomed to failure before it even began' — is no doubt close to the mark. The major Soviet proposals, for the mutual disbandment of NATO and the Warsaw Pact, the withdrawal of all 'foreign' troops from Europe, to be followed by the drawing-up of a European security treaty, did not appeal to the Western governments. The chief Western initiative came in the field of disarmament. President Eisenhower presented his Open Skies proposal, calling for each side to exchange plans of their military installations and allow aerial surveillance of those installations by the other side. The Soviets did not even bother to make a formal reply to this proposal.

Despite meagre results of diplomatic substance, the Geneva Summit did signify an improvement in the diplomatic atmosphere — hence the phrase the 'Spirit of Geneva'. From the vantage point of his retirement Khrushchev himself assessed the summit as an 'important breakthrough':

> 66 As a result of our own showing in Geneva, our enemies now realized that we were able to resist their pressure and see through their tricks. They now knew that they had to deal with us honestly and fairly... They realized that they would have to build their relations with us on new assumptions and on new expectations if they really wanted peace. The Geneva meeting was an important breakthrough for us on the diplomatic front. We had established ourselves as able to hold our own in the international arena. 99

Crankshaw (ed.),
Khrushchev Remembers,
p.400

It is revealing to compare Khrushchev's retrospective commentary on the Geneva Summit with that of President Eisenhower:

> 66 The Summit Conference had been hailed by the world as a great success, even a diplomatic triumph for the West. It had been held in a cordial atmosphere, which represented a sharp departure from the vitriolic recriminations which have characterised so many meetings in the past. Agreements had been reached to study ways of increasing friendship between the peoples of the West and of the Soviet Union, and these contacts could, we thought, presage the beginning of a more open society in the USSR. More surprising had been the Soviet agreement... that 'the settlement of the German question and the reunification of Germany by free elections shall be carried out in conformity with the national interests of the German people and interests of European security,' an agreement which, if acted on, would have done much to re-establish stability and progress among the peoples of the European continent...
>
> Then disillusionment had followed. At the October Foreign Ministers' Conference, held in the same room as the Summit Conference, the Soviets had repudiated every measure to which they had agreed in July. Unfortunately, this received less attention in the press than had the earlier agreements... But to those of us responsible for the conduct of foreign relations, the Soviet duplicity was a grievous disappointment indeed. In the final analysis, however, I believe the Geneva Conference represented a limited success. The record was established: all could now see the nature of Soviet diplomatic tactics as contrasted with those of the Free World. Peoples had been given a glowing picture of hope and, though it was badly blurred by the Soviets, at least the outlines of the picture remained. Moreover, and in spite of what happened thereafter the cordial atmosphere of the talks, dubbed the 'Spirit of Geneva', never faded entirely. Indeed, the way was opened for some increases in intercourse between East and West — there began, between the United States and Russia, exchanges of trade exhibitions, scientists, musicians and other performers... These were small beginnings, but they could not have transpired in the atmosphere before Geneva... 99

Dwight D. Eisenhower, *The White House Years I: Mandate for Change 1953-1956*, Heinemann, London, 1963, pp.529-30

Review and Discuss

- How did Khrushchev and Eisenhower differ in their evaluation of the benefits of the Geneva Summit?

- Why was Eisenhower disappointed with the results?

- How tangible was the 'Spirit of Geneva'?

DEVELOPMENTS IN THE SOVIET CAMP

The new Soviet leaders were not only interested in improving relations with the Western powers but also with the Socialist bloc, particularly Yugoslavia. In late May 1955 a high-ranking Soviet delegation arrived in Belgrade. In a speech at the airport Khrushchev referred to Tito as 'dear comrade' and concluded with the words: 'Long live the fraternal friendship and close co-operation between the peoples of the Soviet Union and Yugoslavia.'

The amazed reaction of the Yugoslav comrades can be imagined. In 1949 the Cominform had declared that the Yugoslav party was 'in the hands of murderers and spies'. Now Yugoslavia was declared to be 'a land of intrepid heroes and tireless workers'. The Soviet delegation received a fairly cool reception, but Khrushchev did succeed in re-establishing relations with Yugoslavia. The Soviet *rapprochement* with Yugoslavia gave practical recognition to the principle that each communist party must find its own way to socialism.

The permissibility of 'many roads to socialism' was announced in Khrushchev's famous public speech at the 20th Party Congress in February 1956. Khrushchev delivered two speeches, one 'open' and the other 'secret', which were to exert considerable influence on Soviet relations with the West and with the Eastern bloc states.

In his open speech, Khrushchev stressed the special significance of the task of improving Soviet–American relations:

> The establishment of firm friendly relations between the two biggest powers of the world, the Soviet Union and the United States of America, would be of great significance for the strengthening of world peace. We think that if the well-known Five Principles of peaceful co-existence were to underlie the relations between the U.S.S.R. and the United States, that would be of truly great importance for all mankind and would, of course, benefit the people of the United States no less than the Soviet peoples and all other peoples. These principles — mutual respect for territorial integrity and sovereignty, non-aggression, non-interference in each other's domestic affairs, equality and mutual advantage, peaceful coexistence and economic cooperation — are now subscribed to and supported by a score of states...
>
> We want to be friends with the United States and to cooperate with it for peace and international security and also in the economic and cultural spheres...
>
> If good relations between the Soviet Union and the United States are not established and mutual distrust continues, it will lead to an arms race on a still bigger scale and to a still more dangerous build up of strength on both sides. Is this what the peoples of the Soviet Union and the United States want? Of course not.

N.S. Khrushchev, Report to 20th Party Congress, 14 February 1956, in Rush (ed.), *International Situation and Soviet Foreign Policy*, pp.178–9

Although Khrushchev's public statements at the 20th Party Congress were significant and indicated a departure from the previous Soviet line, it was in fact his lengthy secret speech attacking Stalin that was to have even greater impact, especially within the Socialist camp. The decision to go beyond the public attack on the 'cult of personality' and to detail the crimes of the Stalin era was part of the intense political struggle within the top leadership.

There seems little doubt that the denunciation of Stalin — particularly of his handling of the relationship with Yugoslavia — and the declaration in the public speech at the 20th Party Congress of the possibility of 'many roads to socialism', were each part of the price Khrushchev had to pay to entice Tito back into the socialist camp. But, as some of Khrushchev's domestic opponents no doubt predicted, the consequences of the de-Stalinisation process, not just in the USSR but throughout the entire socialist world, were to prove difficult for the Soviet leadership to control.

POLAND AND HUNGARY

The effects of the 20th Party Congress were soon felt all over Eastern Europe. At the end of June 1956 workers in the Polish industrial city of Poznan revolted. In the next few months Polish communist Wladyslaw Gomulka implemented a rapid de-Stalinisation programme. On 19 October 1956 a powerful Soviet delegation flew into Warsaw, led by Khrushchev. Soviet military forces moved into striking position, but the Poles were not to be intimidated. Gomulka responded by threatening to call out the Polish people. In the face of united resistance by the Polish communist leadership, Khrushchev backed down. However, the quite considerable freedom achieved in Poland was gradually whittled away by Gomulka, who became one of Khrushchev's most trusted political allies.

The news of the Polish success spread to Hungary. On 23 October Hungarian students, later joined by workers, took to the streets of Budapest to demand that the Stalinist puppets be replaced with Imre Nagy. Khrushchev agreed to give power to Nagy, but that was no longer enough. The Hungarians demanded the removal of Soviet troops and the creation of a non-communist political party. Nagy announced Hungary's withdrawal from the Warsaw Pact and proclaimed the country's complete neutrality in the Cold War. On 4–5 November Soviet forces launched a general offensive against the Hungarians. There was bitter fighting in Budapest, but the fate of the uprising was never in doubt. Nagy was arrested, later to be executed. A new government under Janos Kadar was created at the headquarters of the Soviet Army and forcibly installed.

The Hungarian uprising coincided with the Suez crisis (discussed in Chapter 5). Many contemporaries felt that the concurrent Suez crisis and American presidential campaign diverted Western attention from the Hungarian revolt. However, as historian André Fontaine has asked:

André Fontaine, *History of the Cold War from the Korean War to the Present*, Vintage, New York, 1970, p.231

> ❝ What could the West have done to prevent this denouement? Intervene militarily? They did not consider it for one moment, despite all the appeals for help they received, as it would have meant a head-on confrontation with the Soviet Government and the risk of a nuclear war. The error was to have let the insurgents believe in the possibility of intervention. ❞

A bronze statue was toppled by a crowd in Budapest, Hungary, November 1956 (Wide World). Why was the statue toppled? Why was the crowd's treatment of the statue significant? What developments led to the Hungarian uprising in 1956? Why did the West not help the Hungarians?

It is important to understand why the Soviet leaders responded differently to the Polish and Hungarian developments. The great difference was that in the former the Communist Party retained control of affairs, while in the latter it lost it. Hungary in 1956 (and Czechoslovakia in 1968) showed that the Soviets would intervene militarily where the local Communist Party was in danger of losing its control over the State machinery. Nagy's decision to seek a status for Hungary similar to that of Austria would have meant the exclusion of Soviet influence and an undermining of the defensive barrier the Soviet Union had built around its western borders in the years 1944 to 1948.

The Soviets' brutal use of force in putting down the Hungarian uprising left no doubt about the high priority placed by the leadership on the preservation of its Eastern European sphere. In a sense it also strengthened the Soviet position in relation to the Western powers. After the events in Hungary, the Soviets could feel confident that there would be no American intervention in the affairs of 'their' part of Europe. A more obvious effect of the Soviet actions was that it led many observers in the West, neutral as well as pro-American, to conclude that the messages of peace that had recently been emanating from Moscow were indeed a sham.

FROM SUEZ TO CUBA

CHAPTER FIVE

THE SUEZ CRISIS

I N 1953 US Secretary of State Dulles became interested in organising a collective security pact among the nations on the southern border of the USSR, the so-called 'northern tier' of Middle Eastern countries. Eventually, the pact was completed at Baghdad in April 1955 with Turkey, Iraq and Britain as the signatories, joined a few months later by Pakistan and Iran. The pact drew loud protests from Moscow:

> ...the Soviet Union cannot remain indifferent to the situation arising in the region of the Near and Middle East, since the formation of these blocs and the establishment of foreign military bases on the territory of the countries of the Near and Middle East have a direct bearing on the security of the U.S.S.R.

Joseph L. Nogee & Robert H. Donaldson, *Soviet Foreign Policy Since World War II*, Pergamon, New York, 1981, p.151

The Baghdad Pact and the active role of Iraq in its formulation produced severe uneasiness in Egypt, where Colonel Gamal Nasser aspired to create a united Arab bloc under his own leadership. He sought military aid from the West but it was not forthcoming. The Russians, already interested in the area and suspicious of the Baghdad Pact, were quite ready to arrange for the supply of military equipment to Egypt. The Egyptian arms deal, with Czechoslovakia acting as surrogate for the USSR, was concluded in September 1955. It produced considerable disquiet both in Iraq and in the United States.

In December 1955 the United States and Great Britain agreed in principle to help finance the Aswan Dam, an enormous Egyptian hydroelectricity project. In February 1956 Nasser reached an agreement with the president of the World Bank for funds from America, Britain and the bank. He then formally requested $100 million in aid from the United States. He heard nothing for the next five months.

In the meantime, Dulles' attitude towards Nasser had changed after the Czech arms deal was followed by Egyptian recognition of communist China in May 1956. Dulles reasoned that he could teach Nasser a lesson if he withdrew American support for the Aswan Dam. The President of the World Bank warned that 'all hell might break loose' if Dulles reneged on his promise. On 19 July Dulles bluntly announced that America was withdrawing its support for the dam.

One week later Nasser struck back by nationalising the British-owned Universal Suez Canal Company, an act which restored his lost prestige at a stroke and gave him the $25 million annual profit from the canal operation. The British and French were furious. Nearly all of Europe's oil came through the canal and the Europeans feared that an intense nationalist such as Nasser

The Suez crisis: a British cartoon of 1956 (reproduced by permission of Punch). Identify the schoolteacher and the three pupils writing lines. What action led to their punishment? Who is enjoying their discomfort? Who are the figures in the corner and what are they doing?

might interrupt this flow. At the end of July the British Foreign Secretary let Dulles know that the Europeans would move militarily against Egypt if the crisis were not resolved quickly.

By October Egypt still operated the canal on its own and the British and French secretly adopted a plan for military intervention, allied with the government of Israel, which believed that the European anger at Nasser was the perfect cover for its own desire for preventive action to end repeated border conflicts with Egypt. The Israeli Army crossed the frontier on 29 October and swiftly drove across the Sinai Peninsula, scattering a much larger Egyptian army and approaching the canal within a few days. French and British paratroopers landed in the Canal Zone on 1 November and demanded that the Egyptian and Israeli forces withdraw to a zone eight kilometres on either side of the waterway. The Israelis complied.

The Anglo–French statement of protection for free passage through the canal fooled no one. Opposition parties in France and Britain raised a storm of protest and the British Parliament erupted in shouts. In Washington, Dulles, whose dislike for British Prime Minister Eden was widely known, thought the British had purposely misled him. On 2 November the United States joined with the Soviet Union in condemning the two Western powers and Israel at the United Nations, where the General Assembly voted a resolution demanding a ceasefire.

This alignment between the Soviets and Americans came at a particularly embarrassing juncture, for at that very moment Soviet tanks were crushing the Hungarian uprising in the streets of Budapest. The Soviets sent a strongly worded protest to Britain and France on 5 November, by which time the will and ability of Britain and France to continue the operation had been seriously eroded.

The British and French agreed to a ceasefire on 6 November and their forces were soon withdrawn and replaced by a United Nations peacekeeping force. The Soviets claimed exclusive credit for the Anglo–French backdown since it came within twenty-four hours of their stern warning. However, American pressure and the strength of British public opinion played important roles. Nevertheless the Soviets were able to take comfort in the boost to their own prestige in the Third World in conjunction with the sharp blow delivered to Western unity. Khrushchev described the Suez crisis as an 'historic turning point' and wrote that it marked the end of the notion, long held in Russia and elsewhere, that the Middle East was an Anglo–French preserve.

THE EISENHOWER DOCTRINE AND ITS APPLICATION

The temptation for the United States to fill the 'vacuum' that had been created was strong. Why not take advantage of the position it had adopted during the Suez crisis and of the USSR's isolation in the aftermath of the Hungarian uprising to recruit the Middle East on its side finally, thus ensuring that the region's oil did not fall into the hands of hostile powers?

With this objective Eisenhower went before Congress on 5 January 1957 to ask for a resolution empowering him to use economic aid and, if necessary, military forces to block communist expansion in the Middle East. His pronouncement was soon labelled the Eisenhower Doctrine.

> There is a general recognition in the Middle East, as elsewhere, that the United States does not seek either political or economic domination over any other people. Our desire is a world environment of freedom, not servitude. On the other hand many, if not all, of the nations of the Middle East are aware of the danger that stems from International Communism and welcome closer co-operation with the United States to realize for themselves the United Nations goals of independence, economic well being and spiritual growth.
>
> If the Middle East is to continue its geographic role of uniting rather than separating East and West; if its vast economic resources are to serve the well-being of the peoples there, as well as that of others... then the United States must make more evident its willingness to support the independence of the freedom-loving nations of the area...
>
> The action which I propose would have the following features.
>
> It would first of all authorize the United States to co-operate with and assist any nation or group of nations in the general area of the Middle East in the development of economic strength dedicated to the maintenance of national independence.
>
> It would, in the second place, authorize the Executive to undertake in the same region programs of military assistance and co-operation with any nation or group of nations which desires such aid.
>
> It would, in the third place, authorize such assistance and co-operation to include the employment of the armed forces of the United States to secure and protect the territorial integrity and political independence of such nations requesting such aid, against overt armed aggression from any nation controlled by International Communism.

Dwight D. Eisenhower, Special Message to Congress, 5 January 1957, *Department of State Bulletin*, XXXVI, 21 January 1957, pp.85–6

Review and Discuss

- What was Eisenhower's aim in formulating the Eisenhower Doctrine?
- What kind of programme of support was to be offered to Middle Eastern nations who requested it?

Eisenhower, like Truman before him, had chosen to use fear of Soviet communism to gain his foreign policy objectives and the Eisenhower Doctrine sailed through the Democrat-controlled Congress in early March.

The Eisenhower Doctrine was severely tested in mid-1958. In May of that year Nasser had formed a United Arab Republic of Egypt, Syria and Yemen

(UAR). In mid-July, a nationalist coup occurred in Iraq, where General Kassim toppled the monarchy. Kassim began talks with Nasser about joining the UAR. Suddenly the Baghdad Pact looked like having a gaping hole. Dulles was keen to demonstrate American power in the Middle East and an opportunity presented itself in Lebanon. As news of the Kassim coup reached Washington, the United States received a request from the President of Lebanon for help in the civil war there. Eisenhower immediately ordered 14 000 American marines to Lebanon to quell what was portrayed as a 'Communist-inspired' coup. Sun bathers on the beaches of Beirut watched in astonishment as a division of combat-clad marines waded ashore looking for communists. Eisenhower's orders restricted them to taking the airfield and the capital as he wanted to limit the risks and America's commitment.

The American action had the desired effect on the new government of Iraq and on Nasser in Egypt. Over the next few months, Iraq assured Western oil companies that their properties were safe, and Kassim dropped his bid for membership of the UAR. Nasser had to back down after discovering that the Soviet Union would not move beyond verbal support. Gradually the situation in the Middle East improved. The United States recognised the new regime in Iraq, thus easing Arab fears considerably. American troops were withdrawn from Lebanon in November 1958. The prospects for long-term stability, however, were not bright.

THE IMPACT OF SPUTNIK

Khrushchev's caution in this Middle East crisis surprised some knowledgeable observers as the progress of Soviet science and technology in the previous twelve months had been spectacular. More than one Western military expert had begun to talk in terms of Soviet strategic superiority. In August 1957 the Russians announced that they had successfully tested an intercontinental ballistic missile (ICBM). On 4 October they launched the world's first artificial satellite — Sputnik ('travelling companion' in Russian) — and a month later they launched Sputnik II.

Khrushchev was quick to emphasise the political and military importance of Soviet technological progress:

Khrushchev, quoted in Fontaine, *History of the Cold War from the Korean War to the Present,* pp.284–5

    66 The Sputniks prove that socialism has won the competition between Socialist and capitalist countries... that the economy, science, culture, and the creative genius of the people in all spheres of life develop better and faster under socialism. 99

The Americans were both alarmed and angry. LaFeber describes the American reaction:

    66 Americans were extremely disturbed. Strategic Air Force units were dispersed and placed on alert, short range Jupiter missiles installed in Turkey and

'Dear Boy, Where Have You Been Keeping Yourself?'

The impact of Sputnik: an American cartoon of 1957 (Washington Post). Who is the figure emerging from the cellar? How does he appear to have been treated in the past? Who has unlocked the cellar? Why has that action been taken?

LaFeber, *America, Russia and the Cold War*, p.195

Italy to offset the long-range Soviet weapons, money poured into missile and bomber programs, and 'gaps' were suddenly discovered in everything from missile production to the teaching of arithmetic at pre-school level. **"**

The world's media quickly promoted a Soviet–American 'space race'. With the failure of the first US space shot in February 1958, the impression of a vast Soviet superiority in missile technology soon became established in the popular mind. Khrushchev himself helped create that impression, not only trumpeting Soviet technological superiority but also hammering the fact that the Soviet gross national product had increased at an annual average of seven per cent between 1950 and 1958. (This was twice the American rate.) The economic growth was real, but the Soviet lead in ICBMs was greatly exaggerated and Khrushchev encouraged these exaggerations.

Such exaggerations were the basis for influential US arms experts and politicians to warn that America was on the wrong side of an increasing 'missile gap'. The warnings were reinforced when American newspapers discovered and published in late 1957 the findings and recommendations of a top secret investigating committee, the Gaither Report. The report recommended a vast increase in offensive power, especially missile development, a build-up of conventional forces capable of fighting limited war, and a massive programme of fall-out shelters that would not only supposedly protect Americans from Soviet attack, but permit 'our own air defense to use nuclear warheads with greater freedom'.

Eisenhower refused to panic, believing that the Gaither Report was misguided and that current programmes were sufficient. In his memoirs he stated simply: 'We could not turn the nation into a garrison state.' He seems to have judged that much of the post-Sputnik panic was attributed to ambitious politicians or long-time defence specialists such as Paul Nitze, an author of both the Gaither Report and National Security Council Memorandum 68, and later to become a top Reagan administration official.

While Eisenhower could afford to ignore Khrushchev's missile bluff, the game turned out to be rather more costly for Khrushchev. In a matter of months it contributed to a worsening of Sino–Soviet relations. Differences began to surface after the 20th Party Congress in February 1956. The Chinese communists disagreed with Khrushchev's de-Stalinisation campaign; in their view, the dead dictator's virtues exceeded his faults. Also, Mao was developing his own personality cult and could not have relished seeing a fellow prophet toppled so brutally. Despite these reservations, the Chinese loyally supported Khrushchev during the East European crisis of October–November 1956.

Then came Sputnik. Mao assumed, a Chinese newspaper commented in February 1958, that Soviet missile successes had created

Mao Zedong, quoted in LaFeber, *America, Russia and the Cold War*, p.199

> 66 a qualitative change in the distribution of world power [which] had... torn apart the paper tiger of American imperialism, and shattered the tale of the 'position of strength.' 99

The Chinese urged strong support for 'wars of liberation' in the newly emerging nations, wars that could be safely fanned because Soviet missile development had neutralised the strategic power of the USA. Khrushchev for his part refused to co-operate in any reckless adventures. He knew that the Soviet ICBM programme was considerably more of a 'paper tiger' than US long-range bombers.

Zbigniew Brzezinski (later an adviser to President Carter) has discussed the difference in perspective between Moscow and Beijing developing at this time:

> 66 The Soviets to the Chinese: 'You overestimate the ability of the imperialists to initiate a war, hence war is not inevitable; you underestimate the destructiveness of war and our deterrent capabilities; you underestimate the danger of a total war developing out of local conflicts; you underestimate the world wide appeal of socialism as a powerful force and the global significance of the economic power of the world socialist system.'
>
> The Chinese to the Soviets: 'You overestimate the destructiveness of war; you overestimate the willingness of the imperialists to make peaceful concessions; you underestimate the militant revolutionary opportunities and the dangers of co-existence to the revolutionary zeal of the international Communist movements; you underestimate the ability of the socialist camp to win local wars or to force the imperialists to desist when they start one. Finally, you underestimate the possibility of the imperialists plunging the world into war, either out of despair or duplicity, and hence there is a continuing danger of war.' 99

Z. Brzezinski, *The Soviet Bloc: Unity and Conflict*, rev. edn, Harvard University Press, Cambridge, Mass., 1971, pp.374–5

> **Review and Discuss**
>
> • In what ways would such doctrinal differences between the Soviets and the Chinese have led to different policies with respect to international affairs?

In August 1958 Mao initiated the second Quemoy crisis with renewed shelling of the nationalist positions on the offshore islands. The USA intervened, implying that if the island was sufficiently endangered, then it would bomb the artillery batteries on the Chinese coast. China's Soviet ally was conspicuously silent. After the crisis had gone off the boil, Khrushchev announced the Soviet position in *Tass* on 5 October 1958.

Khrushchev, quoted in Fontaine, *History of the Cold War from the Korean War to the Present*, p.308

> 66 The U.S.S.R. will come to her aid... if China is attacked by the United States... but as for the civil war that the Chinese are waging against Chiang Kai-shek's clique, we did not get mixed up in it and have no intention of doing so. 99

The danger in the Formosa Straits had passed. However, in November 1958 in Berlin, Khrushchev triggered one of the gravest crises of the Cold War and one that was to last, with varying degrees of intensity, for four years.

BERLIN AND BEYOND

By the late 1950s Berlin provided a dramatic illustration of the contrast between East and West. West Berlin under British, French and American occupation and loosely tied to the Federal Republic had a booming economy that reflected the West German 'economic miracle'. East Berlin, under Soviet occupation, was a drab and depressing contrast. An enclave 170 kilometres deep in East German territory, Berlin served as an escape hatch for the East German population. Since 1949 East Germany had lost close to three million people through that escape hatch, most of them young, talented, professionals. West Berlin was also a major source of intelligence concerning the communist world, and its radio stations constantly beamed propaganda into Eastern Europe.

On 10 November 1958 Khrushchev began a series of moves that culminated in the demand that the USA, Britain and France withdraw their occupation forces from West Berlin, make it a 'free city' and negotiate with the German Democratic Republic (which none of the Western powers recognised) for access into Berlin. With the support of the Western allies Dulles rejected Khrushchev's demands, refused to contemplate recognition of East Germany and intimated that in the eventuality of East German control of the access routes and denial of Western access, NATO would retaliate, 'if need be by military force'.

Khrushchev began to back down. In the early months of 1959 the Berlin crisis subsided and the Soviets began to reveal their interest in another summit meeting. Khrushchev accepted an invitation to visit the United States in September 1959 and arranged with Eisenhower for a summit meeting in Paris scheduled for May 1960.

The Soviet leader's two-week visit to the USA in September was highly publicised. Although they produced few diplomatic results, from a public relations point of view the talks with Eisenhower were a great success. Khrushchev stated publicly that his conversations with the American President 'broke the ice', and that it was now up to the diplomats to remove the chunks. On his return to Moscow he described Eisenhower as a man who 'sincerely wants to liquidate the cold war and improve relations between our two great countries'.

Khrushchev's visit to the United States was followed by a visit to China in October 1959. The growing differences between Moscow and Beijing were becoming increasingly obvious. The wider significance of Sino–Soviet differences is highlighted by Stephen Ambrose.

> Mao had become... a problem for Khrushchev... Khrushchev's refusal to support Mao's call for wars of national liberation signified to Mao that the Russians had joined the have powers against the have-nots. There was other evidence, such as Khrushchev's trip to the United States, his willingness to go to the summit again, and the cooling of the Berlin crisis. As the Chinese saw it, the Soviets were selling out both Communism and the Third World. They accused Khrushchev of appeasement. Mao's propaganda increasingly warned of winds blowing from the east instead of the west and of a world wide revolt of the rural peoples against the urbanites, among whom the Chinese counted the Russians. Mao's radicalism, heightened by his emphasis on racism, appealed strongly to the Third World and made it almost as difficult for the Soviets to influence development in Southeast Asia and Africa as it was for the United States. Mao challenged, directly and successfully, Khrushchev's leadership of the Communist world.

Ambrose, *Rise to Globalism*, pp.172–3

On 14 January 1960 Khrushchev delivered a speech to the Supreme Soviet that was, in many ways, one of the most important in the Cold War. The speech was notable not only for its discussion of strategic nuclear issues but also because it seemed to suggest that communism could afford to bring the Cold War to an end. Khrushchev spoke passionately of a peaceful competition between capitalism and communism for the favour of the peoples, a competition in which a warless victory will be won because of the truth and efficacy of communist ideas.

> Peaceful co-existence of all countries irrespective of their internal order, of their social systems, is the fundamental question today, the question of questions in international relations...
>
> As it is, however, there exists [sic] two camps in the world today, each with a different social system. The countries in these camps shape their policies along entirely different lines. In these circumstances, the problem of peaceful co-existence, that is, of safeguarding the world against the disaster of a military conflict between these two essentially antagonistic systems, between the groups of countries in which the two systems reign supreme,

is of paramount importance. It is necessary to see to it that the inevitable struggle between them resolves solely into a struggle between ideologies and into peaceful emulation, or competition, to use a term that the capitalists find easier to understand. Each side will demonstrate its advantages to the best of its ability, but war as a means of settling this dispute must be ruled out. This, then, is co-existence as we Communists see it...

Some Western politicians... misrepresent our aims because they are afraid of the influence which the peace policy of the socialist countries exerts on the peoples. We have never said, of course, that our aim is to conquer the world or a part of it. What does 'conquer' mean? It means forcibly to impose one's terms, one's political system, one's ideology, on the other side. But then that is not co-existence, it is interference in the internal affairs of other countries, it is war. It is something we are most emphatically opposed to.

We consider that it is impossible forcibly to impose on other peoples something they object to, something they do not want. The Communists are firmly convinced that no ideology, including communist ideology, can be implanted forcibly, by war, by bayonets...

No bayonets, no prisons or force, can stem the ideas of communism, for the simple reason that Marxism–Leninism is an expression of the vital interests of the working people, that it is the truth. Communist society is a society based on complete justice, freedom, equality, and genuine respect for man. Whatever guards one may post, however much one may try to fool people, they will in the end see and understand what is true and what isn't, what is good and what is bad. That is why we are confident that the cause of communism will triumph in the end. Communism will win, but not in the sense that the socialist countries will conquer the other countries. No, the people of each country will themselves weigh all the facts and when they have appreciated the essence of Marxism–Leninism, they will of their own free will choose the more progressive social system.

N.S. Khrushchev, Report to the Supreme Soviet, 14 January 1960, in Rush (ed.), International Situation and Soviet Foreign Policy, pp.224-5

99

Review and Discuss

- How did Khrushchev define the struggle between capitalism and socialism?
- Why was Khrushchev at pains to stress the definition? How was it related to what he called Western 'misrepresen-

tation' of Soviet aims?
- How have subsequent events falsified Khrushchev's expectation that social-ism would triumph over capitalism?

REVERSAL AND REWARD

Khrushchev's political career had its ups and downs, but no reversal was more dramatic than the change in his fortunes that occurred in May 1960. After the optimism of the Camp David meeting with Eisenhower and the January speech to the Supreme Soviet, great achievements were expected at the Paris Summit. It was not to be. A few days before the summit meeting convened in Paris, the Soviets announced that an American plane had been shot down over Russia on 1 May. The United States indicated that it was a weather plane that had wandered off course. The Soviet leaders then revealed that the aircraft had been downed nearly 2000 kilometres inside Russia, that it was a high-altitude, photo-reconnaissance plane, and that the pilot, who had safely parachuted but was captured, had conceded the 'spy' character of his mission.

Khrushchev bitterly attacked the United States for its 'aggressive acts'. Eisenhower admitted the validity of Khrushchev's accusations but, contrary to the Soviet leader's expectations, claimed foreknowledge of the flight, defended it and took personal responsibility for it. Eisenhower refused to apologise and Khrushchev cancelled Eisenhower's planned visit to Russia; the Paris Summit was ruined. The best hope for an agreement on Berlin had gone.

The middle of 1960 had been a difficult time for the Soviets, Khrushchev had declared that no further negotiations with the West could take place while Eisenhower was in office and Sino–Soviet quarrels continued to heat up. The Soviets were also engaged in a messy and ultimately unsuccessful operation in the Congo. However, one important development, which the Soviets did turn to their own advantage at this time, was the coming to power of Castro in Cuba.

This turn of events had begun on New Year's Day 1959, when a revolutionary nationalist movement led by Fidel Castro sent the Cuban dictator Fulgencio Batista fleeing from Havana to Miami. Batista had close ties with the American government as well as with organised crime in the United States. The events in Cuba brought the dilemma of America's relationship to the underdeveloped world to a head. At that time, Americans owned eighty per cent of Cuba's utilities, forty per cent of its sugar, ninety per cent of its mining wealth and the island's key strategic location of Guantanamo Bay. Cuban life was controlled from Washington by the simple device of manipulating the amount of Cuban sugar allowed into the American market. Immediately on seizing power, Castro commenced executions of Batista's henchmen, closed down the gambling casinos and threatened to expropriate American sugar holdings.

Liberals in the United States initially welcomed Castro's victory and applauded his democratic reforms. The attitude of the Eisenhower administration, however, was decidedly cool. The Americans began to search for a so-called 'third force'. In Eisenhower's words: 'Our only hope lay with some kind of non-dictatorial "third force" neither Castroite nor Batistiano.'

In February 1960 the Russians signed a trade agreement to exchange Cuban sugar for Soviet oil, machinery and technicians. The Soviets for their part did not then regard Castro as a communist, though they knew that some of his key advisers were (including his brother Raoul and Che Guevara). They were quite happy to provide assistance to Castro (including weapons) in his confrontation with the USA.

The Russian view of the Cuban–American confrontation was outlined by Khrushchev in a speech in July 1960.

> 66 But the time when the United States *diktat* prevailed is over. The Soviet Union is raising its voice on behalf of, and is offering help to, the people of Cuba who are fighting for their independence...
>
> It is clear to everybody that economic blockade by the American monopolists can be a prelude to intervention against Cuba. Therefore we must speak up in defence of Cuba and give warning that the imperialists can no longer rob and divide the world as they please... Today the peoples of the colonial and dependent countries rebel and fight successfully to rid themselves of the shameful colonial yoke and of enslavement by the United States imperialists. 99

N.S. Khrushchev, Speech to RFSR Teachers Congress, Moscow, 9 July 1960, in *Soviet News*, 11 July 1960, pp.28–9

Review and Discuss

- Why was Khrushchev offering to help Cuba in its confrontation with the USA?

- What American action against Cuba did Khrushchev anticipate?

By the time Eisenhower left office he knew that US policy towards Cuba was in deep trouble. He had in fact given the go-ahead to the US Central Intelligence Agency (CIA) to plan an invasion of Cuba and to begin training Cuban exiles to carry it out, with American support. The decision whether to implement such a plan was one of Eisenhower's legacies to his successor.

Although Eisenhower and Khrushchev never met again, the Soviet leader did visit the USA a second time in September 1960 to attend the United Nations General Assembly. Fidel Castro came as well, and was given a warm embrace by Khrushchev. The significance of the gesture was not lost on American officials.

Happy times at the United Nations, New York, October 1960 (Wide World). Identify the two leaders shown embracing. How did friendship between their two countries develop? How was this friendship viewed by the USA?

KHRUSHCHEV AND KENNEDY

CHAPTER SIX

KENNEDY'S 'THOUSAND DAYS'

K HRUSHCHEV'S VISIT to the United Nations in New York coincided with the presidential election of 1960. The Democrat nominee, John F. Kennedy, won the election by one of the narrowest margins in the history of presidential elections, beating the Republican candidate, Vice-President Richard Nixon.

The Soviets made no secret of their delight in the fact that the forty-three-year-old Kennedy, and not Nixon, had succeeded Eisenhower. In congratulating Kennedy on his election, Khrushchev expressed the hope that during his presidency 'relations between the two countries could again be what they had been in Franklin Roosevelt's time'. The new administration came to office determined to pursue an activist policy and to meet the Soviet challenge in Europe and the Third World head on.

The fresh sense of purpose in the Kennedy administration was expressed in memorable phrases in the new President's inaugural address.

> Let the word go forth from this time and place, to friend and foe alike, that the torch has been passed to a new generation of Americans — born in this century, tempered by war, disciplined by a hard and bitter peace, proud of our ancient heritage — and unwilling to witness or permit the slow undoing of those human rights to which this nation has always been committed, and to which we are committed today at home and around the world.
>
> Let every nation know whether it wishes us well or ill, that we shall pay any price, bear any burden, meet any hardship, support any friend, oppose any foe to assure the survival and the success of liberty...
>
> ...to those nations who would make themselves our adversary, we offer not a pledge but a request: that both sides begin anew the quest for peace,

before the dark powers of destruction unleashed by science engulf all humanity in planned or accidental self-destruction.

We dare not tempt them with weakness. For only when our arms are sufficient beyond doubt can we be certain beyond doubt that they will never be employed.

But neither can two great powerful groups of nations take comfort from our present course — both sides overburdened by the cost of modern weapons, both rightly alarmed by the steady spread of the deadly atom, yet both racing to alter that uncertain balance of terror that stays the hand of mankind's final war.

So let us begin anew — remembering on both sides that civility is not a sign of weakness, and sincerity is always subject to proof. Let us never negotiate out of fear. But let us never fear to negotiate.

John F. Kennedy, Inaugural Address, 20 January 1961, *Department of State Bulletin*, XLIV, 6 February 1961, pp.175–6

Kennedy's intellectual qualities and personal attributes were considerable. Arthur Schlesinger, Jr, a Harvard historian who worked on Kennedy's staff, described the President's mind as practical, ironic, sceptical and inexhaustibly curious. Schlesinger has drawn attention to Kennedy's liking for the credo of the British military historian and strategist Liddel Hart.

Keep strong, if possible. In any case keep cool. Have unlimited patience. Never corner an opponent, and always assist him to save face. Put yourself in his shoes — so as to see things through his eyes. Avoid self-righteousness like the devil — nothing is so self-blinding.

B. Liddel Hart, quoted in Arthur M. Schlesinger, *A Thousand Days*, Deutsch, London, 1965, pp.99–100

Kennedy liked that advice. Subsequent events were to give him ample opportunity to try to put it into practice.

Unlike Eisenhower, Kennedy chose to concentrate foreign policy in the White House, instead of leaving it largely to the Secretary of State. For that office he selected Dean Rusk, an urbane southerner who had been Assistant Secretary under Truman, with good connections to the foreign policy establishment. Rusk rarely asserted himself in the councils of the new administration, preferring to listen impassively while the White House 'action intellectuals' discussed the issues.

Kennedy was keen to seek the advice of these action intellectuals. For the previous decade a small but significant group of academic entrepreneurs had told government officials and each other that the Cold War was too important to be left to the politicians, diplomats and generals. They prided themselves on their 'toughmindedness', and 'lack of sentimentality'. In Kennedy's view their 'hard headed realism' was what the USA needed.

Typical was McGeorge Bundy (aged forty-one), Kennedy's National Security Adviser, straight from the deanship of Harvard. Bundy's deputy was MIT professor of economic history, Walt Rostow, shortly to become head of the Policy Planning Staff of the State Department. Earlier Rostow had written an influential book, *The Stages of Economic Growth* (1960), a theory of how underdeveloped countries could achieve 'take off' into industrialism. Its subtitle, *A Non-Communist Manifesto*, gave some indication of Rostow's stance on the Cold War.

Probably the most dazzling of the new group of advisers was the Secretary of Defense, Robert McNamara. McNamara (aged forty-five) was a brilliant statistician who had gone from an academic career at the Harvard Business School to the presidency of the Ford Motor Company. He quickly moved to apply the same state-of-the-art management techniques that had proved a winner at Ford to the work of the Defense Department. Closest of the presidential counsellors was the Attorney-General, Robert F. Kennedy, 'Brother Bobby,' not yet thirty-six.

WAGING COLD WAR IN THE THIRD WORLD

Latin America was the first region in which the Kennedy administration tried to set a new tone. On 13 March 1961 Kennedy announced the Alliance for Progress with the Latin nations. To the foreign aid commitment of the previous administration Kennedy would add $20 billion over the next ten years to supplement the investment of the Latin American nations themselves. Bureaucratic infighting in Washington and corruptions in Latin America were to limit the effectiveness of the alliance.

The Peace Corps, another Kennedy initiative in March 1961, was more successful. It paid special attention to Latin America and the idea proved immensely popular in the USA. It also brought a favourable response from the developing parts of the world. At the same time, the Pentagon and Central Intelligence Agency (CIA) increased the training of Latin American police and paramilitary outfits in order to help them fight guerrilla wars. The Pentagon set up two Jungle Warfare Schools to train Latin American units.

The Alliance for Progress and the training of Latin American police were both designed to prevent the rise of another Castro-like nationalist revolution. But what to do about the revolutionary government in Cuba itself? On assuming office, Kennedy's military advisers endorsed a scheme approved by Eisenhower to train Cuban exiles for an invasion of Cuba, and the CIA assured him the attack would succeed. Although Kennedy, and others, had some qualms about it, he acquiesced in the venture.

A force of about 1600 guerrillas landed at the Bay of Pigs on Cuba's southern coast on 17 April 1961. The CIA's director of operations, Richard Bissell, had assured Kennedy that this force would encourage a general rising of the Cuban population against Castro. No such uprising greeted the invaders. Castro was popular in the island generally and especially in the Bay of Pigs area where he frequently went on holiday. Within forty-eight hours of the landing the brigade was captured by the Cuban army.

At the time, the standard explanation was to lay the blame at the feet of the CIA and the Joint Chiefs. But, as Stephen Ambrose reminds us:

> [Kennedy] believed that Castro had betrayed the Cuban revolution; he... believed that the Cuban people were groaning under the oppressor's heel.

Ambrose, *Rise to
Globalism*, p.183

The President believed there was a liberal alternative between Castro and
Batista and that the exile counterrevolutionary group would supply the
liberal leadership around which the Cuban people would rally. It was not
the experts who got Kennedy into the Bay of Pigs; it was his own view
of the world. **"**

The whole affair was a humiliating disaster for the Kennedy administration.
The Bay of Pigs fiasco resulted in an increase of Castro's domestic support
and strengthened Cuban ties with Russia. It gave Khrushchev an opportunity
to bluster and threaten. It outraged many Latin Americans, revived fears of
Yankee imperialism in the Southern Hemisphere and set back Kennedy's promising attempts to identify the United States with anti-colonialism.

Kennedy was to be luckier in Central Africa. The Congo (now Zaire) was
the scene of some shabby intrigues by both Moscow and Washington. In June
1960 the former Belgian colony gained its independence. Patrice Lumumba,
leader of the ardent nationalist faction became prime minister, announcing
that he was a nationalist not a communist and declaring a policy of 'positive
neutrality'. The Congo's new independence was soon shattered by a mutiny
of the Belgian-trained army, followed not long after by the announced secession
of the mineral-rich province of Katanga. Belgium dispatched paratroopers to
protect its citizens and their economic holdings. Meanwhile Lumumba appealed
to the United Nations for assistance and an emergency peace-keeping force
was created for the Congo. The UN forces were not immediately successful
in expelling the Belgian forces or ending the Katanga secession and Lumumba
turned to the Soviets for assistance. The limited amounts of Soviet aid that
reached the Congo were not sufficient to stabilise Lumumba's regime and in
September 1960 he was ousted from power.

US policy in the Congo continued to have American rather than African
interests at its centre. The USA gave lip service to supporting the UN force
but actually favoured secession. The CIA saw Lumumba as a Moscow puppet
since he had received training in the Soviet capital. In January 1961, a matter
of days after Kennedy assumed office, Lumumba was assassinated. There were
persistent rumours that the CIA had organised the affair. Eventually a new
government under Joseph Kasavubu took power. It soon became dependent
on the West for financial support and the Congo continued to be racked by
civil war.

THE VIENNA SUMMIT AND THE BERLIN WALL

In the weeks following the Bay of Pigs fiasco Kennedy and Khrushchev agreed
to hold a summit meeting in Vienna in early June 1961. The meeting did
result in an agreement to stop the growing conflict in Laos by neutralising
that country, but there was little harmony in their other discussions. Responding to Kennedy's urging of the need to preserve the existing balance of power,

The superpower leaders together at the Vienna Summit, June 1961 (Sovfoto). Identify the two leaders. What were their purposes in attending the Vienna Summit? Why were both sides disappointed with the outcome of the summit?

Khrushchev indicated that the Soviet Union could hardly be expected to co-operate in enforcing stability on a predominantly colonial/capitalist world.

Khrushchev was even more militant on the question of Berlin. He personally handed to Kennedy at Vienna the Soviet *aide-mémoire* that demanded a Berlin solution on Soviet terms with a period of 'not more than six months'. Kennedy sought and accepted the advice of that experienced Cold War campaigner, Dean Acheson. For Acheson, the Berlin issue was a 'simple conflict of wills'. There was no possibility of negotiation until the Soviets lifted their threats. However, as the historian Walter LaFeber points out, Acheson's argument did not address Khrushchev's very real problems. He lists these succinctly:

> …the growing military power of West Germany, its strengthened ties with the West, its attractiveness to technicians and other experts living in East Germany, the very weak position of the East German communist regime, the position of West Berlin as an espionage and propaganda centre within the communist bloc, the growing fear of the Soviet peoples over West Germany's power, and, finally, Khrushchev's realization that with his ICBM braggadocio punctuated as only myth, he needed a major strategic victory.

LaFeber, *America, Russia and the Cold War,* p.218

Tension continued to rise. On 25 July 1961 Kennedy announced a substantial strengthening of US armed forces. Congress was asked to approve an additional appropriation of $3.25 billion for the defence budget. On the same day Kennedy spoke on radio and television to the American people:

> …West Berlin, lying exposed 110 miles inside East Germany, surrounded by Soviet troops and close to Soviet supply lines, has many roles. It is more than a showcase of liberty, a symbol, an island of freedom in a Communist sea. It is even more than a link with the free world, a beacon of hope behind the Iron Curtain, an escape hatch for refugees.
>
> West Berlin is all of that. But above all it has now become, as never before, the great testing place of Western courage and will, a focal point

where our solemn commitments, stretching back over the years since 1945, and Soviet ambitions now meet in basic confrontation...

We do not want to fight, but we have fought before. And others in earlier times have made the same dangerous mistake of assuming that the West was too selfish and too soft and too divided to resist invasions of freedom in other lands... We cannot and will not permit the Communists to drive us out of Berlin, either gradually or by force...

The world is not deceived by the Communist attempt to label Berlin as a hot bed of war. There is peace in Berlin today. The source of world trouble and tension is Moscow, not Berlin. And if war begins it will have begun in Moscow, and not Berlin. For the choice of peace or war is largely theirs, not ours. It is the Soviets who have stirred up this crisis. It is they who are trying to force a change... In short while we are ready to defend our interests we shall also be ready to search for peace...

The Atlantic community... has been built in response to challenge: the challenge of European chaos in 1947, of the Berlin blockade of 1948, the challenge of Communist aggression in Korea in 1950... If we do not meet our commitments to Berlin, where will we later stand? If we are not true to our word there, all that we have achieved in collective security, which relies on these words, will mean nothing. And if there is one path above all others to war, it is the path of weakness and disunity... We seek peace but we shall not surrender.

Department of State Bulletin, XLV, 14 August 1961, pp.267–73

99

Review and Discuss

- Why was Berlin of such special significance to the West?
- Why did Kennedy link his response to the Berlin crisis with the earlier Cold War crises of 1947, 1948 and 1950?

The Vienna Summit: an American cartoon of 1961. (Copyrighted 1961, Chicago Tribune Company, all rights reserved, used with permission.) What do the actions of the two leaders suggest about the cartoonist's view of the main purpose of the summit meeting? How far did the meeting achieve this purpose?

An East German guard crossing to West Berlin, August 1961 (APL/Bettmann). Why would the guard have wanted to jump the barrier? Why would Western sources be keen to use this photograph? What actions did the Soviet bloc subsequently take in regard to this barrier? With what effect?

Nineteen days later, on Sunday 13 August, came the Soviet and East German response. The East German police placed barbed wire entanglements along the fifty kilometre line dividing the two Berlins. By daybreak a concrete wall was under construction, completed by Tuesday — a barrier that was ultimately extended along the entire western border of East Germany. The 'Iron Curtain' was a figure of speech; the Berlin Wall was all too real. The Western powers protested but did not use force against the barricade.

Only gradually did this Berlin crisis abate. Khrushchev asserted in his memoirs that the establishment of 'border control' (the wall) in Berlin stabilised the situation there. The wall, he stated, 'restored order and discipline in the East Germans' lives'. Khrushchev concluded his account of the Berlin crisis with an interesting admission relating to the need to 'guard the gates of Socialist paradise'. He stated quite candidly: 'Unfortunately, the GDR — and not only the GDR — has yet to reach a level of moral and material development where competition with the West is possible.'

The political aftermath of the Berlin crisis yielded a symbolic gesture on the part of the American President. On 26 June 1963, during a highly publicised visit to the divided city, Kennedy proclaimed *'Ich bin ein Berliner'* (I am a Berliner). Nevertheless, the Berlin Wall stood, in silent testimony to the failure of imagination of both Soviet and American diplomacy.

THE CUBAN MISSILE CRISIS

The compromise solution in Berlin did not lead to an end of tension. The American military build up continued, having been accelerated during the crisis. There was little Khrushchev could do about US strategic nuclear superiority, but public American boastfulness does appear to have been a significant factor in Khrushchev's search for a dramatic strategic victory. As Ambrose observes, there were a number of factors leading him in that direction.

> 66 Khrushchev, frustrated in the nuclear field, unable to push the West out of Berlin, incapable of matching the United States in I.C.B.M.S., and increasingly irritated by the Chinese harping about Soviet weakness, began to look elsewhere for an opportunity to alter the strategic balance. He found it in Cuba. 99

Ambrose, Rise to Globalism, pp.191–2

In August 1962 the Soviets began construction of intermediate range ballistic missile sites in Cuba, despite a warning from Kennedy not to provide Cuba with offensive weapons. What did Khrushchev hope to achieve? The account that he gives in his memoirs repays careful examination.

> 66 We were sure that the Americans would never reconcile themselves to the existence of Castro's Cuba. They feared, as much as we hoped, that a Socialist Cuba might become a magnet that would attract other Latin American countries to Socialism... America would not leave Cuba alone unless we did something...
>
> One thought kept hammering away at my brain: what will happen if we lose Cuba? I knew it would have been a terrible blow to Marxism–Leninism. It would gravely diminish our stature throughout the world, but especially in Latin America. If Cuba fell, other Latin American countries would reject us, claiming that for all our might the Soviet Union hadn't been able to do anything for Cuba except to make empty protests to the United Nations... We had to establish a tangible and effective deterrent to American interference in the Caribbean. But what exactly? The logical answer was missiles...
>
> I had the idea of installing missiles with nuclear warheads in Cuba without letting the United States find out they were there until it was too late to do anything about them... My thinking went like this: if we installed the missiles secretly and if the United States discovered the missiles were there after they were already poised and ready to strike, the Americans would think twice before trying to liquidate our installations by military means... The installation of our missiles in Cuba would, I thought, restrain the United States from precipitous military action against Castro's government. In addition to protecting Cuba our missiles would have equalized what the West liked to call 'the balance of power.' The Americans had surrounded our country with military bases and threatened us with nuclear weapons, and now they would learn just what it feels like to have enemy missiles pointing at you; we'd be doing nothing more than giving them a little of their own medicine. And it was high time America learned what it feels like to have her own land and her own people threatened... 99

Khrushchev Remembers, pp.493–4

Review and Discuss

- What did Khrushchev advance as the main reason for the Soviet decision to place missiles in Cuba?
- How was Cuban security important within the broader Latin American context?
- What was Khrushchev's thinking in relation to the American reaction once the emplacement of the missiles was discovered?

Although the account in Khrushchev's memoirs emphasises his desire to protect Cuba from another American-sponsored invasion, the other reasons he cites — 'equalizing the balance of power' and 'giving the Americans a taste of their own medicine' — are clearly more credible. The political and psychological impact of Soviet missiles just 140 kilometres off American shores was a factor of great significance to the Americans. As Theodore Sorensen, Kennedy's speech writer, later put it:

> 66 To be sure these Cuban missiles alone, in view of all the other megatonnage the Soviets were capable of unleashing upon us did not substantially alter the strategic balance in fact... But that balance would have been substantially altered in appearance; and in matters of national will and world leadership... such appearances contribute to reality. 99

T.C. Sorensen, quoted in Ambrose, *Rise to Globalism*, p.193

In September 1962 Soviet Ambassador Dobrynin assured Kennedy that Moscow would not cause trouble in Berlin or Cuba in the lead-up to the November Congressional elections. On 14 October a U–2 overflight of Cuba provided clear evidence that missile installations were being constructed. Kennedy was immediately informed, and he convened a series of secret meetings with close advisers in an atmosphere of the utmost tension. A variety of alternatives was explored, but gradually two possible courses of action came to the fore. One group of advisers urged an immediate air strike against the missiles, even though such an attack would almost certainly have resulted in the deaths of Soviet technicians working on the sites. A second group supported Under Secretary of State George Ball's recommendation that some form of blockade be instituted against Cuba, which would give the Russians maximum opportunity to back down without humiliation. Ball thought that if the blockade failed, an air strike could always be ordered later. Kennedy listened carefully to the discussion of the merits and demerits of each option and chose the blockade as the initial American response.

On the evening of 22 October, Kennedy went on television to break the news to the American people.

> 66 The urgent transformation of Cuba into an important strategic base — by the presence of... large, longrange, and clearly offensive weapons of sudden mass destruction — constitutes an explicit threat to the peace and security of all the Americas...

Photograph taken from a U–2 aircraft flying over Cuba, released by US Department of Defense, 28 October 1962 (Wide World). What does the photograph reveal about Soviet activities in Cuba? Why did the Soviets undertake these activities? Why would the US authorities have released such a top secret photograph so quickly? How was the Cuban missile crisis resolved?

This action... contradicts the repeated assurances of Soviet spokesmen, both publicly and privately delivered, that the arms build-up in Cuba would retain its original defensive character...

Neither the United States of America nor the world community of nations can tolerate deliberate deception and offensive threats on the part of any nation, large or small... This sudden, clandestine decision to station strategic weapons for the first time outside of Soviet soil — is a deliberately provocative and unjustified change in the status quo...

The 1930s taught us a clear lesson: aggressive conduct, if allowed to grow unchecked and unchallenged, ultimately leads to war. This nation is opposed to war. We are also true to our word.

Our unswerving objective, therefore, must be to prevent the use of these missiles against this or any other country, and to secure their withdrawal or elimination from the Western hemisphere.

Our policy has been one of patience and restraint, as befits a peaceful and powerful nation, which leads a world-wide alliance... We will not prematurely or unnecessarily risk the costs of world-wide nuclear war in which even the fruits of victory would be ashes in our mouth — but neither will we shrink from the risk at any time it must be faced.

Department of State Bulletin, XLVII, 12 November 1962, pp.715–20

"

Review and Discuss

- What interpretation did Kennedy place on the Soviet installation of missiles on Cuba?
- In what terms did Kennedy justify the need for an American response?
- How did Kennedy present the risks that accompanied the proposed US response?

Even as the President spoke, the Strategic Air Command was beginning a massive airborne alert, 156 ICBMs were in combat readiness, a fleet of Polaris submarines was on guard at sea, the US Navy was establishing a 3300 kilometre 'quarantine' circle around Cuba and hundreds of thousands of men were placed on combat alert.

Khrushchev's initial reaction was belligerent. On 23 October he declared that the Soviet Union would not observe the illegal blockade. He accused Kennedy of pushing mankind 'to the abyss of a world missile-nuclear war' and declared that Soviet ship captains bound for Cuba would not be obeying US Navy orders. Soviet ships continued to steam towards Cuba, although about a dozen vessels suddenly turned back (presumably they were carrying missiles). Secretary of State Dean Rusk was prompted to remark: 'We're eyeball to eyeball and I think the other fellow just blinked.'

On 26 October Khrushchev started to back off. First through an unofficial channel and on the same day in a rambling and emotional letter to Kennedy, Khrushchev outlined a possible solution. The letter implied that Russia would remove the missile bases if the United States would end the blockade and give an assurance not to invade Cuba. Before the USA had a chance to respond, next day a second letter, quite different in tone and substance from the first, arrived. This second letter offered to dismantle Soviet missile sites in Cuba if the USA agreed to remove American missiles from Turkey (a suggestion that had in fact been made by newspaper columnist Walter Lippmann).

On 28 October, the American administration adopted Robert Kennedy's suggestion of deliberately ignoring the second letter altogether and accepting the offer conveyed in Khrushchev's first letter (and the unofficial channel). This rather ingenious expedient worked. The United States promised not to invade Cuba if the missiles were promptly withdrawn, and a number of medium-range Soviet bombers were returned to the USSR. (UN observers were to monitor this process.)

President Kennedy lost no time in hailing that decision as 'worthy of a statesman' and in replying to Khrushchev that his message made 'an important contribution to peace'. Khrushchev later reflected on Kennedy's handling of the crisis in his memoirs:

> **“** In our negotiations with the Americans during the crisis, they had, on the whole, been open and candid with us, especially Robert Kennedy... It had been, to say the least, an interesting and challenging situation. The two most powerful nations of the world had been squared off against each other, each with its finger on the button. You'd have thought that war was inevitable. But both sides showed that if the desire to avoid war is strong enough, even the most pressing dispute can be solved by compromise... The episode ended in a triumph of common sense. I'll always remember the late President with deep respect because, in the final analysis, he showed himself to be sober-minded and determined to avoid war. He didn't let himself become frightened, nor did he become reckless. He didn't overestimate America's might, and he left himself a way out of the crisis. He showed real wisdom and statesmanship... **”**

Khrushchev Remembers,
p.500

Review and Discuss

- Why did Khrushchev hold Kennedy's handling of the Cuban missile crisis in high regard?

Thirty years later, with the declassification of Russian and American documents relating to the crisis, it became frighteningly clear just how close the world had come to nuclear war. Early in 1992 the Russians revealed that thirty-six intermediate-range missiles with nuclear warheads were already in place during the crisis. Further, there were nine short-range nuclear missiles ready to be used against any US invasion force. Kennedy's advisers were unaware of the readiness of these nuclear warheads. When Secretary of Defense Robert McNamara learned of this in 1992 he declared: 'This... meant that had a US invasion been carried out... there was a 99 percent probability that nuclear war would have been initiated.'

However, at the time the Cuban missile crisis turned out better than Kennedy and his advisers had dared to hope. Kennedy became more moderate and less strident, at least in his dealing with the Soviet Union. He also understood that the missile withdrawal suggested no universal formula for dealing successfully with the Russians. For Khrushchev, the missile crisis played an important role in undermining his power in Moscow and within the Soviet bloc. The Chinese, in particular, were angered by the events in Cuba. They called Khrushchev foolish for putting missiles into Cuba ('adventurism') and cowardly for removing them ('capitulationism'). In October 1964 he was ousted from all his posts.

THE DOWNWARD SLOPE IN SOUTH-EAST ASIA

Upon taking office one of the first briefings Kennedy had received concerned the new insurgency of the remnants of the Vietminh in South Vietnam. The President's newly appointed Chairman of the Joint Chiefs of Staff, General Maxwell Taylor, believed that Vietnam would be an ideal testing place for the new counter-insurgency fighters being trained at Fort Bragg, North Carolina — the special forces called the Green Berets. As Stephen Ambrose points out, the idea appealed to the President as well.

> Kennedy set out to build a counter-insurgency force that could stamp out insurrection or revolution in the jungles of Asia or the mountains of South America. With his counter-insurgency force Kennedy would prove to the world that the so-called wars of national liberation did not work...
>
> The great opportunity came in South Vietnam... Vietnam was an ideal battle ground for the Green Berets. Small-unit actions in the jungles or

rice paddies suited them perfectly, as did the emphasis on winning the hearts and minds of the people through medical and technical aid. From JFK's point of view Vietnam was an almost perfect place to get involved. There he could show his interest in the Third World, demonstrate conclusively that America lived up to her commitments (the 1954 SEATO Treaty had extended protection to South Vietnam if it were attacked from without), and play the exciting game of counter-insurgency.

Ambrose, Rise to Globalism, pp.201–3

"

Review and Discuss

- Why did Kennedy welcome Vietnam as a 'great opportunity'?
- What kind of tone does Ambrose adopt

in describing Kennedy's support for continuing involvement in Vietnam?
- How fair is the treatment of Kennedy?

In May 1961 Kennedy sent Vice-President Johnson to investigate conditions in South Vietnam. He came back with some ominous impressions. Johnson recommended an increase in American assistance to Diem, whom he characterised as the 'Winston Churchill of Asia'. In October 1961 Kennedy sent another mission to Saigon, headed by General Maxwell Taylor and presidential aide Walt Rostow. They reported that South Vietnam had enough vitality to justify a major US effort and their recommendations tended towards a military solution.

In May 1963 public attention was riveted by the sight of a Buddhist monk in Hué who poured petrol over his body and set himself alight. This self-immolation climaxed a series of demonstrations by the Buddhists, some eighty per cent of South Vietnam's population, who deeply resented the control exercised by the Catholic twenty per cent who backed Diem. While world television news audiences watched the burning with horror, Madame Nhu, Diem's sister-in-law and wife of the head of the South's secret police, accused American reporters of having staged the suicide.

For Kennedy and his advisers the Buddhist rebellion indicated that the Diem government no longer had the support of the country. To American diplomats the complaints against Diem were depressingly similar to those voiced in China against Jiang Jie-shi's corruption before 1949. CIA operatives in Saigon thought that the replacement of Diem with a group of less corrupt military men would improve ARVN (the South Vietnamese army) morale. The US Ambassador, Henry Cabot Lodge, forwarded these hopes and fears to Washington with the recommendation that the USA provide tacit support for a coup to oust Diem. In the White House, National Security Adviser McGeorge Bundy agreed.

Word went back to Saigon and, on 1 November, Diem's government was toppled. The President and his brother were taken to the outskirts of Saigon and executed. Historians are still uncertain whether the CIA ordered or knew about the plan to eliminate the Vietnamese President. What is certain is that the American Ambassador and National Security Adviser had decided that the government of Vietnam had to be replaced.

On 22 November 1963, barely three weeks after Diem's murder, John F. Kennedy was himself cut down by an assassin's bullet in Dallas. A week before his death he had expressed misgivings about the American build-up in Vietnam, commenting that the process was like an 'alcoholic who takes a drink. The effect wears off, and you have to take another one'. Theodore Sorensen, Kennedy's principal speech-writer and biographer, lamented that the President 'had only begun, he was given so little time'. Given Kennedy's capacity to learn from his mistakes, Vietnam was seen by Sorensen as part of an emerging knowledge of the limitations of American power. Nevertheless, the fact remains that Kennedy did not mention quitting the war to his foreign policy advisers. Indeed, he saw Vietnam as an exemplary test case of US policy. Vietnam would provide a demonstration of American toughness and ability to win a war of national liberation.

A successful application of 'counter-insurgency', however, was naturally dependent on the expert advisers having correctly analysed the 'reality' of the situation in Indo-China. This they failed to do, as the English historian Hugh Brogan makes clear.

> America's participation in the Indo-Chinese wars was a mistake with many roots, some of which have yet to be disentangled by historians... Yet the most important single cause can be stated in a sentence. It was the failure to understand the nature and consequences of the great movement which dismantled the European empires. Obsessed with the Cold War, and imagining that all the rest of the world shared their obsession, American policy-makers and their supporters simply did not notice that reality was in large part organized round different concerns, and they forced such facts as could not be denied into their preconceptions, instead of modifying the preconceptions to fit the facts. In 1961 Soviet Russia and Red China were perceived as a united threat to the peace of the world and the liberty of the United States, and were likened to the German danger of the first half of the century. The steady divergence of Russian and Chinese policies was ignored, and when the two great communist powers began openly to quarrel experienced men could be heard warning that it was all a pretence to lull the West into false security... The idea that a nationalist movement, such as that led against the French Empire in Indo-China by Ho Chi Minh, was exceedingly unlikely to let itself become a simple tool of Soviet or Chinese expansionism, was often put forward but Washington paid no attention to such arguments (which have been amply vindicated by events since 1975). Ho Chi Minh, said Washington, was a communist; he was therefore a tool of the Kremlin; he was therefore an enemy of the United States. The syllogism was as perfect in form as it was worthless in content.

Hugh Brogan, *Pelican History of the United States of America*, Penguin, Harmondsworth, 1986, pp.667–8

THE HAZARDS
OF GLOBALISM

CHAPTER SEVEN

THE KENNEDY LEGACY

L ESS THAN one month after Kennedy's assassination, the new President, Lyndon B. Johnson addressed the United Nations General Assembly.

> " We meet in a time of mourning but in a moment of dedication ... the assassin's bullet which took his [Kennedy's] life did not alter his nation's purpose. We are more than ever opposed to the doctrines of hate and violence in our own land and around the world. We are more than ever committed to the rule of law — in our own land and around the world. We believe more than ever in the rights of man, all men of every colour — in our own land and around the world. And more than ever we support the United Nations, as the best instrument yet devised to promote the peace of the world and to promote the well being of mankind ...
>
> If there is one commitment more than any other that I would like to leave with you today, it is my unswerving commitment to the keeping and to the strengthening of the peace. Peace is a journey of a thousand miles and it must be taken one step at a time.
>
> The United States of America wants to see the cold war end ... wants to press on with arms control and reduction ... wants to co-operate with all the members of this organization to conquer everywhere the ancient enemies of mankind — hunger, and disease and ignorance ... wants sanity and security and peace for all, and above all ...
>
> And therefore any man and any nation that seeks peace — and hates war — and is willing to fight the good fight against hunger, and disease, and ignorance and misery will find the United States of America by their side, willing to walk with them — walk with them every step of the way. "

Lyndon B. Johnson,
Address to UN General
Assembly, 17 December
1963, *Department of State
Bulletin*, L, 6 January 1964,
pp.1–4

Johnson's administration was confronted with a series of difficult international problems. The 1960s generally was a time of increased diffusion of world power and, as a consequence, some slippage of American authority. Although United States relations with the Soviet Union were improving when Johnson assumed the presidency, a number of thorny foreign affairs problems — with NATO, in Latin America, the Middle East, the Third World generally — were on the horizon. The question of America's role in South-East Asia was only a small cloud on the horizon when Johnson took office, but during his five years in the White House it consumed his energies, his ambitions, and ultimately his reputation.

In responding to changes in the international scene, US policy-makers tended to cling to the past, still thinking that Uncle Sam could direct events through the carefully directed use of arms and aid. Johnson himself shared that perception. He accepted implicitly the threat of international communism, the wisdom of containment, the need to honour commitments to one's allies, and the special obligations to maintain an American presence in East Asia.

By the mid-1960s, although the ideological conflict between American liberal democracy and Soviet communism was no longer the kind of obsession it had been in earlier times, it nevertheless remained the most important factor in shaping American policy. Khrushchev's sudden departure from the scene in October 1964 caused some concern in Washington, but his successors, Premier Alexei Kosygin and First Party Secretary Leonid Brezhnev, soon revealed their desire to continue the policy of 'peaceful co-existence'.

The beginnings of Soviet–American détente — relaxation or lessening of international tension — in the latter part of the 1960s did not mean that the two superpowers had abandoned their rivalry for the support of Third World and unaligned nations. The explosive situation in the Middle East made

"HE ATE TOO MUCH"

The politics of US economic aid: an American cartoon of 1962 by Poinier. (Reprinted with permission of the Detroit News, *a Gannett newspaper, copyright 1962.) What does the horse in the cartoon represent? What action has been taken by the US Congress? Why? How does the cartoonist relate this action to US strategy in the Cold War?*

that clear. Following Israel's spectacular military victory in the Six Day War of 1967, the Arab nations were drawn more closely into alignment with the Soviet Union. In the aftermath of the Six Day War, Soviet Premier Kosygin went to New York to attend a special session of the United Nations.

While in America Kosygin met Johnson for their only conference at the small college town of Glassboro, New Jersey (June 1967). No real progress was made in the talks on either the Middle Eastern or Indo-China conflicts. Johnson at least came away from the conversations with the view that the Soviets did wish to avoid direct military confrontation with the USA in Vietnam. Further, the Glassboro discussions did lead to a commitment by both leaders to do more to limit the race in strategic arms between the two superpowers.

In Western and Central Europe Johnson hoped to advance the Kennedy administration's plans for the strengthening of defence and trade relations within the Atlantic community. He made little progress in this regard, however, particularly with the French, and the NATO alliance continued to lose cohesiveness.

INTERVENTION IN LATIN AMERICA

In Latin America, smouldering nationalism, the frequency of military coups and Castro's continuing and irritating survival all helped to define Johnson's policies. Johnson was determined to prevent a recurrence of Castroism in the Western hemisphere, not only because of his commitment to the containment of communism, but also because he remembered how the Republican Party opposition had made political capital out of the Cuban situation in the early sixties. It soon became clear that US policy was to be based on stabilising Latin American politics, protecting the private interests of US capital in the area and waging war against communism in any shape or form. The USA was more interested in supporting anti-communist governments through economic assistance than in opposing undemocratic military regimes.

The major crisis in Johnson's Latin American diplomacy occurred in the Dominican Republic. The Dominican Republic had emerged from thirty years of despotism when Rafael Trujillo (dictator since 1931) was assassinated in 1961. After a series of provisional governments, the Dominican people elected Juan Bosch as their President with sixty per cent of the vote. Ten months later a military coup ousted Bosch and a conservative junta under Reid Cabral took power. In April 1965, an odd coalition of democrats, radicals and junior military officers launched a counter-coup, with the object of restoring constitutional government under Bosch. Johnson and his advisers assumed that the revolt was 'communist or Castroite'-inspired and 33 000 US troops were dispatched to crush the rebellion. American newspaper reporters accompanying the troops gave wide publicity to Bosch's complaint that 'this was a democratic revolution smashed by the leading democracy in the world'.

Johnson's critics pointed out that American unwillingness or inability to distinguish between nationalism and communism meant that the United States was forfeiting the support of liberal reformers in the Third World. Someone who saw this very clearly was Senator J. William Fulbright, Chairman of the influential Senate Foreign Relations Committee. Fulbright, who opposed the Dominican venture, complained:

> We have made ourselves the prisoners of the Latin American oligarchs who are engaged in a vain attempt to preserve the status quo — reactionaries who habitually use the term communist very loosely, in part... in a calculated effort to scare the United States into supporting their selfish and discredited aims...
>
> Many North Americans seem to believe that, while the United States does indeed participate in Latin American affairs from time to time, sometimes by force, it is done with the best of intentions... and therefore cannot really be considered intervention. The trouble with this point of view is that it is not shared by our neighbours to the south. Most of them do think they need protection from the United States... 'Good intentions' are not a very sound basis for judging the fulfilment of contractual obligations. Just about everybody, including the Communists, believes in his own 'good intentions'.
>
> In the eyes of educated, energetic, and patriotic young Latin Americans... the United States committed a worse offence in the Dominican Republic than just intervention; it intervened against social revolution and in support... of a corrupt, reactionary military oligarchy... The tragedy of Santo Domingo is that a policy that purported to defeat communism in the short term is more likely to have the effect of promoting it in the long run...
>
> We are not, as we like to claim in Fourth of July speeches, the most truly revolutionary nation on earth; we are, on the contrary, much closer to being the most unrevolutionary nation on earth.

Congressional Record, 89th Congress, 2nd Session, 15 September 1965

Review and Discuss

- How did North Americans perceive US intervention in Latin America?
- How did Latin Americans perceive that same US intervention?

- What did Fulbright see as the 'tragic' aspect of US intervention in the Dominican Republic?

ESCALATION OF THE VIETNAM WAR

Shortly after the Dominican intervention Johnson stated publicly: 'Now I am the most denounced man in the world.' There certainly was a surge of anti-American feeling around the world, but the criticism was directed more against

American actions in Vietnam than against those in Latin America. Soon after Diem's death, the National Liberation Front, UN Secretary General U Thant, France, and many concerned Americans called for the formation of a coalition government in Saigon and the neutralisation of South Vietnam. The time did seem propitious for negotiation. Johnson, however, declared that the United States sought 'victory' because the 'neutralization of South Vietnam would only be another name for a communist take over'.

In February 1964 the American-advised South Vietnamese forces began covert commando raids and sabotage missions into North Vietnam. By mid-year American ships, heavily laden with sophisticated electronic gear, monitored North Vietnamese communications while the South Vietnamese vessels raided the coast. On the night of 2 August, the American destroyer *Maddox* was fired on by North Vietnamese patrol boats while engaged in espionage in the Gulf of Tonkin. Two days later the *Maddox* and a second destroyer were allegedly fired upon during a night so dark and stormy that the two US ships could not even see each other. No physical evidence of an assault was found. Hanoi admitted attacking the *Maddox* on 2 August but not on 4 August, in retaliation for the *Maddox*'s participation in offensive actions against North Vietnam.

It hardly mattered what actually happened in the Tonkin Gulf, for the Johnson administration wanted a reason for some dramatic gesture against North Vietnam. As soon as news of the incident reached Washington, Johnson interpreted the attack as 'open aggression on the high seas' and insisted 'the attacks were unprovoked'. That very night Johnson went on television to announce retaliatory air strikes against North Vietnamese targets. SEATO and NATO allies and the US Congress had not yet been consulted. The next day Johnson did address Congress and ask for its approval of the blanket Gulf of Tonkin Resolution, which authorised the President to 'take all necessary measures to repel any armed attack against the forces of the United States and to prevent further aggression'.

The debate on the Gulf of Tonkin Resolution was led by the Chairman of the Senate Foreign Relations Committee, J. William Fulbright. Fulbright later became one of the harshest critics of the Vietnam War and he subsequently apologised to the two senators who dissented from the resolution, saying it was 'the dumbest thing I've ever done'. The resolution was quickly passed in the House and for the next six years, until it was repealed by Congress in 1970, the Gulf of Tonkin Resolution was used as the legal basis for the American war in Vietnam.

After the Tonkin Gulf affair, American advisers drew up plans for bombing raids on North Vietnam and after Johnson's overwhelming victory in the November 1964 election these plans took on increased significance. The Joint Chiefs of Staff recommended a commitment of US combat troops and bombing of the North to stem the flow of supplies to the South and boost morale in Saigon. Johnson approved the bombing of North Vietnam and Operation Rolling Thunder — the sustained bombing of the North — began in February 1965.

On 7 April 1965 Johnson outlined his war aims in a speech at Johns Hopkins University.

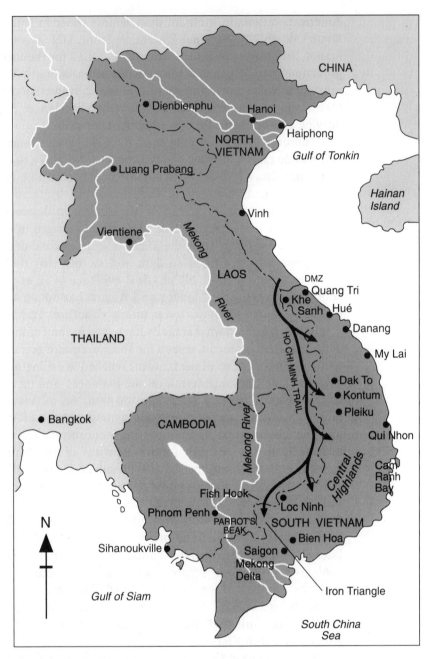

CHINA

Dienbienphu   Hanoi
                Haiphong

NORTH
VIETNAM   Gulf of Tonkin

Luang Prabang   Hainan
                                     Island

Vientiene   Vinh

             Mekong

                    LAOS   DMZ
                                   Quang Tri
THAILAND   River   Khe Hué
                                 Sanh
                                      Danang

                                         My Lai

                                    Dak To
                                    Kontum
                                    Pleiku

Bangkok   CAMBODIA   Qui Nhon

                    Mekong River   Cam
                                              Ranh
                                              Bay

                                    Central
             Fish Hook   Highlands
Phnom Penh   Loc Ninh
             PARROT'S
             BEAK   SOUTH VIETNAM
Sihanoukville   Bien Hoa
                    Saigon
N   Mekong
                    Delta
                                    Iron Triangle
    Gulf of Siam
                                    South China
                                    Sea

HO CHI MINH TRAIL

*Indo-China during
the Vietnam War*

> ❝ The contest in Vietnam is part of a wider pattern of aggressive purpose...
> Why are we in South Vietnam? We are there because we have a promise
> to keep. Since 1954 every American President has offered support to the
> people of South Vietnam. We have helped to build, and we have helped
> to defend. Thus over many years, we have made a national pledge to help
> South Vietnam defend its independence. And I intend to keep that promise.
> To dishonour the pledge, to abandon this small and brave nation to its
> enemy, and to the terror that must follow, would be an unforgivable wrong.
> We are also there to strengthen world order. Around the globe from Berlin

to Thailand, are people whose well-being rests, in part, on the belief that they can count on us if they are attacked. To leave Vietnam to its fate would shake the confidence of all these people in the value of American commitment, the value of America's word. The result would be increased unrest and instability, and even wider war.

We are also there because there are great stakes in the balance. Let no one think for a moment that retreat from Vietnam would bring an end to conflict. The battle would be renewed in one country and then another. The central lesson of our time is that the appetite for aggression is never satisfied. To withdraw from one battlefield means only to prepare for the next. We must say in South-East Asia as we did in Europe, in the words of the Bible: 'Hitherto shalt thou come, but no further'.

Department of State Bulletin, 26 April 1965, p.607

99

Review and Discuss

- How did Johnson justify American involvement in Vietnam?
- What assumption was behind Johnson's belief that American withdrawal from Vietnam would not end conflict in the region?

Johnson's speech at Johns Hopkins University was widely interpreted at the time of its delivery as an indication of US willingness to negotiate a conclusion to the Vietnam War. Johnson did offer to negotiate with the North Vietnamese about their withdrawal of troops from the South. He held out the prospect of more bombing and more American troops if they refused. The North Vietnamese leader, Ho Chi Minh, pointed out that the Americans had simply taken over from the French as the major imperial power. Ho's position, consistent throughout the war, was that the United States should stop bombing and withdraw its troops and then negotiations could begin. In February 1967, Ho replied to a further offer from Johnson, suggesting peace talks, in the following terms:

66 Vietnam is a thousand miles away from the United States. The Vietnamese people have never done any harm to the United States. But contrary to the pledges made by its representative at the 1954 Geneva Conference, the US Government has ceaselessly intervened in Vietnam, it has unleashed and intensified the war of aggression in South Vietnam with a view to prolonging the partition of Vietnam and turning South Vietnam into a neo-colony and military base of the United States...

The Vietnamese people deeply love independence, freedom and peace. But in the face of the U.S. aggression, they have risen up, united as one man, fearless of sacrifices and hardships: they are determined to carry on their Resistance until they have won genuine independence and freedom and true peace...

President Ho Chi Minh's Reply to President Lyndon B. Johnson, February 1967, quoted in Against the U.S. Aggression for National Salvation, Foreign Languages Publishing House, Hanoi, 1967

The Vietnamese people will never submit to force; they will never accept talks under the threat of bombs.

99

Review and Discuss

• How did Ho Chi Minh view the purpose of American involvement in Vietnam?

• What did Ho indicate would be the response of the Vietnamese people 'in the face of US aggression'?

The heaviest build up of American forces in Vietnam occurred after July 1965 when Johnson accepted his generals' request for more ground troops. US forces numbered 50 000 at the beginning of 1965; the peak level of 542 000 was reached in February 1969. In the period 1965–68 the Pentagon dropped the fiction that US personnel were advisers to the army of South Vietnam. It became America's war fought by draftees, who quickly learned to despise all Vietnamese, both friend and foe alike. Small contingents from South Korea, the Philippines, Australia and New Zealand fought alongside the Americans and South Vietnamese.

The new American commander in Vietnam, General William C. Westmoreland, favoured a strategy of 'search and destroy' in which American and South Vietnamese troops scoured the countryside looking for the Vietcong and killing them. The use of bombs, napalm and defoliant destroyed hundreds of villages, denuded the landscape and created thousands of refugees. By the end of 1967 as many as 4 million people, or twenty-five per cent of the population, were refugees.

Responsibility for the nightmare in South Vietnam cannot be attributed exclusively to the United States, for the Vietcong and the North Vietnamese were certainly shooting back. However, the overwhelming American fire power and clearing operations strategy were direct causes of much of the horror and devastation. The fact that many of these military operations were televised into American homes every evening was an important element in the growing public questioning of America's role in Vietnam.

COLLAPSE OF THE COLD WAR CONSENSUS

As the war in Vietnam escalated, critics of US policy became more outspoken. One of the most significant defections from the bipartisan foreign policy of the Johnson administration was that of Senator J. William Fulbright. Fulbright decided in 1965 that the USA was 'losing its perspective on what is exactly within the realm of its power and what is beyond it'. In early 1966 he denounced 'the arrogance of power' of American diplomacy since World War II.

In February 1966 Fulbright's Senate Foreign Relations Committee conducted publicly televised hearings into the purpose and extent of US participation in Vietnam. Administration spokespeople defended the war, citing the traditional need to contain communism. Secretary of State Dean Rusk explained that the USA was involved in 'the process of preventing the expansion and extension of Communist domination by the use of force against the weaker nations on the perimeter of Communist power'.

Several important members of the foreign policy establishment who testified before the committee — George F. Kennan, father of containment, James Gavin, former army general, and Hans Morgenthau, Jr, University of Chicago professor of international relations — questioned the wisdom of US policy. Kennan forcefully insisted that his containment doctrine, designed for a stable European nation-state context in the 1940s, was not applicable to Asia. Gavin and Morgenthau also thought the United States was diverting precious resources from Europe, the proper focus of diplomatic attention, by waging a costly and unwinnable war in South-East Asia. All three urged a gradual US withdrawal from Vietnam.

In later Senate Committee hearings, widely respected historian Henry Steele Commager emphasised the wider context of the Vietnamese revolt when he stated that the rebellion 'is against two or three hundred years of exploitation and of imperialism... And by what seems to me to be a most unfair, but perfectly understandable process, a great many of the antagonisms against the European West are focused on us'. America had stepped into a traditional struggle over which it could not exert control. Continuing his testimony before the committee, Commager stated:

> 66 It is my feeling that we do not have the resources, material, intellectual, or moral to be at once an American power, a European power and an Asian power...
>
> It is not our duty to keep peace throughout the globe, to put down aggression whenever it starts up, to stop the advance of Communism or other isms which we may not approve of. It is primarily the responsibility of the United Nations to keep the peace, to settle disputes, to discourage aggression, and if that organization is not strong enough to do the job we should perhaps bind our major energies to giving her the necessary authority and the tools. 99

US Senate Foreign Relations Committee, *Changing American Attitudes Toward Foreign Policy*, 90th Congress, 1st Session, 20 February 1967

The Johnson administration lashed out at this apparent defection from the Cold War consensus. Polls were cited that showed most Americans would not tolerate a Vietcong victory. Yet doubt grew within the administration's own ranks. Walt Rostow tried to reassure Johnson with statistical charts showing the 'enemy's' heavy loss of life and property. Secretary of Defense McNamara, racked with doubts about the morality of the bombing campaign in the North and the South, asked an assistant, Leslie Gelb, to compile a documentary history of US involvement in the war. The outcome of the Defense Department enquiry, published in condensed form as *The Pentagon Papers* in 1971, is a crucial and revealing study, which concludes that American leaders since Roosevelt had deceived the public into supporting an unwinnable war. In November 1967, McNamara, convinced that the war could not be won and ashamed of his own participation in it, decided to resign.

The last hope the administration had of persuading the public that the war could be won vanished when the Vietnamese launched the Tet (New Year)

The legacy of Vietnam: a British cartoon of 1967 (reproduced by permission of Punch). Who is the figure with the axe? What is he doing? Why is he doing this? What is the cartoonist's view of the effect of these actions?

The Train Robbery

offensive on 31 January 1968. In two weeks of bitter fighting the North Vietnamese captured eight provincial capitals and actually took temporary possession of the American embassy in Saigon.

By March 1968 Johnson was severely shaken. His new Secretary of Defense, Clark Clifford, widely considered to be a hawk, organised a high-level review of US policy in Vietnam. The group of top advisers he consulted (including former Secretary of State Dean Acheson) let Johnson know that they believed the war could not be won. On 31 March 1968 the President went on national television and announced that he was stopping the bombing of North Vietnam at the 19th parallel and was withdrawing from the presidential race, so that he could devote himself full time to negotiating a settlement.

> 66 It was a humiliating end. Certainly L.B.J. had been the most powerful man in the world, and quite possibly he had the strongest will, yet a relative handful of V.C. [Vietcong] had resisted and overcome his power and broken his will... He had wanted to bring democracy and prosperity to South-East Asia but he had brought only death and destruction. By early 1968 he had learned the painful lessons that the power to destroy is not the power to control, and that he had reached and passed the limits of his own power. As he retired to his beloved hill country of central Texas, two questions remained. How long would it take his country to also recognize that it had reached and passed the limits of its power? How long before the United States retired from South-East Asia? 99

Ambrose, *Rise to Globalism*, pp.229-30

PART THREE

Détente and Beyond

THE STRUGGLE FOR DÉTENTE

CHAPTER EIGHT

BREZHNEV AND THE SEARCH FOR DETENTE

THE SOVIET UNION was the nation that benefited most from American involvement in the Vietnam War. With American attention and resources tied up in South-East Asia, the USSR made a dramatic recovery in world affairs between 1965 and 1970. The ousting of Khrushchev and his replacement by Premier Alexei Kosygin and First Party Secretary Leonid Brezhnev occurred as the United States was stepping up its military effort in Vietnam. As Soviet influence in Hanoi grew, Moscow was not inclined to mediate. For one thing the two sides seemed irreconcilable. More significantly, as long as the conflict remained limited, it would continue to severely drain US resources and thereby benefit the Soviet Union.

The seeds of détente were sown in 1967–68 in the context of the war in Vietnam. The Johnson administration began to pursue the idea of détente with the new Soviet leaders in the hope that they might be able to put some pressure on North Vietnam's leader, Ho Chi Minh, to agree to peace negotiations.

Two factors were significant in Brezhnev's move towards détente with the West. The first of these was the emergence of a fundamental change in the relationship between the two superpowers. In the aftermath of the 1962 Cuban missile crisis a Soviet official had warned an American: 'You'll never be able to do that to us again.' By the end of the 1960s the Russians had achieved strategic parity with the Americans. The United States remained ahead in many categories of arms, but in overall military capability the United States could no longer be considered pre-eminent. The political implications of this strategic parity were very important. In matters of arms control the Soviet Union could now negotiate from a position of equality. This situation was to open the way for genuine efforts at arms control in the 1970s.

The second factor fundamental to an understanding of Brezhnev's desire for détente was the state of the Soviet economy. Although Russia's military power had increased sharply in the 1960s, its economic growth rate had dropped drastically. In 1965 the Soviet leadership introduced a series of economic reforms to modernise the economy, stimulate growth and improve the quality and quantity of consumer goods. By the late 1960s it was clear that these reforms were a failure. To the Soviets the idea of détente made sense since it offered economic relief. The slowing down of the arms race would mean a 'peace dividend' for the Soviet economy.

SOVIET INTERVENTION IN CZECHOSLOVAKIA

The détente process was temporarily derailed in August 1968 by the Soviet invasion of Czechoslovakia. Given the example of the poor Soviet economic planning record, during the 1960s some Eastern European governments experimented with more liberal economic policies. In Czechoslovakia, what began as a limited set of measures to improve productivity broadened into a major reform movement that challenged the monopoly on decision-making essential to the communist system.

The Czech leadership, mindful of the bitter experience of the Hungarians in 1956, went out of its way to assure Moscow of its loyalty. In April 1968 the Czechoslovak government declared:

> 66 The Czechoslovak Socialist Republic is a socialist country. The permanent foundation of Czechoslovak foreign policy is friendship and close co-operation with the Soviet Union and the other socialist countries. Our alliance with the Soviet Union belongs to those permanent, firm values whose purity has been fully confirmed by the critical examination of all values in our current revival process. This is so because our friendship with the Soviet Union arises organically from a number of experiences paid for so dearly by our nations, because we were brought to it by the very logic of historical development, the vital interests and needs of our homeland, because it is supported by the will, needs and feelings of our people. 99

Robin A. Remington,
Winter in Prague, MIT
Press, Cambridge, Mass.,
1969 (Document 20)

Review and Discuss

- What assurance was given by the Czechoslovak government? Why was such an assurance considered necessary?

Despite the Czech assurance, the Soviet leaders grew anxious. In their eyes the developments associated with the so-called 'Prague spring' were undermining the foundations of communist society in Czechoslovakia. After strong pressure from the military, who feared that demand for Prague-type reform might spread to the entire Eastern bloc, Moscow decided to resort to force. In August 1968 the Red Army, together with token forces from the other members of the Warsaw Pact, invaded Czechoslovakia, toppled and arrested the reformist government and installed in its place a hand-picked regime entirely subservient to Moscow.

Partly in response to the hostility of the communist parties in Western Europe (who displayed greater outrage than did their capitalist governments), and partly to 'explain' Soviet policy to its Eastern European allies, Moscow published in *Pravda* in September 1968 a major policy statement that subsequently came to be known in the West as the Brezhnev Doctrine. The document asserted that the interests of the 'socialist community' as a whole superseded those of its individual members and whenever these were threatened, the socialist community had the right, indeed the duty, to intervene to set matters straight.

> There is no doubt that the peoples of the socialist countries and the Communist Parties have and must have freedom to determine their country's path to development. However, any decision of theirs must damage neither socialism in their own country nor the fundamental interests of other socialist countries... This means that every Communist Party is responsible not only to its own people but also to all the socialist countries and the entire Communist movement. Whoever forgets this is placing sole emphasis on the autonomy and independence of Communist Parties, lapses into one-sidedness, shirking his internationalist obligations... Just as, in V.I. Lenin's

Anti-Soviet slogans in Prague, Czechoslovakia, August 1968 (Popperfoto). Why did the Soviets crush the Czechoslovak reform movement? What messages are conveyed by the graffiti?

S. Kovalev, 'Sovereignty and the international obligations of Communist countries', *Pravda*, 26 September 1968, quoted in Remington, *Winter in Prague* (Document 65)

> words, someone living in a society cannot be free of that society, so a socialist state that is in a system of other states constituting a socialist commonwealth cannot be free of the common interests of that commonwealth. **"**

Review and Discuss

- On what grounds did the Brezhnev Doctrine justify Soviet intervention in Czechoslovakia?

- Were there other advantages in the doctrine from Moscow's point of view?

The Brezhnev Doctrine violated international agreements signed by the Soviet Union (such as the United Nations Charter) as well as its own frequently proclaimed doctrine that each socialist country had the right to choose its own path to communism. It left no doubt that what had happened in Czechoslovakia in 1968 was not in any way an 'accident' but a deliberate decision grounded in political philosophy and for that reason likely to happen again.

NIXON, KISSINGER AND 'LINKAGE'

The movement towards détente began to gather momentum in 1969. There was a new administration in Washington that appeared ready to accept the implications of Soviet nuclear might. President Richard Nixon and National Security Adviser (and later Secretary of State) Henry Kissinger believed that there was a path to peace in Vietnam, if not with honour then without defeat, and that the path led through Moscow and Beijing. Kissinger presented his ideas as a new concept in diplomacy, one which he called 'linkage'. As perceived by Kissinger, the development of economic, political and strategic ties between the USA and the USSR, equally rewarding to both, would bind the two in a common fate, thereby lessening the incentive for conflict and war. Nixon explained the concept of linkage at the start of his administration in a letter to the Secretaries of State and Defense and the Director of the CIA:

> **"** ...the previous administration took the view that when we perceive a mutual interest on an issue with the USSR, we should pursue agreement and attempt to insulate it as much as possible from the ups and downs of conflicts elsewhere. This may well be sound on numerous bilateral and practical matters such as cultural or scientific exchanges. But on the crucial issues of our day... I believe that the Soviet leaders should be brought to understand that they cannot expect to reap the benefits of cooperation in one area while seeking to take advantage of tension or confrontation elsewhere. Such a course involves the danger that the Soviets will use talks on arms as

Henry Kissinger, *The White House Years*, Weidenfeld & Nicolson and Michael Joseph, London, 1979, p.136

a safety valve on intransigence elsewhere... I believe I should retain the freedom to ensure, to the extent that we have control over it, that the timing of talks with the Soviet Union on strategic weapons is optimal... Indeed it means that we should — at least in our public position — keep open the option that there may be no talks at all. **99**

Review and Discuss

- What role did Nixon see arms negotiations playing in USSR–US relations? How does this illustrate the concept of linkage?

In Moscow, Brezhnev was receptive to the idea that the superpowers should engage in serious arms limitation talks. At the 24th Party Congress in March 1971 he launched a 'peace program' that was to shape Soviet foreign policy throughout the 1970s. He emphasised a dual approach: peaceful co-existence combined with a resistance to imperialism.

Leonid Brezhnev, Report of the Central Committee of the CPSU to the 24th Congress of the Communist Party of the Soviet Union, Novosti, Moscow, 1971

66 Our policy has always combined firm rebuffs to aggression with the constructive line of settling international problems and maintaining normal, and, whenever the situation allows, good relations with states belonging to the other social system. As in the past, we have consistently stood up for the Leninist principle of peaceful co-existence of states, regardless of their social system. This principle has now become a real force of international development. **99**

WINDING DOWN THE VIETNAM WAR

Meanwhile Kissinger was convinced that the Soviet Union held the key to peace in Vietnam. He was prepared to make concessions to the Kremlin in trade, credits, technology, arms reduction talks and more, if Moscow would use its influence with Hanoi to negotiate an end to the war. This was what linkage was all about.

The Nixon administration for its part had adopted a policy of 'Vietnamization', i.e. building up South Vietnam's army so that it could replace departing American troops, whose phased withdrawal Nixon had announced in 1969. Simultaneously, the administration announced a Nixon Doctrine: as the United States pulled back from some of its military commitments, certain friends would take up the burden of containment of communism, helped by American advisers and armaments. In Asia, the friend would be Japan; in the Middle East, Iran; and in Africa, Zaire (the former Belgian Congo) and white-dominated South Africa. Historian Walter LaFeber outlines some of the problems created by the application of the Nixon Doctrine.

> 66 In all, the Nixon Doctrine encouraged a dangerous military build up in the Middle East and southern Africa; nearly bankrupted some nations and encouraged others, such as Iran, to raise oil prices to pay for the inflation-priced United States equipment; made these nations more likely to use force rather than negotiations to settle disputes; helped create dangerously strained relations with Japan when it refused to become an Asian policeman; and caused Nixon to become a political bedfellow of the Shah and white supremacist regimes in Africa. The doctrine's only redeeming virtue was that it gave the President a rationale for pulling back from Vietnam. 99

LaFeber, America, Russia and the Cold War, p.263

Withdrawal from Vietnam proved to be a most difficult operation for the USA. As Nixon pulled out the troops he secretly escalated the bombing, including neutral Cambodia, which had managed to stay out of the war thus far. The bombing only drove the communists deeper into Cambodia and destabilised the government. In May 1970 American and South Vietnamese troops invaded Cambodia to clean out the communist camps. Nixon's televised announcement of the operation stressed that the purpose was to gain time for the American withdrawal. The results of the invasion of Cambodia were overwhelmingly negative. It turned Cambodia into a battleground and widened the communist insurgency there. By 1971 the communists controlled half the country. By 1975 they had all of it. The United States invasion of Cambodia had the effect of making the domino theory come true.

In 1971 Nixon authorised South Vietnamese troops to clean out communist sanctuaries in Laos. As in Cambodia, the United States operation contributed to the domino effect. By mid-1971 the communists were in a stronger position in Laos than at any time since 1962.

In July 1971 Kissinger announced in Beijing that the US President would be coming to China to open 'normal' relations between the two countries. Such a visit represented a major change in United States policy toward China.

Vietnam on the receiving end of 'liberation': an American cartoon by Pat Oliphant of 1972 (reproduced with permission Universal Press Syndicate). Who is the figure in the cartoon? What action does she take in each of the six frames? What happens to her in the process of liberation?

'Greetings, French Liberators!'

'Greetings, Nationalist Liberators!'

'Greetings, Viet Cong Liberators!'

'Greetings, American Liberators!'

'Greetings, Government Liberators!'

'Greetings, North Vietnamese Liberators!'

Why did the sudden turnabout in American diplomacy occur? Historian Stephen Ambrose offers the following explanation:

> " Why had it been done? Who stood to gain from it? Commentators speculated that perhaps Nixon and Kissinger wanted to use the opening to China as a way to squeeze both Moscow and Hanoi.
>
> It appeared that Nixon saw vast possibilities for the United States in a Sino–Soviet split. He specifically believed that he could so manage the split as to force both Communist powers to abandon North Vietnam, which in turn would let the United States safely exit from Vietnam. The way to get Russia and China to cooperate, Nixon reasoned, was to keep them guessing about actual United States intentions. Nixon's active pursuit of détente could not help but make China worry about a possible U.S.–U.S.S.R. alliance against China. Nixon's opening to China, meanwhile, made Russia's leaders fearful of a U.S.–China alliance directed against them. "

Ambrose, Rise to Globalism, p.239

In February 1972 Nixon flew to Beijing. His trip proved a huge success. He met with the ageing Mao and accepted the Chinese leader's complaints about the 'hegemonism' of the Soviet Union. The two pledged to end their thirty years of hostility and move towards the establishment of normal relations. Within months the People's Republic of China entered the United Nations, while Jiang Jie-shi's delegation was expelled. (Before the decade was out America and China had full diplomatic exchanges.)

During 1972, the critical year of negotiations between the Americans and the North Vietnamese, the Soviet Union did agree to act as an intermediary between Washington and Hanoi. Kissinger made several trips to Moscow to enlist Soviet support to put pressure on Ho Chi Minh to accept a compromise settlement. Brezhnev insisted that Hanoi's policies were not subject to Soviet control. The North Vietnamese continued their offensive and the United States responded by carrying out heavy bombing raids over Hanoi and planting mines in the harbour at Haiphong.

An American in Beijing, February 1972 (Wide World). Identify the three leaders in the photograph. Why was this meeting of historic significance for US–China relations? How did this development affect Soviet–US relations?

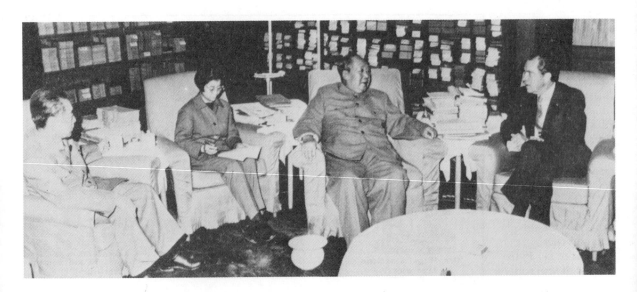

Nixon's escalation of the war was a calculated risk coming as it did only weeks before the first scheduled summit meeting in Moscow. But Nixon had calculated correctly. Regardless of events in Vietnam, the Soviets wanted to negotiate, and in May 1972 Nixon became the first American President to visit the Soviet capital. Although Brezhnev and his colleagues were not willing to concede any substantive points, they made it clear that they did not consider the Vietnam War an obstacle to the process of détente. They agreed to continue their intermediary role in a complex shuttle of proposals and counterproposals between Washington and Hanoi. In October 1972 Hanoi agreed for the first time to a ceasefire without demanding President Thieu's removal as a prior condition. This concession paved the way for a truce that was finally signed in January 1973. The Americans firmly believed that Soviet pressure had played an important part in softening Hanoi's negotiating position.

THE FRUITS OF SUMMITRY

The major outcome of the Moscow Summit was agreement on a number of arms control measures that had been under negotiation for some time. In the last week of May 1972, two important agreements were signed by Brezhnev and Nixon. The first was a Strategic Arms Limitation Treaty (SALT I), which set upper limits on the number of offensive missiles each side could hold. The pact also ended the race to develop a defensive anti-ballistic missile (ABM) system. (These arms control measures are examined in Chapter 13.) The second agreement was a document entitled Basic Principles of Relations Between the USSR and the USA. Brezhnev told Nixon that he considered this statement even more important than the SALT agreement. The following extract gives some idea of the diplomatic sentiment underlying the agreement:

> 66 The Union of Soviet Socialist Republics and the United States of America ... have agreed as follows.
>
> *First.* They will proceed from the common determination that in the nuclear age there is no alternative to conducting their mutual relations on the basis of peaceful co-existence. Differences in ideology and in the social systems of the USSR and the USA are not obstacles to the bilateral development of normal relations based on the principles of sovereignty, equality, non-interference in internal affairs and mutual advantage.
>
> *Second.* The USSR and the USA ... will do their utmost to avoid military confrontations and to prevent the outbreak of nuclear war. They will always exercise restraint in their mutual relations, and will be prepared to negotiate and settle differences by peaceful means.
>
> *Third.* The USSR and the USA have a special responsibility to do everything in their power so that conflicts or situations will not arise which would serve to increase international tensions. Accordingly, they will seek to promote conditions in which all countries will live in peace and security and will not be subject to outside interference in their internal affairs ... 99

'Basic Principles of Relations Between the USSR and the USA', signed in Moscow, 29 May 1972, in Leonid Brezhnev, *Peace, Détente and Soviet-American Relations*, Harcourt Brace Jovanovich, New York/Novosti, Moscow, 1979, pp.225–6

Brezhnev's high regard for the Basic Principles statement is evident both from his remarks to Nixon at the time and his subsequent references to it in many of his speeches. The Americans, however, did not appear to appreciate the symbolic and psychological value of such a statement for Moscow. This is evident from Kissinger's account in his memoirs:

> 66 The Soviets are much addicted to declarations of principle. Probably they see in them an acknowledgement of equality and a device to create the impression that major progress is being made in bilateral relations. Perhaps there is something in Russian history that leads them to value ritual, solemn declarations, and visible symbols. 99

Kissinger, *The White House Years*, p.1132

Kissinger goes on to comment on the equality aspect:

> 66 Equality seemed to mean a great deal to Brezhnev... He expressed his pleasure when in my brief opening remarks I stated the obvious: that we were approaching the summit in a spirit of equality and reciprocity. What a more secure leader might have regarded as cliché or condescension, Brezhnev treated as a welcome sign of seriousness. 99

Kissinger, *The White House Years*, p.1141

Review and Discuss

- How did Kissinger interpret Brezhnev's attitude toward the summit negotiations?

- What do Kissinger's comments reveal about his own attitude towards the summit negotiations?

One area of negotiation not completed at the first summit was Soviet-American trade — a subject of vital importance to the Soviet Union. The Nixon administration, desperate for Soviet help on the Vietnam issue, was prepared to bargain generously with the Soviet Union on trade. A new era in Soviet-American trade relations was thought to be under way with the signing of a trade agreement in October 1972. As it turned out this was one agreement that did not survive the downturn in Soviet-American relations following Richard Nixon's resignation from office. In 1974–75 the United States Senate struck at the heart of Kissinger's détente policy by attaching conditions to the Soviet-American trade treaty that made the pact unacceptable to the Soviets. The Soviets angrily charged the United States with violating the terms of the 1972 trade treaty and in January 1975 the Kremlin formally repudiated the agreement.

From the Soviet point of view the most important of the measures negotiated at the second Brezhnev-Nixon Summit, in Washington in June 1973, was the Agreement... on the Prevention of Nuclear War. The Soviet Politburo resolved that, if implemented, this agreement 'will have a truly historic significance for all mankind'. At a news conference Kissinger commented that the agreement 'could mark a landmark on the road toward the structure of peace'. The most important commitment in the agreement was Article 4:

'Agreement Between the USSR and the USA on the Prevention of Nuclear War', 22 June 1973, in Brezhnev, *Peace, Détente and Soviet–American Relations*, p.229

66 If at any time relations between the Parties or between either Party and other countries appear to involve the risk of a nuclear conflict, or if relations between countries not parties to this Agreement appear to involve the risk of nuclear war between the Union of Soviet Socialist Republics and the United States of America or between either Party and other countries, the Soviet Union and the United States, acting in accordance with the provisions of this Agreement shall immediately enter into urgent consultations with each other and make every effort to avert this risk. 99

TESTING SUPERPOWER COMMITMENT: THE YOM KIPPUR WAR

Article 4 of the Agreement ... on the Prevention of Nuclear War had potentially enormous implications for Soviet–American relations. It depended, however, on how the article would be interpreted. The constant danger of the Cold War had always been that the superpowers could be drawn into a confrontation because of the actions of their allies or clients, over which neither superpower had full control. On paper the agreement committed the USSR and the USA to co-operate with each other, if necessary, against the interests of an ally. Within less than four months Article 4 of the agreement would be put to its first test in the Arab–Israeli war of October 1973. It did not pass that test.

War broke out between Israel and its neighbours when Syria and Egypt attacked on 6 October 1973, on the holiest day of the Jewish year, Yom Kippur. In the first three days of the war, Egyptian troops crossed the Suez Canal, forcing the surrender of hundreds of surprised Israeli soldiers. In the north the Syrian army posed an even graver threat to the Jewish state. It nearly broke through the Israeli defences on the Golan Heights to cut the country in two. Israeli Prime Minister Golda Meir sent urgent requests for American military aid and considered using the Israeli atomic bomb against the Arabs.

Nixon and Kissinger devised a strategy of helping Israel repel the attack, while simultaneously pressing the Meir government to acknowledge its dependence on the United States. On 21 October Nixon authorised an air lift of replacement military equipment to Israel. Sure that they would receive additional supplies, the Israelis committed the remainder of their equipment and turned the tide. They threw the Syrians back beyond the original line of the Golan Heights and then crossed the Suez Canal and surrounded the Egyptian Third Army. At this point (24 October), Brezhnev proposed a joint Soviet–American expeditionary force to save the Egyptian army from the Israelis and threatened to go in alone if the Americans were not interested. Nixon responded in the strongest possible terms. He ordered a worldwide alert of American armed forces, including nuclear strike forces. Kissinger informed Brezhnev that a UN peacekeeping force drawn from the armies of non-nuclear powers be used. Brezhnev agreed. In late October both the Soviet Union and the United States joined in a United Nations Security Council resolution demanding a

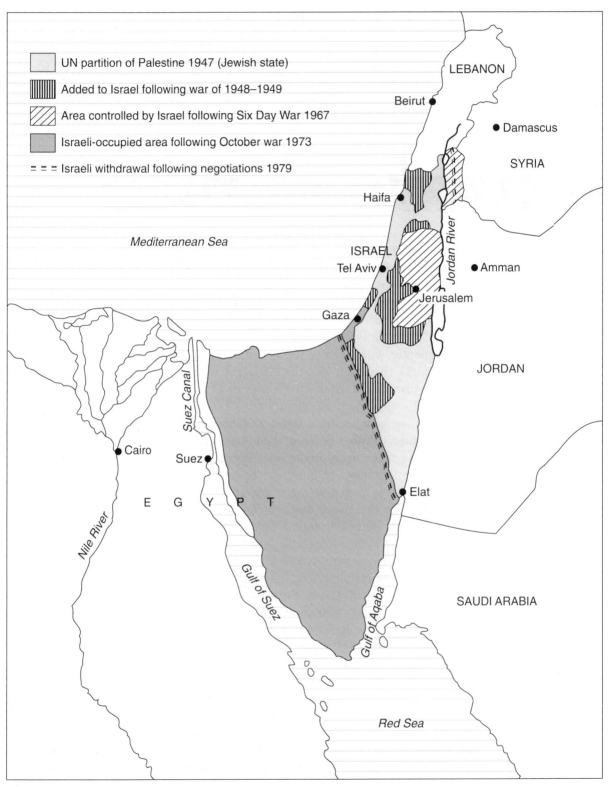

UN partition of Palestine 1947 (Jewish state)

Added to Israel following war of 1948–1949

Area controlled by Israel following Six Day War 1967

Israeli-occupied area following October war 1973

= = = Israeli withdrawal following negotiations 1979

LEBANON

Beirut

Damascus

SYRIA

Haifa

Mediterranean Sea

ISRAEL
Tel Aviv

Jerusalem

Jordan River

Amman

JORDAN

Gaza

Suez Canal

Cairo

Suez

E G Y P T

Elat

Nile River

Gulf of Suez

Gulf of Aqaba

SAUDI ARABIA

Red Sea

*The Arab-Israeli
conflict*

The Arab–Israeli conflict: a British cartoon of 1973 (Les Gibbard, the Guardian). Who are the two doctors in the cartoon? What action are they taking? Why? What is the cartoonist suggesting about the effect of this action on the combatants?

ceasefire. The Israelis reluctantly agreed despite the fact that they were in a position to deliver a telling blow to the Egyptians.

In mid-December a United Nations peace conference on the Middle East opened in Geneva, jointly sponsored by the United States and the Soviet Union. For the first time in the history of the Arab–Israeli conflict, both sides sat down at the same table. However, this icily correct meeting had only one session. Neither the Israelis nor the Egyptians wanted the Soviet Union involved in the dispute. Instead, Kissinger began a process of 'shuttle diplomacy' early in 1974, flying from Cairo to Tel Aviv and back to obtain a disengagement between the two armies. After months of subtly shading what each had to say, Kissinger prodded them to an agreement in May. Negotiations between Israel and Syria were harder to carry off as the Syrians were closer to Moscow and their hatred of the Israelis ran deeper.

THE ACHIEVEMENTS OF DÉTENTE

By the time of the third Brezhnev–Nixon Summit in Moscow in July 1974, the mood had darkened considerably. Richard Nixon's position at home had plummeted dramatically and Brezhnev was too much of a realist to link his own fate too closely with the American President. The Yom Kippur War in the Middle East had threatened to bring about the kind of confrontation that détente had been specifically designed to prevent, revealing the hollowness of some of the agreements signed at previous meetings, notably the Basic

Principles Statement and the Agreement... on the Prevention of Nuclear War.

One further area of negotiation remains to be commented on. At the Moscow Summit of May 1972 President Nixon made a formal commitment to participate in a European Security Conference. The Conference on Security and Cooperation in Europe opened in Helsinki in July 1973 and went on, in Helsinki and Geneva, until the Final Act was signed in Helsinki on 1 August 1975. Thirty-five heads of state or government signed that Final Act, commonly called the Helsinki Declaration. The Final Act linked three so-called 'baskets'. The first was the security basket: a multilateral recognition of the existing frontiers of Europe — a follow-up to Brandt's *Ostpolitik* negotiations with the Soviet bloc. The second was the co-operation basket: the act called for closer economic, scientific and cultural collaboration — for the 'web of interests' that Kissinger believed would lead to wider political agreement.

For Basket Three of the Final Act the signatories pledged: to respect human rights and fundamental freedoms, including freedom of thought, conscience or religion; to facilitate freer movement and contacts for persons individually or collectively; to permit travel for family visits; to permit family reunification; to facilitate the free and wider dissemination of information of all kinds, including newspapers and publications from other states. Brezhnev's reservations in relation to Basket Three were publicly stated to the conference:

> 66 No one should try, on the basis of foreign policy considerations of one kind or another, to dictate to other peoples how they should manage their internal affairs. It is only the people of each given State, and no one else, who have the sovereign rights to decide their own internal affairs... A different approach is flimsy and perilous ground for the cause of international cooperation. 99

Brezhnev, Speech at Helsinki Conference... 31 July 1975, in *Peace, Détente and Soviet-American Relations*, p.97

Review and Discuss

- What did Brezhnev's statement suggest about the likely impact of the human rights provisions of Basket Three on Soviet domestic affairs?

- Given his publicly stated intentions, why was Brezhnev prepared to sign a Final Act that included Basket Three?

It is obvious that Brezhnev was weighing up carefully the value of the first and second baskets. Basket Three was the price he had to pay for what was uppermost in his mind: the recognition in the Final Act of the existing frontiers in Eastern Europe and the affirmation that the signatories agreed to 'broaden, deepen and make continuing and lasting the process of détente'.

Brezhnev summarised the aims and achievements of Soviet foreign policy during this period in his report to the 25th Party Congress in February 1976:

Brezhnev, Report to the 25th Congress of the Communist Party of the Soviet Union, 24 February 1976, in *Peace, Détente and Soviet-American Relations*, pp.103-4

“ Struggle to consolidate the principles of peaceful co-existence, to assure lasting peace, to reduce, and in the longer term to eliminate, the danger of another world war has been, and remains, the main element of our policy toward the capitalist states. It may be noted that considerable progress has been achieved in this area in the last five years.

The passage from 'cold war', from the explosive confrontation of the two worlds, to détente was primarily connected with changes in the correlation of world forces. But much effort was required for people — especially those responsible for the policy of states — to become accustomed to the thought that not brinkmanship but negotiation of disputed questions, not confrontation but peaceful cooperation, is the natural state of things...

Though world peace is by no means guaranteed as yet, we have every reason to declare that the improvement of the international climate is convincing evidence that lasting peace is not merely a good intention, but an entirely realistic object. And we can and must continue to work tirelessly in the name of achieving it. ”

THE DECLINE

OF DÉTENTE

I N A NUMBER OF WAYS Washington and Moscow had remarkably similar views of the nature and purposes of détente. Kissinger hoped that the United States could build up a web of relationships with Moscow through trade, political dialogue and arms control to lock the Soviets into a pattern of collaborative behaviour with the West that would be more 'compliant' and 'manageable' and less 'adventurist'. For their part, the Soviets regarded the Americans as aggressive and bullying. Détente would help to modify this behaviour by getting Washington accustomed to regular consultation and agreement with Moscow. Brezhnev talked of 'making détente irreversible' — a phrase that he frequently used in speeches of the period.

AMERICA COUNTS THE COST

However, as Jonathan Steele points out in a study of Soviet foreign policy under Brezhnev and his successors, détente involved costs for both sides as well as benefits.

" When détente eventually broke down… the pressure against it came from forces in the United States… Three factors ultimately caused its death. One was the imbalance in its ideological costs, which were greater on the American side. In the Soviet Union the danger of 'contamination' by Western ideas as a result of the slight opening of Soviet society which détente might entail was contained without serious internal upheaval by tightening the pressure on certain Soviet dissidents and pressing others into exile abroad…

Most Soviet citizens welcomed détente wholeheartedly. As for the notion that the Soviet Union had reached parity with the United States, this fitted the concept of historical progress that every Russian had learned and most wanted to believe.

Americans, by contrast, found it a threatening notion. Taught that their country was the world's most powerful nation and 'the last, best hope' of mankind they found it hard to accept that their major ideological enemy had become their military equal and seemed immune to the liberalizing tendencies that détente was expected to bring.

America's emotional reaction to its loss of global superiority was compounded by the second and third major factors that wounded détente — ambiguity over the area that it was meant to cover, and unrealistic expectations of its scope. Was détente meant to include the Third World? Nixon and Kissinger hoped that it would... Brezhnev and his colleagues never saw East–West détente as a binding commitment to Third World restraint...

American policy makers were never able to come to terms with this... The record shows that the Soviet Union has largely been cautious and slow to intervene in the Third World, but to expect it to refrain from ever acting at all, either by agreement or through fear of the consequences, is unrealistic. **99**

Jonathan Steele, *The Limits of Soviet Power*, rev. edn, Penguin, Harmondsworth, 1985, pp.58–63

Review and Discuss

- Why did Americans find détente 'threatening'?
- How realistic were Kissinger's expectations that détente would lead to Soviet 'restraint' in the Third World?

The nature of détente: a British cartoon of 1976 (source unknown). What cartoon format has been used for the 'détente is...' sequence? Why? Identify the two figures in the cartoon. What point is the cartoonist making in each of the frames?

In spite of these differing perceptions the two sides continued to maintain a dialogue on arms control. This was all the more remarkable since each side went on competing actively in the Third World, in the Middle East, Latin America and Africa.

CARTER'S AMBIGUOUS YEARS

By 1976 the complexities and contradictions of détente had become explosive. Caretaker President Ford even instructed his staff not to use the word 'détente' in the 1976 presidential campaign. Jimmy Carter's election victory did not resolve this debate. In fact, it sharpened it, since the question of how to deal with Moscow received two quite different answers from within the new administration. The differing viewpoints were personified by Cyrus Vance, the détente-minded Secretary of State, and Zbigniew Brzezinski, the hawkish National Security Adviser. Carter himself wavered from one side to the other.

The clash between the world views of Vance and Brzezinski soon became obvious. Brzezinski saw the world very much in bipolar terms, with the Soviets posing immediate global dangers. A Polish immigrant who had lectured on totalitarianism at Columbia University, Brzezinski enjoyed being, according to one White House colleague, 'the first Pole in 300 years in a position to really stick it to the Russians'. Cyrus Vance, in stark contrast, accepted the views of Marshall Shulman, himself a former Columbia professor and expert on Soviet affairs. Shulman had been a critic of Brzezinski's views for a quarter of a century.

Vance and Shulman believed that peace with the Soviets could only be arrived at on the basis of negotiation and building up economic ties. They saw SALT II as the central diplomatic issue of the moment and were of the view that no problem, even aggressive Russian behaviour in the Middle East, should be allowed to stand in the way of arms talks. In Shulman's view, the approach most likely to influence Soviet behaviour was that of 'soft linkage'. This meant saying quietly to Soviet officials that they stood a better chance of receiving badly needed American economic help if they were more attentive to human rights in their own country and peace elsewhere.

DIPLOMATIC UPS AND DOWNS

Carter did manage a number of diplomatic successes, which were achieved when the Vance–Shulman approach was followed. (Vance and Shulman believed that trouble in newly emerging nations could usually be handled as a problem of emerging nationalism, not as an occasion for superpower confrontation.) Two such successes warrant specific mention. The first came in 1978 when Carter took a courageous stand on the Panama Canal Treaty, which returned to Panama full sovereignty over the Canal Zone. With the support of Gerald Ford and Henry Kissinger and the authority of the presidency behind him, Carter pressed for ratification and the treaty was narrowly passed in the Senate.

The second diplomatic triumph was of greater significance: Carter played a central role in bringing about a peace treaty between Israel and Egypt. In September 1978 he invited Egyptian President Anwar Sadat and Israel's leader Menachem Begin to meet with him at the presidential retreat in Camp David, Maryland. The United States acted as a full partner in the difficult negotiations. The treaty, finally signed in March 1979, was essentially an agreement for Egyptian recognition of Israel and peace between the two nations in return for a staged Israeli withdrawal from the Sinai. There was a general reference to the future of the Palestine Liberation Organization (PLO), but the vague language allowed for a difference of interpretation. No mention was made of Jerusalem, the West Bank or the Golan Heights. The treaty was unacceptable to the other Arab states, all of whom vigorously denounced Sadat and broke relations with Egypt. This animosity was no doubt a factor in Sadat's assassination by Egyptian soldiers in October 1981.

After the high point of Camp David, internal divisions and uncontrollable external events contributed to a downturn in American fortunes. The Camp David meeting itself was a factor in the deterioration in Soviet–American relations, expressly because the Soviets were not invited. In October 1977 Carter had agreed to a joint Soviet–American statement proposing the reconvening of the Geneva Conference on the Middle East under their joint sponsorship. The Russians made significant concessions in return for Carter's assurance that they could help construct a Middle East peace. Under pressure

The signing ceremony for the Egyptian-Israeli Peace Treaty, Washington, March 1979 (Wide World). Identify the three leaders in the photograph. What were the main areas of agreement between Egypt and Israel? Why did this agreement not lead to peace between Israel and its other Arab neighbours?

from Israel and American Jewish leaders, the Carter administration shelved the document. Sadat was also anxious to avoid Brezhnev's unsubtle hand in the settlement of the Egyptian–Israeli differences. Carter's bowing to the Israeli lobby and the Sadat–Begin Camp David talks could only be interpreted by Moscow as a humiliation. In disappointment and frustration the Soviet leaders rushed more arms to their friends in the region, including Israel's arch-enemy, Syria.

On 1 January 1979 the United States gave full diplomatic recognition to the People's Republic of China. In late January, Deng Xiaoping, Vice Chairman of the Chinese Communist Party and the guiding hand behind the movement away from Maoist revolutionary orthodoxy, visited the United States. After his return home, China launched an attack on Vietnam. (Vietnam, friend of the Soviet Union, had recently invaded Cambodia, friend of China.) By his timing Deng made it appear to Moscow that the United States was a silent partner in the invasion.

The only bright moment for Moscow in 1979 was the Vienna Summit in June at which Brezhnev and Carter signed the SALT II Pact. (For discussion see Chapter 13.) Carter appeared to have doubts about the treaty almost before he arrived home. He allowed the sudden 'discovery' of a Soviet brigade in Cuba to be used as evidence that Moscow and Havana were testing US will. The Soviet brigade had been in Cuba for many years but its 'discovery' could be used as a lever with the Russians being asked to 'get out of Cuba' before SALT II was ratified.

Of more significance was opposition to the treaty by a group called the Committee on the Present Danger. Established in 1976, the committee was

The superpower leaders and their advisers at the signing of SALT II, Vienna, June 1979. (Copyright by Interfoto MTI, Hungary, supplied by Keystone.) Identify the two leaders. What were the main provisions of SALT II? What happened to the treaty in the US Congress? What effect did this have on Soviet–US relations?

headed by Paul Nitze and Eugene Rostow, both with long Washington experience and both driven by the fear that Americans were losing their will to fight communism. Nitze resurrected the old rhetoric from the National Security Council Memorandum 68: 'The principal threat to our nation, to world peace, and to the cause of human freedom is the Soviet drive for dominance based on unprecedented military buildup.' Norman Podhoretz, editor of the influential US magazine *Commentary*, blamed 'isolationism' and 'the culture of appeasement' for producing SALT II. His magazine published an article by Harvard historian Richard Pipes with the provocative title 'Why the Soviet Union Thinks it Could Fight and Win a Nuclear War', which warned that commercial societies like the United States were unable to devote 'serious attention to military strategy'. In the face of such opposition the Carter administration hesitated about asking for a vote on SALT II in late 1979 and then withdrew the treaty in January 1980.

AMERICA'S IRANIAN BONDAGE

Toward the end of Carter's presidency external events were to play an even bigger role in undermining US prestige. Events beyond Carter's control in Iran were to dominate the last year of his first term and torpedo any chance of his gaining a second term as President.

Since 1953, the year in which the Shah of Iran was restored to his throne, as a result of a CIA coup, American relations with the government of Iran had wavered. The Eisenhower administration had enthusiastically supported the Shah's regime, but during the Kennedy–Johnson years there had been limitations in arms sales and economic assistance to Iran. Nixon and Kissinger dramatically accelerated US assistance to the Shah. They saw Iran as a principal partner in containing the Soviets, as well as being the most reliable supplier of oil to the West. The Shah was both a staunch foe of communism and a valued customer of American military equipment. He had allowed the CIA to place sophisticated electronic listening devices along the Iranian–Soviet border and the CIA was also involved in training the Shah's notorious secret police SAVAK. On the surface relations between the United States and Iran were close.

This was deceptive, because it described America's relationship with the Iranian ruling elite. In the wider community anti-American feeling was strong and growing stronger. The Moslem leaders (the mullahs) were rapidly becoming implacable foes of the Shah. By early 1978 the Shah was losing control to the religious leaders and political fanatics (moderate leaders were in prison or dead) and he was suffering from cancer.

United States, and probably Soviet, officials understood few of these developments. At the Shah's insistence American intelligence had virtually no contact with opposition parties. As the revolution gathered momentum, in Washington Brzezinski and Vance differed over how to respond. Brzezinski urged helping the Shah to establish military rule to crush any revolt or, if that failed, mobilising US paratroopers for actual intervention.

Vance urged Carter to make contact with the revolutionary leaders, distance himself from the Shah, and assume that any military move could lead to the disintegration of the weakened Iranian army. Carter could not make a decision. In February 1979 the Ayatollah Khomeini, having recently returned in triumph from exile in Paris, led forces that drove the Shah from power.

The Shah's fall was clearly a major defeat for United States foreign policy. By the same token, the Russians who publicly applauded the US setback could not take too much comfort because Khomeini led a violently anti-communist group whose fanaticism could easily spread to Russia's expanding Moslem population.

In late October, on humanitarian grounds and under pressure, Carter agreed to the deposed Shah's admission to an American hospital for cancer treatment. On 4 November 1979 enraged Iranian 'students' overran the United States embassy in Teheran and seized sixty-nine hostages. Khomeini authorised the release of sixteen women and blacks but refused to release the remaining fifty-three. Carter announced that he would not leave the White House until he secured the release of the hostages, no easy task since no responsible Iranian official could be found to negotiate with the United States. The new Prime Minister resigned at the beginning of the crisis and Khomeini was adamant: either the USA returned the Shah or he would execute the hostages as 'spies'.

In April 1980 Carter gave the go-ahead for a military attempt to rescue the hostages. Equipment failure led Carter to cancel the operation and this failed mission prompted Secretary of State Vance's resignation. Vance had opposed the use of force, and stated that even if successful it would almost certainly lead to the loss of some hostages' lives as well as further poisoning US–Iran relations. Vance thought it might also tempt Soviet intervention. More generally he had seen his own view of world order gradually lose ground to Brzezinski's over the previous year. Six weeks later, as he accepted an honorary degree from Harvard University, he warned Americans against looking for the 'quick fix' in foreign policy and decried 'nostalgia for the day when the United States had enormously great influence in the world'.

The impasse on the hostage crisis continued throughout the middle of 1980. Even when the Shah died, in Egypt in late July, Iranian negotiating conditions remained stiff: the United States must return the Shah's wealth, cancel all financial claims against Iran, free Iranian assets frozen in the United States and promise never to interfere in Iran's affairs. Two events finally drove the Iranians toward a negotiated settlement. In September 1980 Iraq invaded Iran's Khuzistan province and full-scale war erupted between the two countries. Second, on 4 November Ronald Reagan won the US presidential election. Khomeini could hardly expect the incoming Reagan administration to offer a deal as favourable as the outgoing Carter administration. In December and January a deal was hammered out and the hostages flew out of Teheran on Carter's last day in office.

SOVIET INTERVENTION IN AFGHANISTAN

Soviet actions in Afghanistan, simultaneous with the hostage crisis in Iran, were to focus world attention on the nature of Soviet intentions and completed Carter's conversion to the need for adopting a hard line with Moscow. Some American experts nominate the Soviet invasion of Afghanistan in late December 1979 as the major cause of the breakdown of détente. Political commentator Jonathan Steele offers some thoughtful observations on Soviet reasoning:

> Détente had been dying for more than two years when the Kremlin found itself confronted by a crisis in Afghanistan... The Kremlin was uncertain what to do about a country on its southern border that had been friendly to Moscow for more than fifty years. The decision in December 1979 to save the [Marxist] revolution must have been finely balanced. On the one hand it would provide a good chance, certainly the only chance, of preserving a Marxist–Leninist regime, although there was bound to be fierce local resistance. On the other hand it would provoke a storm of international protest since there could be no easy explanation...
>
> Nevertheless, the intensity of the reaction of the non-aligned movement... seems to have surprised Moscow. More than a hundred countries condemned the Soviet invasion. The Western reaction was more predictable. Moscow seems to have calculated that Western Europe would forget soon, while the Americans were so hostile that Afghanistan would make little difference.

Steele, *Limits of Soviet Power*, pp.65f.

The 'official' Soviet statement of the Kremlin's rationale for intervention in Afghanistan was presented by Alexander Bovin, *Izvestia*'s political correspondent, in April 1980.

> The point is that the developments forced us to make a choice: we had either to bring in troops or let the Afghan revolution be defeated and the country turned into a kind of Shah's Iran. We decided to bring in the troops. It was not a simple decision to take. We weighed the pros and cons before taking it. We knew that the victory of counter-revolution and of religious zealots and revenge-seeking feudal lords would result in a bloodbath before which even the crimes of the Chilean junta would pale. We knew that the victory of counter-revolution would pave the way for massive American military presence in a country which borders on the Soviet Union and that this was a challenge to our country's security. We knew that the decision to bring in troops would not be popular in the modern world even if it was absolutely legal. But we also knew that we would have ceased to be a great power if we refrained from carrying the burden of taking unpopular but necessary decisions, extraordinary decisions prompted by extraordinary circumstances... History and politics cannot always be fitted into legal formulas. There are situations when non-intervention is a disgrace and a betrayal. Such a situation developed in Afghanistan. And when I hear the voices of protest from people who claim to be democrats, humanists and even revolutionaries, saying they are outraged by Soviet 'intervention' I tell them this: it is logic that prompted us. If you are against Soviet military aid to Afghanistan, then you are for the victory of counter-revolution. There is no third way.

Quoted in Jonathan Steele, *Superpowers in Collision*, 2nd edn, Penguin, Harmondsworth, 1984, pp.73f.

Review and Discuss

- How do the above two accounts explain the reasoning behind the Soviet decision to intervene militarily in Afghanistan?

- How far did the Soviets anticipate the reaction to their intervention? How did the Soviets view that reaction?

The Soviet invasion of Afghanistan seriously jolted Carter. He stated that the invasion of Afghanistan could pose the most serious threat to world peace since World War II. In early January 1980 he withdrew SALT II from the Senate, where it was doomed anyway. He slapped an embargo on American grain and high technology electronic equipment bound for the Soviet Union and forbade Americans to participate in the Moscow Olympics the following July.

Carter's critics saw this response as an overreaction. In the view of US Secretary of State Cyrus Vance, the Soviets had invaded Afghanistan because they had a 'dangerous problem' on their border and because they also felt they had little more 'to lose in [their] relationship with the United States'. Carter did not see it that way and in any case, as we have already noted, Vance resigned in April 1980 after the abortive attempt to rescue the US hostages in Teheran.

Carter insisted that the Red Army was on the march. (It was indeed true that this was the first time that the Kremlin had moved Soviet troops out of the sphere of influence inherited at the end of World War II.) He backed away from SALT II and promised to increase defence spending by five per cent in real terms for each of the next five years. Young men were ordered

Soviet policy objectives, this time in Africa: an American cartoon of 1978 (copyrighted 1978, Chicago Tribune Company, all rights reserved, used with permission). Identify the two figures in the cartoon. What are they doing? How does the cartoonist suggest that they are working together towards a common purpose? How and why have Cuban forces been used to further Soviet policy objectives in Africa?

to register for a potential draft. Finally, the President announced a Carter Doctrine, that pledged American intervention — unilaterally if necessary — if the Soviets threatened Western interests in the Persian Gulf. At Brzezinski's suggestion Carter introduced the doctrine by directly comparing the crisis to Truman's in 1947. There were some significant differences, however. There had been no American consultation with the Persian Gulf states themselves or indeed with America's NATO allies before the promulgation of the Carter Doctrine.

A brief assessment of the diplomacy of the Carter years is appropriate. The following Soviet account offers a thoughtful perspective:

> " There were intense struggles in the American power elite at that time over foreign policy. Carter gave some hopes to the hard-liners, but his emerging administration as a whole was not committed to wrecking arms control and détente. So the Right began portraying Carter as a liberal and creating new groups to put pressure on the administration, trying to block any positive move in Soviet–American relations...
>
> If the Carter administration had been unequivocally committed to détente, it would have been able to withstand those pressures and provide constructive leadership both in the Congress and in the realm of public opinion. But the problem was, first, that Carter himself did not have either an indubitable position or clear-cut commitments. Second, the antidétente camp had rather prominent representatives within the administration, like Zbigniew Brzezinski and James Schlesinger. Third, Carter overestimated his ability to forge a broad consensus that would have satisfied all groups. As a result, Carter's approach to foreign policy was initially characterized by attempts to include in his policy important elements of both the prodé tente and antidétente positions. This ambivalence not only damaged Soviet–American relations, but created a justified impression that Carter indeed did not have a coherent foreign policy. "

Georgi Arbatov, *Cold War or Détente? The Soviet Viewpoint*, Zed, London, 1983, p.71

REAGAN AND RENEWED CONFRONTATION

With the coming to office of the Reagan administration, American foreign policy took a significant turn to the right. The new administration of President Ronald Reagan, former Hollywood movie actor and Governor of California, and Secretary of State Alexander Haig, former general, NATO commander and assistant to Kissinger, believed in taking a far tougher line with the Soviets. This was clear from Reagan's first press conference in the White House.

> " So far détente's been a one-way street which the Soviet Union has used to pursue its own aims. I know of no leader of the Soviet Union, since the Revolution and including the present leadership, that has not more than once repeated in the various Communist congresses they hold their determination that their goal must be the promotion of world revolution and a one-world Socialist or Communist state... Now, as long as they do

that and as long as they, at the same time, have openly and publicly declared that the only morality they recognize is what will further their cause, meaning they reserve the right to lie, to cheat in order to obtain it, I think that when you do business with them — even in détente — you keep that in mind. **99**

International Herald Tribune, 31 January 1981

The new Republican administration emphasised its determination to restore shattered American prestige around the world. Reagan hoped to accomplish this goal by taking a tough stand with the Soviets, by taking a firm anti-communist line in Central America and the Middle East, and by dramatically escalating the arms race.

The arms race is looked at in Chapter 12. Reagan's contribution can be summarised briefly as follows: he ordered the B-1 bomber to be put into production, he stepped up preparations for the deployment of Pershing II missiles in Western Europe, he sharply increased US government expenditures for both conventional and nuclear forces and he encouraged American arms manufacturers to sell arms at a record level. In the early 1980s the amount of military spending, especially by Third World countries, reached unprecedented proportions.

Reagan's arms build up and militarist foreign policy were aimed at restoring US superiority and at building forces to counter Soviet influence in the Third World. The forces proved incapable, however, of imposing American solutions in the two crucial Third World areas to which they were applied. The first was the Middle East; the second was Central America.

PROBLEMS IN THE MIDDLE EAST

In the Middle East the main problem area was Lebanon. The war in Lebanon continues to be one of the most complex situations of recent times — Lebanese Moslems pitted against Lebanese Christians, Syria against Lebanon, the PLO against everyone and, of course Jew against Arab. The aims of American Middle East policy were still dominated by the perceived need for containment of the Soviet Union. The US administration saw Syria as a client state of the Russians and Israel as a potential Cold War ally in the Middle East. Secretary of State Alexander Haig and Secretary of Defense Caspar Weinberger regarded Israel as the strongest and most reliable power in the region and were keen for close military ties. The Israelis, for their part, were eager enough to accept American arms and co-operate with the Americans on military intelligence but they saw Arab nationalism and the PLO as the main threat — not the Russians.

In June 1982 Israel invaded Lebanon. The Israeli army blasted its way to the outskirts of Beirut in an effort to eliminate the PLO. Reports of thousands of civilian casualties among Lebanese and Palestinian refugees turned American and world opinion sharply against the Israelis. New US Secretary of State George

Shultz and special envoy Philip Habib worked out a plan for the PLO to evacuate Beirut under the protection of a force made up of American, French and Italian soldiers. Soon after the PLO leader Yasser Arafat led his fighters from Beirut in late August, the Israeli army moved into Beirut again, following the assassination of President Basir Gemayel, and took control of the city. Three days after Gemayel's assassination his Christian militia, presumably with Israeli collusion, entered two Palestinian refugee camps and slaughtered hundreds of women and children. An international outcry over the incident seemed to shake the Israeli government. The multinational force returned, this time for an indefinite stay.

A US-sponsored agreement of May 1983 envisaged Israeli withdrawal from Lebanon in return for 'normalisation' of relations between the two countries. That, however, depended on Syrian and Lebanese Moslem compliance, which was not forthcoming. This made national reconciliation impossible and the civil war broke out again with the multinational force caught in the middle. The government began to collapse and in February 1984, after the Americans and French had suffered severe casualties, the multinational force was withdrawn. Israel's forces continued to occupy territory in southern Lebanon and still suffered at the hands of the terrorists. As they began to withdraw in 1985, they left behind a much more hostile and divided population than they had found on arrival.

PROBLEMS IN CENTRAL AMERICA

In July 1979 the revolutionary Sandinista forces had overthrown the dictatorial Somoza regime that had ruled Nicaragua (with United States support) since the 1930s. By the late 1970s Somoza's corrupt rule had turned the bulk of the population to the Sandinista side. The new regime was wary of moving too close to Washington and was initially determined to follow a non-aligned foreign policy. However, the Sandinistas turned to Cuba, whose support had been welcome in the final months of the civil war and who then sent thousands of teachers, health experts and, of course, military advisers.

Convinced that Cuban and Soviet support was helping to sustain the Sandinista effort and that the Sandinistas were aiding rebel forces in El Salvador, the Reagan administration determined to support the anti-Sandinista forces led by former Somoza officers (the Contras). Reagan terminated an aid programme for Nicaragua that Carter had pushed through Congress and began a policy of military confrontation by CIA-sponsored support of the Contras. In December 1982 the US Congress forbade the CIA from arming counter-revolutionaries 'for the purpose of overthrowing the government' of Nicaragua. The administration chose to interpret the Congressional form of words to suit its already preferred policies — its guns were designed to intimidate not overthrow the Sandinistas. Congress resented this double talk. Between 1981 and 1984 the CIA invested at least $70 million in the Contra's cause, although there were few victories to show for their efforts. Meanwhile the Sandinistas increased their own military and political power in spite of economic hardship caused by the CIA's illegal mining of Nicaraguan harbours. The CIA continued to fund their opponents by an illegal and politically damaging diversion of funds from American arms sales to Iran to the Contra cause. This 'Iran–Contra scandal' is likely to be seen as one of the most ill-conceived and politically damaging episodes in American diplomatic history.

Part of the reason for the United State's tough line with Nicaragua was the belief that without Sandinista support the left-wing rebels in El Salvador would be unable to maintain their struggle. In November 1979 a coup had overthrown the oppressive regime of General Romero. The new leaders were in turn overthrown by conservative officers and the regime moved steadily toward the right. By 1982 the victims of the ruthless right-wing 'death squads' were running at 10 000 a year. Under pressure from the US administration this was reduced. In fact the US Congress made progress on human rights a condition of military assistance to the Salvadoran government. In May 1982 the heavily US-supported José Napoleon Duarte won the presidential election. He faced a difficult task inasmuch as he occupied a centrist position between the extremes of left and right in Salvadoran politics, but at least a compromise seemed possible.

In the meantime the Contadora group of nations — Venezuela, Columbia, Panama and Mexico — worked patiently for negotiated settlements in Nicaragua and El Salvador. Although a friend of the United States, the Contadora group continued to condemn its military approach to Central American affairs.

Another brief but dramatic conflict in Grenada clearly demonstrated the nature of US policy in the region. In March 1979 a coup had brought a leftward-leaning government to power. It soon alarmed the US administration by signing

US Foreign policy in the 1980s: an American cartoon of 1986 (reproduced with permission Universal Press Syndicate). Who is the figure on the horse? How is he represented? Who/ what is he looking for? What is the cartoonist's message about the gang that is being ignored?

'NO, THAT'S NOT THE GANG I'M LOOKING FOR, MA'AM — I'M AFTER COMMUNISTS!'

military agreements with communist bloc countries and inviting Cuban construction workers to help build an international airport. In October 1983 a further coup installed a new military leader thought by the United States to be even more communist-inclined. The US decided to intervene. On 25 October, 1900 marines invaded Grenada and established a new government more congenial to US wishes. Such an action did not help further Anglo-American relations since Britain was not even consulted. (Grenada was a member of the British Commonwealth of Nations.)

Despite the success of Reagan's Grenada operation, his Central American policies were coming under increasing criticism. Stephen Ambrose highlights the main points.

> 66 Too many politicians and too large a segment of the public, believed that Reagan was seeing the wrong threats and applying the wrong solutions... His critics thought that it was precisely the governments themselves, the ones Reagan was supporting with military aid, that were the danger and the problem. Narrowly based military regimes that perpetuated right wing violence and a grossly unfair *status quo* based on a colonial relationship with the United States such as the governments of El Salvador, Honduras and Guatemala could never bring stability to an area that cried out for change... The critics thought that the United States should be working with the Sandinistas, not against them, in order to promote the kind of social and economic democracy that is a prerequisite for stability. Economic aid to the forces of the left rather than military aid to the forces of the right, was the proper policy. 99

Ambrose, *Rise to Globalism*, pp.336-7

Review and Discuss

- What criticisms were levelled at Reagan's Latin American policies?
- Given the conduct of American foreign policy since 1945, what obstacles might stand in the way of implementing the policies advocated by Reagan's critics?

THE MAIN CONTEST

In his relations with the Soviet Union Reagan had clearer goals than he had in the Middle East and Latin America: he wanted good relations with the Russians including peace, arms limitations and an actual reduction in the size of each country's nuclear arsenals. However, Reagan's tactics for achieving peace and controlling the arms race included 'talking tough' to the Russians. In a speech to the British Parliament on 8 June 1982 he chose to mock the Soviets by paraphrasing their own terminology:

Quoted in Strobe Talbott, *The Russians and Reagan*, Vintage Books, New York, 1984, p.102

> ❝ ... The march of freedom and democracy ... will leave Marxism–Leninism on the ash heap of history as it has left other tyrannies which stifle the freedom and muzzle the self-expression of the people. ❞

In another major address in March 1983, Reagan characterised the Soviet Union as an 'evil empire' and 'the focus of evil in the modern world'. Although many Americans might have agreed with Reagan's sentiments, they must have wondered how such accusations could further the cause of peace or détente.

One commentator has described the difference between the Carter and Reagan approach to Soviet–American relations in the following terms:

> ❝ For all his tendency to scold and preach at the Soviets, Carter came into office with dreams of conciliation and disarmament. For all the trouble he had in getting to the summit, there was never any doubt that he wanted one. Reagan was quite another matter. Not only did he allow Soviet-American relations to deteriorate seriously (in doing that he had plenty of help from the Soviets themselves), but he also conveyed the impression, certainly during his first two years in office, that the relationship ought to be bad: the Soviets were such murderous, deceitful scoundrels that competition and confrontation were the only appropriate forms for the relationship; the Soviets did not deserve détente, by that or any other name. ❞

Talbott, *The Russians and Reagan*, p.70

Reagan's name-calling reached its peak after the Soviets shot down a South Korean airliner on 31 August 1983, which flew into Soviet airspace over the strategically sensitive submarine bases and missile sites in the Soviet Far East. The Soviet Union claimed the plane was on a CIA spy mission but did not make it clear whether Moscow had distinguished it as a civilian Boeing 747 rather than a military RC–135, a type that frequently flies close to the Soviet Union for the purpose of electronic surveillance. Western analysts later concluded that the Russians had probably mistaken it for an RC–135. (An RC–135 was operating in the area at the time.)

The Reagan administration made an immediate outcry over what it called Moscow's callous and brutal attitude to human life. Washington's campaign of outrage led to the collapse of opposition in the US Congress to Reagan's proposals for the deployment of the powerful new mobile intercontinental missile (the MX). Another result was the stiffening of the NATO allies' resolve to take the Cruise and Pershing II missiles by the November 1983 deadline. On the Soviet side the Korean airliner episode led the Politburo to conclude that it was impossible to conduct any business with the Reagan administration.

On 28 September 1983 General Secretary Yuri Andropov issued one of the most important statements in the history of Soviet-American relations. Strobe Talbott describes Andropov's statement as 'a polemical *tour de force*, the most comprehensive, categorical denunciation of a US administration by a top Soviet leader since the darkest, coldest days of the Cold War'.

> ❝ The Soviet leadership deems it necessary to make known to Soviet people, other peoples and all those who are responsible for shaping the policy of state its assessment of the course pursued in international affairs by the present U.S. Administration.

Briefly speaking, it is a militarist course which poses a grave threat to peace. Its essence is to try to assure for the United States dominant positions in the world without reckoning with the interests of other states and peoples.

Precisely these aims are served by the unprecedented build up of the U.S. military potential, the large scale programs of manufacturing weapons of all types — such as chemical and conventional. Now it is planned to project the unrestricted arms race into outer space as well.

American military presence thousands of kilometres from U.S. territory is expanded under spurious pretexts of all kinds. Bridgeheads are set up for direct armed interference in the affairs of other states, and for the use of American weapons against any country which rejects Washington's *diktat*. As a result, tensions have grown the world over — in Europe, Asia, Africa, the Middle East and Central America...

If anyone had any illusions about a possible evolution for the better in the policy of the present American Administration, such illusions have been completely dispelled by the latest developments. For the sake of its imperial ambitions, that Administration goes to such lengths that one begins to doubt whether Washington has any brakes at all to prevent it from crossing the line before which any soberminded person must stop.

Yuri Andropov, 'Statement', 28 September 1983 (in *Pravda*, 29 September), in Talbott, *The Russians and Reagan*, pp.119-20

Alexander Bovin, *Izvestia*'s influential political commentator and a close friend of Andropov, had arrived at the same conclusion somewhat earlier. A few weeks before Brezhnev's death he commented rather gloomily:

Alexander Bovin, *Izvestia*, 5 August 1982, quoted in Steele, *The Limits of Soviet Power*, p.69

It is now difficult to do business with the Americans. They are dodging, resorting to subterfuges, are saying one thing and doing another. They show a lot of ambition and conceit but little responsibility. But what can be done? Partners are not chosen. They are given by destiny, by history, and we have to talk to them and conduct negotiations.

Review and Discuss

- What do the statements of Andropov and Bovin reveal about the underlying Soviet concern over the policies of the Reagan administration?

- How does the authoritative position of their authors lend these statements special significance?

Reagan's economic policies towards the Soviet Union were contradictory and contributed to the difficulties in Soviet–American relations. Originally Reagan had supported Carter's decision to impose an economic blockade against the USSR in response to the invasion of Afghanistan. He also imposed economic sanctions on those corporations that sold American-produced equipment to the Soviets for construction of a gas pipeline from Siberia. The sanctions were insufficient to deter the Europeans — or the Soviets. In any case Reagan himself was soon eager to trade. For all his 'evil empire' talk Reagan was faced with a high grain surplus and a serious balance of payments problem. In September 1983, the Reagan administration concluded the biggest grain deal in history with the USSR. The European allies found Reagan's action totally contradictory. He was selling wheat to the Soviets while insisting that they *not* sell the pipeline technology. In the USA many Americans were also confused. If the USSR was their enemy, why was the USA selling it badly needed commodities and goods? If the USSR was *not* their enemy, why was the USA spending enormous amounts of money on military technology directed against Russia?

Reagan delivered a major foreign policy address in January 1984, on the eve of a European disarmament conference in Stockholm. It contains some clues to his reasoning:

> 66 …Over the last ten years, the Soviets devoted twice as much of their gross national product to military expenditures as the United States, produced six times as many ICBMs, four times as many tanks, and twice as many combat aircraft. And they began deploying the SS–20 intermediate range missile at a time when the United States had no comparable weapon.
>
> History teaches us that wars begin when governments believe the price of aggression is cheap. To keep the peace, we and our allies must be strong enough to convince any potential aggressor that war could bring no benefit, only disaster. So, when we neglected our defenses, the risks of serious confrontation grew.
>
> Three years ago, we embraced a mandate from the American people to change course. And we have. With the support of the American people and the Congress, we halted America's decline. Our defenses are being rebuilt, our alliances are solid and our commitment to defend our values have never been more clear.
>
> America's recovery may have taken Soviet leaders by surprise. They may have counted on us to keep weakening ourselves. They've been saying for years that our demise was inevitable. They said it so often they probably started believing it. Well, if so, I think they can now see they were wrong… America's deterrent is more credible, and it is making the world a safer place. Safer because there is less danger that the Soviet leadership will underestimate our strength or question our resolve. 99

Ronald Reagan, Foreign Policy Address, 16 January 1984, quoted in Talbott, *The Russians and Reagan*, pp.129–31

Review and Discuss

- How might Reagan's use of military data be open to question? (The material presented in Chapter 12 will be helpful in answering this and the next question.)
- What grounds might there be for doubting that Reagan's policy was likely to make the world 'a safer place'?
- Have subsequent events at the end of the 1980s confirmed the wisdom of Reagan's policy (see discussion in Epilogue)?

THE END OF
THE COLD WAR

S OVIET FOREIGN POLICY in the early 1980s was presided over by three ailing leaders and was primarily defensive, leaving the field open to the USA to take initiatives. Moscow seemed prepared to wait for a change in US priorities and no doubt hoped for a change in leadership. The election of Mikhail Gorbachev as Party General Secretary in February 1985 ended this seeming paralysis decisively and realised some of the hopes aroused after Brezhnev's death. Not only was Gorbachev a younger, more energetic leader, he quickly moved to replace many entrenched officials with younger people.

GORBACHEV SEIZES THE INITIATIVE

Gorbachev's coming to power was not, in itself, capable of solving the many problems faced by the USSR. The entrenched position of the party bureaucracy, the slowing down of the economy, overall inferiority vis-à-vis the United States — these were all problems that no Soviet leader could resolve easily. Nonetheless, Gorbachev seized the initiative on several fronts.

The first such front was arms control. Gorbachev made a number of major arms control proposals to the West including a unilateral freeze on testing (the 'moratorium') which lasted beyond the initial date nominated but which was not matched by the USA. He also offered to withdraw intermediate range nuclear forces (INF) missiles from Eastern Europe. Negotiations on the elimination of INF weapons made good progress. Gorbachev also offered to hold summit talks with Reagan without preconditions. The two leaders met in Geneva in November 1985, without substantial progress. A second summit in October 1986 at Reykjavik in Iceland also ended without agreement, but after wide-ranging discussions of the most sweeping arms control proposals in history. Although the Reykjavik discussions reached an impasse over Reagan's Star Wars programme (the Strategic Defense Initiative), arms control talks between the two powers since then continued to progress. At the Washington

Summit in December 1987 an INF treaty was signed and progress was made in discussion on the reduction of strategic arms. Further progress was made at the Moscow Summit in June 1988 and in subsequent summit meetings both in the USA and USSR (see Chapter 13).

Gorbachev also moved to clarify and formally state Soviet policy with respect to the Third World. Soviet advances in the Third World in the latter part of the 1970s had still left it in a situation relatively inferior to the United States. There were only six Third World members of the Soviet bloc: Mongolia, Vietnam, Laos, Cambodia, Afghanistan and Cuba. These were ruled by pro-Soviet communist parties and together they received eighty-five per cent of Soviet development aid. While the Soviet Union provided military aid to them, it carefully avoided any formal commitment to defend them in the event of attack. Soviet policy was even more cautious when it came to the wider group of 'states of socialist orientation'. Soviet economic and military aid to such embattled allies as Nicaragua, Ethiopia, Mozambique and South Yemen was limited and did not involve any military commitment to defend them.

The principles governing Soviet foreign policy under Gorbachev's leadership were publicly stated in the new Communist Party of the Soviet Union (CPSU) Party Program announced in October 1985. This was the fourth such programme in the history of the party and revised the one promulgated by Khrushchev in 1961. The 1985 programme modified the 1961 programme in a number of important respects, particularly foreign policy. First, in discussing relations with other communist parties, no attempt was made to establish unity under Soviet leadership. A degree of diversity, unacceptable under Brezhnev's leadership, was now allowed. The second modification was related to Third World countries. Khrushchev's 1961 programme had enthusiastically supported the newly independent countries of Asia and Africa, particulary Egypt, but in discussion of the 'newly-free' countries in the 1985 programme, continued Soviet support was pledged but it was emphasised that Soviet aid would be limited and that these countries had to rely mainly on their own efforts.

These themes were reinforced in Gorbachev's Report of the CPSU Central Committee to the 27th Party Congress in February 1986. That report was notable for its emphasis on the use of political means in the pursuit of foreign policy and national security objectives. It argued that security cannot be achieved without taking into account the security interests of your adversary as well as your own. The ideas were not new. They built on Khrushchev's notion of 'peaceful co-existence'. But the stress on political means and mutuality of interests was new.

This new direction in Soviet foreign policy was confirmed at the special nineteenth party conference in June 1988, which was characterised by vigorous debate shown live on Soviet television. The conference confirmed a 'political approach' to resolving conflicts, approved 'improving Soviet–U.S. relations' and withdrawing troops from Afghanistan. It also explicitly drew the link between foreign policy and *perestroika* (restructuring) at home. There was also increasingly open admission that Soviet behaviour had itself contributed to the creation of the 'threat' perceived in the West. What was needed was a set of policies that would change the West's perception of a Soviet threat — in other words, a strategy for devillainising the Soviet Union.

THE BUSH ADMINISTRATION'S RESPONSE TO THE GORBACHEV CHALLENGE

When President George Bush took office in January 1989 he moved very cautiously in his dealings with the Soviet Union. His administration included a number of senior officials of the Nixon–Ford years, notably Secretary of State James Baker and National Security Adviser Brent Scowcroft, who had learned by bitter experience the political dangers of overestimating the possibility of permanent improvement in Soviet–American relations.

The key question asked by the new administration was whether Gorbachev was genuine. Might not *perestroika* be part of a wider strategy of *peredyshka* (a 'breathing space'), which would allow the Soviet Union to reconstitute itself as a more efficient and formidable adversary? Even if the answer turned out to be yes and the Soviets were indeed changing for the better, in its first months of office the Bush team believed that the onus was on the Soviets to keep changing and making concessions. The USA was under no obligation to adjust its own thinking or behaviour accordingly. Further, it would be unwise to peg American policy to the fortunes of one particular Soviet leader. After all, Gorbachev might die tomorrow or be overthrown by reactionaries, who would have at their disposal the military wherewithal to engage once again in the old thinking and the old behaviour.

Secretary of State James Baker played a key part in nudging Bush toward 'engagement' with Gorbachev. Baker developed a close and productive relationship with Eduard Shevardnadze, then Gorbachev's foreign minister. In their various discussions the two men spent almost as much time on Soviet internal problems as on international relations. As Baker came to appreciate the immensity of the social, economic and political challenges facing Gorbachev, he realised how much leverage the USA had over the USSR in everything from arms control to regional conflict. Baker opposed the wait-and-see attitude toward Soviet reform advocated by some presidential advisers and argued repeatedly that the USA should move quickly to 'lock in' what it liked about what was happening on the Soviet and East European political scene.

In fact, the pace of events in Eastern Europe was gathering speed so fast that in retrospect we can see 1989 as the most momentous year in world history since 1945.

In January 1989 Gorbachev reduced the Soviet military budget by fourteen per cent. In mid-February the last Soviet soldiers withdrew from Afghanistan. Meanwhile, the Estonian Parliament voted to give preference to Estonian over Russian as the official language. In April the Polish government legalised the Solidarity labour union and promised elections for June. In the same month Gorbachev called for more arms reductions in Europe.

In May the Hungarian government dismantled the barbed wire fence on the border with Austria. The Iron Curtain was beginning to come down. Hundreds, then thousands of East Germans fled to Hungary, crossing over to Austria on their way to West Germany. An exodus of gigantic proportions was underway. In the USSR itself ethnic unrest led to riots in many of the republics, with increasing demands for more freedom from Moscow.

Speaking on a visit to West Germany in May, President Bush called for the demolition of the Berlin Wall and an end to the political division of Europe. Gorbachev responded on a brief visit to Bonn by saying that the wall 'can disappear when those conditions that created it fall away'. On a visit to France in June Gorbachev expanded on this when he told reporters that the political future of Poland and Hungary was 'their affair'. These words effectively signalled an end to the Brezhnev Doctrine and invited the East Europeans to take their affairs into their own hands.

In June Solidarity candidates won a decisive victory over the communists in elections for the Polish Parliament and took government in August. General Jaruzelski remained President, but a Solidarity leader became Prime Minister. When postwar Poland's first ever non-communist government asked the USA for economic aid, Bush responded that the $119 million already promised was sufficient.

The pace of events continued to quicken. In October demonstrations in Prague, Budapest, East Berlin and Leipzig swelled to immense size, with more than half a million Czechs, Hungarians and East Germans taking over the streets and chanting 'We are the people'.

In the Soviet Union the three Baltic republics were demanding their independence, while ethnic and economic unrest threatened the break up of the

Events in Eastern Europe: an American cartoon of August 1989 (Tony Auth, the Philadelphia Inquirer). What does the stricken aircraft represent? Who are the passengers? Who is about to jump from the aircraft and with what support?

Soviet empire. Foreign Minister Shevardnadze told the Supreme Soviet that the invasion of Afghanistan by the Red Army was a violation of Soviet and international law. He also admitted that the radar complex in Siberia was 'an open violation' of the ABM Treaty with the USA. Even KBG (Russian secret police) headquarters was the scene of demonstrations as Soviet citizens demanded democratic changes.

Demonstrations in Moscow and Soviet admissions of wrongdoing were unprecedented events. But more was to follow. November 1989 was a climactic month. In Czechoslovakia, dissident playwright Vaclav Havel was released from prison and a week of massive demonstrations led to the resignation of the communist leader Milos Jakes and the end of the communists' constitutionally guaranteed monopoly of power. In December a new coalition government with a non-communist majority was sworn in with Vaclav Havel as President. The Warsaw Pact nations, including the USSR, issued an official statement condemning the 1968 Soviet invasion of Czechoslovakia as 'illegal' and promising not to interfere in each other's internal affairs. In February 1990 Havel visited the USA and Canada. He told an enthusiastic joint sitting of the US Congress that the rise of democracy in the crumbling Soviet bloc was an historically irreversible process.

Meanwhile, on 9 November the most unexpected and most welcome event of all took place. The East German government, completely incapable of stemming the tide of the flight of its people, announced the easing of travel and emigration restrictions. Within hours tens of thousands of jubilant East and West Germans massed at the Berlin Wall, which symbolically, if not physically, came tumbling down that night. In the weeks that followed the calls for reunification grew increasingly vociferous, a move supported by West German Chancellor Kohl. In January 1990 Gorbachev told the East German leadership that reunification was to be expected. On 24 February 1990 Kohl and President Bush endorsed the concept of a united Germany within NATO, a move that complicated matters for the Soviets. After months of negotiations between the two Germanys and the World War II Big Four victor powers, the Unification Treaty was signed in Berlin on 31 August and came into effect at midnight on 2–3 October 1990.

> 66 At the beginning of 1989, the Communists had been in complete — and seemingly permanent — control of Eastern Europe. At the end of the year, they were gone. Democratic coalitions, promising free elections in the immediate future, had taken power in East Berlin, Prague, Budapest, Warsaw, and even Bucharest (where the Rumanian tyrant Nicolae Ceaucescu was overthrown on December 22, then executed on Christmas Day). As a result, the Warsaw Pact had been, in effect, dismantled. The Soviet Union had withdrawn inside its borders. The Cold War in Europe was over. 99

Ambrose, *Rise to Globalism*, 6th edn, 1991, p.378

THE GULF WAR AGAINST IRAQ

On 2 August 1990 Iraq invaded Kuwait. A moment of decision faced the world community: would it stand by and allow Iraq to swallow its neighbour? If Iraq's aggression succeeded, might not Saddam Hussein send his army into Saudi Arabia or intimidate the lightly defended kingdom and its neighbours into obeying his dictates? Such action would give control to fifty-six per cent of the world's oil supplies to the ruthless dictator.

President Bush moved quickly. Executive orders were signed freezing the assets of Iraq and Kuwait in the USA and prohibiting trade. Immediate moves were made to get US allies to follow on the asset freeze, to encourage other Arab states to condemn Iraq, to keep Israel calm, to work through the United Nations and to seek Soviet support for these actions.

Initially Bush turned to the UN, largely to provide a diplomatic umbrella for the Soviet Union and Saudi Arabia, as well as other Arab states reluctant to be seen on the same side as the 'US imperialists'. The UN showed considerable resolve — first condemning Iraq's invasion of Kuwait, then imposing a powerful trade embargo and authorising the use of military force to back it up. US Secretary of State James Baker, who was travelling in the Soviet Union, stood with Eduard Shevardnadze, his Soviet counterpart, and issued a joint declaration demanding Iraq's withdrawal from Kuwait. Algeria, Egypt and Morocco publicly condemned the invasion. The Arab League, to the surprise of many, did likewise.

The Saudis wanted reassurance. If US troops were sent to protect the kingdom, would they stay there until the threat from Hussein was removed? Would US troops be withdrawn immediately the threat was removed? Would the USA sell the advanced warplanes and other weapons Saudi Arabia would need to defend itself? Bush's reply: yes to all three questions.

These diplomatic moves constituted one half of Bush's strategy. The agreement reached with the Saudi government opened the way to the other half of that strategy — this was to present Saddam Hussein with a stark choice: withdraw from Kuwait or be driven out by military force. To that end Bush set in train the largest US military deployment since the Vietnam War. Five days after the Iraqi invasion 210 000 US troops were dispatched to Saudi Arabia.

The consistency of Soviet co-operation in opposing Hussein's invasion of Kuwait was welcomed in the West. Moscow voted yes four times in the UN to condemn Iraq and impose stiff sanctions. Soviet diplomats repeatedly urged Hussein to withdraw and to free all hostages, at the same time rejecting Iraqi pleas to soften their support for the international opposition. As the UN was debating the crucial fifth vote authorising the use of force to back up sanctions, Gorbachev publicly told Hussein to pull out of Kuwait or face further UN action. Within hours the Soviets joined the USA in approving the historic resolution.

The most public demonstration of US–Soviet co-operation in the Gulf crisis was the summit meeting specifically devoted to that issue between President Bush and President Gorbachev in Helsinki on 9 September 1990. There was full agreement on their objective: an unconditional Iraqi withdrawal. *Time* magazine commented:

George J. Church, 'A New World', *Time Australia*, 17 September 1990, p.13

> 66 Moscow so far has played a role that looks as if it might have been scripted in the White House. It has been fully supportive of U.S. efforts — cutting off arms to Iraq, voting for U.N. resolutions establishing a world-wide embargo — without claiming any major part for itself. And it has rebuffed all attempts to drive a wedge between itself and Washington... The days when every Third World clash threatened to bring on a confrontation between nuclear super-powers backing rival clients seem to be over. At best, there is hope for continued U.S.–Soviet collaboration to maintain international order. The gulf crisis, says Georgi Arbatov, a leading Soviet Americanologist, 'will make quite a few people — those who may also have adventurous desires and who would act in a restless way — aware that they won't be able to play the U.S. and the Soviet Union against each other any more. Instead they will probably face co-operation between the Soviet Union and the U.S.'. 99

Once Bush had vowed to liberate Kuwait, General Colin Powell, Chairman, US Joint Chiefs of Staff, urged him to deploy a force so massive that if war became necessary, it could be fought all out and won quickly, unlike Vietnam. By November 1990 Bush had approved a doubling of the US forces to 430 000. This would give the allies the capacity to go on the offensive if Hussein refused to withdraw from Kuwait by the 15 January 1991 deadline set by the UN.

Meanwhile, the Soviets continued to maintain diplomatic pressure on Iraq. Early in October 1990 (and again in February 1991), Yevgeni Primakov, selected by Gorbachev as his personal envoy in this crisis because of his considerable

The changing military threat: an American cartoon of September 1990 (reproduced with permission Universal Press Syndicate). What sequence of events is being depicted (a) in the first three frames, (b) in the second three frames? How does the reaction of the US military guard in each of the frames reflect changing American foreign policy concerns in recent years?

Middle Eastern experience and prior dealings with Hussein, visited Baghdad to attempt to work out a settlement, but without success.

After six weeks of bombing, the USA and its allies began the ground war on 24 February 1991. In four days the world's fourth largest army was humiliated in the most decisive defeat in modern military history. The wider American aim of overthrowing Saddam Hussein in Iraq remained unfulfilled. Nevertheless, Operation Desert Storm was a remarkable achievement and President Bush summed up the feelings of many Americans when he declared: 'It's a proud day for Americans and, by God, we've kicked the Vietnam syndrome once and for all.'

Time magazine's Strobe Talbott, discussing the consequences of the war and the challenging task of keeping the peace, offered the following comment:

Strobe Talbott, 'White Flags in the Desert', *Time Australia*, 11 March 1991, p.15

> Now that both the cold war and the gulf war are over, the United Nations, with the U.S. more than ever its senior partner, will be more credible when it vows to punish — and thus deter — would be aggressors. However, in almost every other respect, the happy ending of the gulf crisis does little, in and of itself, to advance the much vaunted new world order. Whatever challenges to international security and stability lurk in the future, chances are they won't be so morally stark and politically compelling as this one was.

RUSSIA, THE COMMONWEALTH OF INDEPENDENT STATES AND THE WEST

CHAPTER ELEVEN

THE FALL OF GORBACHEV

D URING THE EARLY YEARS of his leadership President Gorbachev was able to steer a middle course between conservative and liberal forces — and used that position to tactical advantage. However, once the conservatives, whose core values and privileges were threatened, became more bitter and desperate, and liberal forces turned to nationalism to further their cause, Gorbachev's room for manoeuvre was restricted. He believed the only way out of his difficulties was by strengthening his formal powers as President so that he could impose his views on the warring factions.

This was a dangerous approach. It was inevitable that a union presidency with extraordinary powers would be opposed by the liberal and nationalist forces. Further, it was a direct challenge to Boris Yeltsin, who had been elected to the leadership of the Russian Federation in May 1990. Yeltsin — once a rising star of the Communist Party, who was sacked from the Politburo when he became too outspoken — had lost any hope that the party could be reformed. Fundamental, not superficial change was needed. For Yeltsin that meant not a strong union, or union presidency, but powerful republics capable of responding directly to the needs of their people without interference from above. Yeltsin was transformed from one of Gorbachev's closest allies into his most serious political rival.

Gorbachev's hopes were in many respects closer to those of the liberals, but his fear that bold steps would provoke a disastrous conservative backlash appear to have made him shrink from decisions. From mid-1990 to early 1991 it seems he considered the liberals, in the short term, to be his more serious problem. Certainly Gorbachev was gradually moving closer to the conservative camp. His tactical plan, it would appear, was to use the conservatives — who still held the key positions in the state apparatus (Army, internal security forces, KGB) — to stop the nationalist leanings of the liberals. From a strengthened power base he could then implement much of the liberal programme.

Gorbachev's plan to manipulate the conservatives was dangerous. The conservative ascendancy and the danger of the drift toward dictatorship were condemned by Foreign Minister Eduard Shevardnadze in his shock resignation in December 1990. His worries were soon realised. In mid-January 1991, with the world distracted by the deepening crises in the Gulf, a new crackdown was launched in the Baltic republics by Soviet interior ministry troops (the notorious 'black berets' or Soviet elite troops). Fifteen people were killed in Lithuania and five in Latvia when public buildings were attacked. Yeltsin condemned the actions (Gorbachev was silent). Describing them as the beginning of a union offensive against the republics, Yeltsin signed a mutual security treaty with the Baltics.

The brutal and unpunished use of force in the Baltics emboldened the conservatives. They moved to impeach Yeltsin in the Supreme Soviet of the Russian republic. A mass rally of pro-Yeltsin supporters in Moscow on 28 March 1991 coincided with and no doubt contributed to the failure of the conservatives to push the no confidence motion through the Supreme Soviet.

In June 1991 Yeltsin became the first popularly elected head of government in Russia's 1000-year history. His standing in Russia — and on the international scene — received an enormous boost. After a triumphant visit to the USA he set about transforming Russia. He immediately placed a ban on communist activity in the workplaces and institutions of the republic. Such a threat to the communists' hold on power led to rumours of an imminent coup.

In July 1991, faced with increasing demands for independence from the fifteen republics, Gorbachev reached an historic agreement with the republican leaders, including Yeltsin, on a treaty for a new, looser union in which the republics

US President George Bush and Soviet President Mikhail Gorbachev at the Group of Seven Economic Summit in London, July 1991. What circumstances led to Gorbachev being invited to the G7 Summit? What were Gorbachev's objectives in attending the summit? To what extent did he achieve these objectives?

A statue falls in Riga, the Latvian capital, August 1991 (Reuters). Whose statue is it? Why is its toppling symbolic? In what ways did the move toward independence in the Baltic republics gather momentum in August 1991? Why did other republics within the USSR also want to break away from Moscow's control?

would be termed 'sovereign' instead of 'socialist' states. The treaty was to be signed on 20 August 1991.

The day before the ceremony was due to take place, the conservatives struck. They placed Gorbachev under house arrest and tried to impose Stalinist restrictions on the press and people. Yeltsin and his Russian government defied the coup leaders, holding out in the Russian Parliament building not far from the Kremlin. When the Army was ordered to take control of the building and other outlying areas where opposition was rising, the military split. The Army refused to fire on Yeltsin and the tens of thousands of supporters who had gathered to defend the building. The coup leaders had miscalculated. They had believed they would meet with little resistance from Gorbachev. Gorbachev refused to join the plotters. They had also assumed that a demonstration of power would intimidate the populace. Here, too, they miscalculated. Least of all did they calculate the effect of international telecommunications. The new technology of CNN (Cable News Network — an American-based news service) news, fax machines and satellite pictures kept the world's eyes focused on the streets of Moscow.

The coup collapsed. Some plotters tried to flee but were captured. Others committed suicide. Gorbachev appeared, tired but triumphal. It was Yeltsin, however, who emerged with a new decisive power. Gorbachev was publicly forced to acknowledge that it was he who had placed the coup plotters in their government positions. As Yeltsin began systematically to uproot Communist Party strength, Gorbachev finally resigned from the party and moved to disband the powerful Central Committee.

The end of the coup signalled the end for the CPSU and for the USSR as well. The party and the central union institutions had been irrevocably discredited. By contrast the positions of Russia and Boris Yeltsin had been profoundly strengthened. The Russian government took *de facto* control.

This became increasingly obvious to Gorbachev as he tried to salvage some form of association for the rapidly dissolving USSR. In the midst of the coup the three Baltic republics (Estonia, Latvia and Lithuania) had declared their full independence, a step rapidly acknowledged by the West and reluctantly by the State Council of the USSR on 6 September 1991. In the months that followed it became clear that Gorbachev had lost whatever support remained for the concept of a unified state and that the leaders of the various republics were looking to Yeltsin for direction. Yeltsin advocated a federation.

In December 1991 the leaders of eleven of the former USSR republics established the Commonwealth of Independent States (CIS) (see below). This effectively marked the end of the USSR. On 25 December an embittered Gorbachev resigned as President of the USSR and the next day a poorly attended meeting of the Supreme Soviet of the USSR voted itself out of existence. The traditional white-blue-red Russian flag replaced the Soviet red flag flying over the Kremlin.

> 66 It was a sad exit for a leader who had profoundly altered world history. Gorbachev had not only recognised that the survival of the Soviet Union depended on fundamental reforms, but had actually initiated them. It was his policy of *glasnost* that had created the men and the mood which ensured that the conservative coup, when it eventually came, would founder. He embarked on a path that would end the Cold War, free Eastern Europe, bring about German unity and profoundly change East-West relations. The world owes much to Gorbachev. 99

International Institute of Strategic Studies (IISS), *Strategic Survey 1991–1992*, Brassey's for IISS, London, 1992, p.22

THE COMMONWEALTH OF INDEPENDENT STATES

When the Soviet Union collapsed after the abortive 19 August 1991 coup against Gorbachev, hopes soon faded for the preservation of what remained of the crumbling union through a Union of Sovereign States (Gorbachev's draft Union Treaty). The leaders of the constituent states of the USSR, notably Russian President Boris Yeltsin, were wary of a union that in many aspects simply replaced the Soviet state and its institutions.

Yeltsin met Ukrainian President Leonid Kravchuk and Byelorussian President Stanislau Shushkevich in Minsk, Belarus, on 7 December 1991. The three agreed to the formation of the Commonwealth of Independent States (CIS). The new confederation was quite distinct from Gorbachev's proposed union. It assumed the form of an alliance between states with a view to preserving certain military and economic functions on a common basis without impinging on the independence of its component republics. Minsk would be the official centre for the co-ordinating bodies of the CIS.

All of the former republics of the USSR were invited to join. On 21 December 1991 the leaders of eleven former Soviet republics met in Alma-Ata, Kazakhstan, and signed an agreement on the formation of the CIS. Four of the former republics (the Baltic states and Georgia) chose not to join. (Georgia joined later in December 1993, however.) The signatories pledged to assume the Soviet Union's international obligations, with the Russian Federation taking over the USSR's seat in the UN Security Council.

In its early meetings mechanisms were established to deal with the most pressing problem of succession — that of the military, and especially the Soviet nuclear arsenal, elements of which were now spread among Russia, Ukraine, Belarus and Kazakhstan. A CIS military command was created under Russian General Yevgeny Shaposhnikov, and a structure devised for ensuring control of nuclear weapons, which effectively remained in Russian hands. Strategic forces remained under CIS command (until June 1993, when Russia assumed direct control). The officer corps and equipment of the bulk of the Army were shared out among the new nations.

In February 1992 the former Soviet states were offered membership in the North American Cooperation Council (NACC), a NATO forum in which they could share a joint dialogue with NATO members on security matters. In late April 1992 most of the former Soviet republics joined the World Bank and the IMF, signalling their intention to embrace free market economies.

With the break up of the Soviet Union and formation of the CIS there has been debate in the USA about which successor states the USA should back. Some advocates (such as deceased former President Richard Nixon) favour a Moscow-centred approach. Their 'pro-Russian' argument points to Russia's predominance among the successor states in terms of territory, population, and military power; the historical centrality of Russia; and Russia's more advanced economic development. At a more sophisticated level the argument stresses that it is Russia's fate that is most important for US national security and that democracy and a healthy economy in Russia are preconditions for democracy and a healthy economy in virtually all the other post-Soviet states. The reverse is scarcely the case. Contributing to this viewpoint is the fact that American officials and scholars tend to be far more at home dealing with Russia to the virtual neglect of non-Russian areas, languages and cultures.

The opposing argument holds that over the centuries Russia has been an expansionist and imperial power and that only coalitions around its boundaries have constrained its outward thrust. Thus politicians who prefer the *realpolitik* approach, such as former National Security Adviser Zbigniew Brzezinski, tend to stress the importance of ties to the new independent Ukraine, as do British and German specialists. Support for the non-Russians has gained favour among those who consider a collapse of the Russian economy or a return to authoritarian rule as possible scenarios. Proponents of a balance between Russia and the non-Russian republics tend to regard international support for the weaker states as necessary to make such an equilibrium viable.

Officially the Bush administration denied the need to choose between Russians and non-Russians. All were 'evenhandedly' recognised. All were admitted to international bodies. All qualified as recipients of aid. But this belies the continued, and perhaps natural, focus on Moscow, whether in regard to security matters or central banking or archival access.

Nevertheless, it would not do to think of the non-Russians as an homogenised, united front. Armenians were bitterly battling Azerbaijanis. Ukraine sought to forge links with potentially anti-Russian entities from Georgia to Tatarstan. Kazakhstan saw its interests served by continued close links to Russia as well as by new Central Asian connections.

The most difficult policy quandary for the USA in relation to the post-Soviet states remained the complex of economic problems. The question of humanitarian aid was relatively straightforward, since there was widespread agreement on the population's short-term needs of food and medical supplies. There was a significant American effort to help, but it was not as massive as had been expected. Nor was it as substantial on a per capita basis, as the contribution of other countries, such as Germany and Britain.

Economic answers were far more questionable, political and expensive when it came to long-term capital assistance, credits and loans that were meant to stabilise the rouble. Similarly with attempts to promote foreign investments, international trade and joint ventures. Although the Yeltsin government favoured far-reaching marketisation of the economy, no models existed for such a transformation. The sequence of steps, the speed with which changes could be introduced and long-term costs were unknowns. Russian economic advisers produced one plan after another for stabilising the currency, replacing planning with market forces, and privatising large segments of industry and agriculture. American and other Western specialists joined to support and elaborate on alternative schemes.

At many levels of post-Soviet society, foreign non-government agencies and individuals are likely to have more impact than official Western government projects. Foreign corporations will often be in a better position to provide needed investments than governments. McDonalds and Pepsico and a range of American experts from the private sector are increasingly in evidence in the former Soviet Union.

Unfortunately there is also ample evidence of naivety, foolishness and bitterness on both sides. There are American sharp operators totally lacking in sensitivity to the local scene, just as there are Russians and others in the former USSR ready to take advantage of the goodwill of outsiders. Only gradually will a supporting structure of business law, dispute arbitration and predictable judicial practice come into being there.

> The United States cannot begin to solve the problems of the Soviet successor states; at the same time, it cannot afford to ignore them. Once it decides that the outcome of the political and economic upheaval in the 15 formerly Soviet societies matters to it — as indeed it does in a great many ways — the United States must be prepared to do more than offer pious advice. It must work with others, and it must do so without delay...
>
> One can argue about the wisdom of the particular reform effort begun in Russia. But a comprehensive reform is under way, and its failure would be a serious set back both for the Russian government and its Western friends and advisers. And while the American contribution is perhaps marginal, it is important both financially and symbolically — and not only to avoid future debate over who lost Russia if all goes wrong.

Alexander Dallin, 'America's Search for a Policy toward the Former Soviet Union', *Current History*, October 1992, pp.325–6

FROM BUSH TO CLINTON

In his quest for a second term of office George Bush thought his foreign policy credentials would stand him in good stead against the Democratic contender Bill Clinton. As it turned out, Clinton convinced the American people that domestic issues were more important, that he appreciated the magnitude of the economic and social problems facing the nation, had a credible programme for economic recovery, and could provide stability and continuity in foreign policy.

On taking office the Clinton administration soon confirmed the continuity of foreign policy with that of the Bush administration. Here it was building on the strong consensus in the USA about national interests and the role the country should play in international affairs. This consensus amounted to the realisation that the USA must remain actively engaged — politically and militarily — in Europe and Asia. It has lasted for some fifty years. In his first press conference after his election victory, Clinton went out of his way to emphasise that 'America's fundamental interests' would not be redefined by his new administration.

Clinton's choice of executives for top foreign policy and national security positions suggested the centrist, consensual direction which would guide policy-making. Secretary of State Warren Christopher and National Security Adviser Anthony Lake both served in the State Department during the Carter administration, as did Ambassador to the UN Madeleine Albright. Secretary of Defense Les Aspin was also Chairman of the House Armed Services Committee for many years.

Clinton himself indicated his commitment to active US involvement in international affairs when he asserted on 8 December 1992:

International Herald Tribune, 9 December 1992, quoted in A. Hartley, 'The Clinton Approach: Idealism with Prudence', *The World Today*, February 1993, p.27

> 66 I am convinced, more than I ever was before, that only the United States can play the leadership role that we ought to be playing, to try to stick up for the alleviation of human suffering, the continued march of democracy and human rights and the continued growth of market economies. 99

On taking office the Clinton administration gave continued support to Bush initiatives in three local crises. The first of these was in Iraq. In 1990 America led UN-sponsored resistance to aggression by that country against its neighbour, Kuwait. US policy had to ensure the observance by Saddam Hussein of the armistice imposed on Iraq at the end of the Gulf War. There was also careful monitoring of the Iraqi dictator's treatment of Shiite Moslems in the south and the Kurdish minority in the north.

In the former Yugoslavia, the USA has largely left it to the European community to cope with the consequences of the break up of the federal state, followed by civil war, and Serb determination to carve a 'Greater Serbia' out of the ruins. Americans were critical of what they saw as European procrastination. The European nations opposed the preferred US policy in Bosnia, which was to supply arms to the predominantly Moslem Army under the command of the government in Sarajevo and bomb the artillery positions of the advancing Serbian forces.

E. Ions, 'Clinton's Conversion', *The World Today*, August/September 1993, p.163

> ❝ It remains one of the more tragic questions before the bar of history as to whether American policy would not have been more effective than the policy insisted on by the European nations. Certainly, air strikes against Serbian artillery and mortar batteries would at the least have given pause to the aggressors at an early stage, checked the advance, and given much greater urgency — not to mention a cold shower of reality — to the Serbs negotiating under the Vance–Owen proposals. But that is now past history. ❞

The third crisis was in Somalia. During the election campaign Clinton had been critical of Bush's handling of the humanitarian aid crisis there. A couple of weeks after the election Bush sent a large contingent of US marines to Somalia to provide escorts for UN and other food relief convoys. Bush insisted that the marines were not there to re-establish political order. Clinton's policy was to reduce the US military presence as soon as possible. However, he appeared more inclined to keep some US troops as part of a UN multinational force to help restore some kind of political order.

Of greater importance than these localised exercises was the Clinton administration's sustained attention to major long-term US interests: America's relations with Europe, expressed in the Atlantic alliance, its involvement in the Middle East peace process, its relations with China, Japan, and Korea and its concern for events in Latin America.

With the military threat from the Soviet Union now extinguished for the foreseeable future, it is clear that the US military presence in Europe will continue to be reduced. However, the Clinton administration, like its predecessors, wishes to preserve its influence in Europe. The possibility of instability in Eastern Europe and in the CIS looms too large for the USA to withdraw a presence that most Europeans regard as reassuring. The new democracies of Eastern Europe also appear to regard the US presence as a stabilising factor in European security. A further reason for continued American involvement in European security is the need to continue the 'nuclear dialogue' with the former Soviet republics where ICBMs are based — Russia, Belarus, Kazakhstan and Ukraine. The objectives have included monitoring the process of arms reduction and preventing nuclear weapons falling into the wrong hands.

The primary interest of the USA in the Middle East has been in the uninterrupted export of oil from the Persian Gulf. Political conflicts in the Middle East continue to be notoriously difficult to settle, but Western policy aims at mitigating conflict where resolution is not possible. US encouragement of the Middle East peace process (between Israel and the Arab states) and the enforcement of armistice terms on Iraq were different facets of one policy designed to prevent any upheaval that might stop the flow of oil.

America continues to be concerned about developments in the Far East. Can US forces be withdrawn from Korea? This will depend on future relations between North and South, but continuing US concerns over North Korea's nuclear programme render a withdrawal most unlikely for the present. US

US President Bill Clinton and Russian President Boris Yeltsin at the Vancouver Summit, April 1993 (APL/ Bettmann). Why was the meeting important to both leaders? What was the main achievement of the summit?

relations with Japan are likely to be influenced by economic, commercial, and competitive considerations and by Japanese willingness (or otherwise) to cut its huge trade surplus with the USA. China is likely to be Clinton's biggest challenge. Too moralistic an approach to the application of human rights criteria to Sino–American relations would give deep offence in Beijing. On the other hand US and world opinion over human rights abuses in China will also influence Clinton's judgement. He is proceeding cautiously: 'We have a big stake in not isolating China, in seeing that China develops a market economy.'

Finally, relations with Latin America will be influenced for the better by US Congress ratification of the North American Free Trade Area (NAFTA) Treaty with Mexico. Put together in the Bush years, the treaty strengthens the position of the USA in future world trade negotiations but also initiates a more creative American policy in Central America whereby growing economic co-operation may open the possibility of improving political relations. The successful settlement of the Uruguay round of the General Agreement on Tariffs and Trade (GATT) negotiations (in December 1993) will also significantly enhance the economic prospects of the USA and its trading partners.

CLINTON'S FOREIGN POLICY

On 27 September 1993 President Clinton addressed the UN General Assembly. This event was preceded by a carefully orchestrated series of speeches outlining the principles of the Clinton administration's foreign policy. Some extracts give the flavour.

Warren Christopher, Secretary of State, 20 September:

> The first issue is really the latest round in a century-old debate between engagement and isolation. The United States chooses engagement.
>
> The second issue... is whether America should exercise its power alone or with others... Let me be clear: multilateralism is a means, not an end. It is one of the many foreign-policy tools at our disposal. And it is warranted only when it serves the central purpose of American foreign policy: to protect American interests.

Anthony Lake, head of the National Security Council, 21 September:

> Our interests and ideals compel us not only to be engaged, but to lead...
>
> The successor to a doctrine of containment must be a strategy of enlargement — enlargement of the world's free community of market democracies...
>
> There will be relatively few intra-national ethnic conflicts that justify our military intervention. Ultimately... we will have to pick and choose...
>
> The simple question in each instance [whether to act multilaterally or unilaterally] is this: what works best?

Madeleine Albright, Ambassador to the UN, 23 September:

> This administration has wisely avoided the temptation to devise a precise list of the circumstances under which military force might be used... Too much precision in public, however well-intentioned, can impinge on the flexibility of the commander-in-chief, or generate dangerous miscalculations abroad...
>
> We will choose means... on a case-by-case basis, relying on diplomacy whenever possible, on force when absolutely necessary.

Bill Clinton, 27 September:

> Domestic renewal is an overdue tonic; but isolationism and protectionism are poison. We must inspire our peoples to look beyond their immediate fears toward a broader horizon...

All quotes from the *Economist*, 2 October 1993, p.32

> The United Nations simply cannot become engaged in every one of the world's conflicts. If the American people are to say 'yes' to UN peacekeeping, the UN must know when to say 'no'. **"**

The two buzz words of the emerging foreign policy are clearly 'engagement' and 'enlargement'. 'Engagement' is a rejection of the notion that, now the Soviet threat has gone, the USA can forget about the outside world. In a world of inter-connected economies and instant communications, isolationism is not a serious option. As the world's largest economy and greatest military power, America must not only be engaged, it must lead. The goal of US leadership is to be enlargement. This means facilitating the spread of free market democracy by strengthening the rich democracies (e.g. through GATT), fostering countries turning to democracy and the market, countering states that are hostile to those freedoms, and providing humanitarian relief where it can do the most good.

All this should be applied within a selective context. For America will now be choosier about where and how it gets engaged. It will decide whether it acts alone or multilaterally, depending on which course looks like working best in the particular situation. It will be more selective about which countries get American aid and in what form. It will also ask harder questions about proposals for UN peacekeeping missions.

It seems a reasonable start for articulating a post-Cold War foreign policy. Nevertheless, the handling of events, rather than the delivering of speeches, will probably provide the clearer definition of American foreign policy.

Bosnia: see no evil. Russia: hear no evil. China: 'speak no evil'. Why is the China message different?

DEBATE ON THE FUTURE OF NATO

The collapse of communism in Eastern Europe and the break up of the Soviet Union have generally reduced the threat that gave rise to the formation of NATO in 1949.

However, other threats have arisen. Brutal ethnic and xenophobic nationalist violence has erupted in formerly communist Europe. Several armed conflicts on Russia's southern borders have led to active intervention by the Russian military. Moscow recently announced that it reserves the option to intervene on behalf of threatened Russians and Russian interests in adjacent ex-Soviet republics.

Fears of revived Russian imperialist ambitions have prompted several Eastern European countries — Poland, Hungary, the Czech Republic, Slovakia, and most recently Lithuania — to seek protection via NATO membership. The fear has been heightened by the unexpectedly strong showing of the racist, ultra-nationalist Vladimir Zhirinovsky and his inappropriately named Liberal Democratic Party in Russia's 12 December 1993 parliamentary elections.

NATO has ruled out immediate membership for the Eastern European countries. In 1991 it had established the North American Cooperation Council (NACC), a forum which invited former communist countries to share in joint dialogue with NATO members on security matters. At the NATO Summit in Brussels in January 1994 the sixteen NATO nations formally endorsed US President Clinton's Partnership for Peace (PFP) proposals aimed at deepening NATO's engagement with the East. The partnership (open to all members of the NACC) envisages co-operative military planning, training exercises and peace keeping operations. The PFP also obligates NATO members to consult with NACC members who feel threatened by an external adversary.

NATO as insurance: an Australian cartoon of January 1994 (Moir, the Sydney Morning Herald). Who is represented as ringing the insurance company? Why? With what response? What events were taking place at the time?

In a recent article in the *Washington Post*, US Secretary of State Warren Christopher outlined the role of the PFP in preparing those partners seeking NATO membership:

> 66 The partnership is central to the task of transforming NATO to meet the tests of the post-Cold War era. It offers nations that seek to join NATO a means to prepare for the obligations of membership. Each state can determine its level of involvement.
>
> Those that choose active engagement in the partnership will begin to develop the habits of co-operation and routines of consultation that are the lifeblood of the alliance...
>
> As a logical corollary to the Partnership for Peace proposal, the United States will seek a clear statement of principle that the door is open to expanding the alliance. We envision an evolutionary process of expansion from which neither Central and Eastern Europe, nor Russia, Ukraine and other states of the former Soviet Union would necessarily be excluded.
>
> We believe that a step-by-step approach to expansion will achieve the twin objectives of increasing the confidence of Central and Eastern European states while not inflaming the passions of extremist elements, particularly in Russia, that perceive an expanded NATO as a military threat...
>
> A prospective member will have to demonstrate adherence to the principles of democracy, individual liberty, and respect for human rights, the rule of law, the peaceful settlement of disputes, the inviolability of national boundaries — the values that NATO embodies and that have made the alliance endure...
>
> We want Russia to take its place in the new European security architecture.
>
> But Russia must assume its share of responsibility, both in how it defines its statehood and in its relationship with the states of the former Soviet Union. Russia must avoid any attempt to reconstitute the USSR. Its conduct towards other states must conform to international standards, avoiding the temptation to rely on the old Soviet practices of intimidation and domination. Should Russia turn away from this new path, we can re-evaluate our approach to transatlantic security and NATO's strategic priorities. 99

Warren Christopher, 'Expanding NATO — the key to securing a long-term peace', the *Washington Post*, reprinted in the *Sydney Morning Herald*, 18 January 1994, p.11

Secretary Christopher was also anxious to reply to the critics of the Clinton administration's approach to gradual NATO expansion. Some critics feared the proposals went too far, potentially diluting the alliance's effectiveness. Other critics feared the partnership would do too little and leave Central and Eastern Europe exposed to what they perceived as Russia's imperial ambitions.

> 66 These fears are misplaced. The partnership we propose will in no way supplant the alliance. NATO's strength is rooted in its political and military cohesion and in the solid commitment of the US to European security. The alliance will never add members at the expense of military readiness or effectiveness.
>
> At the same time, we should attach no talismanic significance to the present number of NATO members. If the alliance fails to reach out to the East and ultimately embrace it, NATO may well sow the seeds of the very instability it seeks to prevent.
>
> But if there is long-term danger in keeping NATO as it is, there is

immediate danger in changing it too rapidly. Swift expansion of NATO eastward may make a neo-imperialist Russia a self-fulfilling prophecy. It would risk redividing Europe by drawing new lines and unintentionally replicating, a bit further to the east, the line of confrontation that we persevered for four decades to overcome. **"**

Christopher, the *Sydney Morning Herald*, p.11

The critics of Clinton's 'Russia-first emphasis' argued that a policy more supportive of the Eastern European democracies is needed. Thus Martin Woollacott, reflecting on the message sent to the Eastern Europeans by the NATO summit, warns:

" The problem with the argument for a cautious NATO and European Union approach to the east Europeans [is that] it ignores the fact that rightly or wrongly there already is a Russian bloc, a Russian sphere, wanted by the Russians and already conceded by the Americans, and that the question is what is in it and what is not.

If NATO can only bring itself to offer the Poles, Hungarians and Czechs a vague right of future entry, we can be sure that the Baltic States, Ukraine and Belarus will never enter the organisation as full members.

Martin Woollacott, 'NATO nations haunted by ghosts of Cold War', the *Guardian*, reprinted in the *Sydney Morning Herald*, 13 January 1994, p.11

That is probably right, practical, and even proper. But it shows that there already is a line of demarcation between the States on the 'Russian' side and those on the 'European' side; and it underlines the fact that we have unwisely left the status of the east Europeans unclear as between the two. **"**

What concerns some critics of the 'gradual NATO expansion' scenario is the potential effect on the internal stability of the Central and Eastern European states. Surely this is as important a concern as the stability of Yeltsin's Russia. It is certainly the main concern of the Central Europeans themselves.

" For their part, the Central Europeans' primary motivation for NATO membership has little to do with the possibility of Russian troops swarming to reannex them. 'It's not to defend against a Russian attack,' explains former Polish Defense Minister Janusz Onyskiewicz. 'We see that as a virtual impossibility. The key reason we want to be in NATO is to secure our own democracies. We need to keep down in our country the very same kind of nationalists Yeltsin's contending with, the same kind that have destroyed Yugoslavia.' ...

Nationalism and ethnic conflict 'have already led to two world wars in Europe,' says Stephen Larrabee, a former U.S. National Security Council staff member now at the Rand Corp. in California. 'The time to act is now, and not with hollow promises.' What Larrabee and others know is that NATO has always been more than a security alliance. 'We understood this at the beginning,' says Larrabee. 'West Germany wasn't a stable democracy before it was allowed into NATO. Belonging to the alliance helped it become one. It's silly to insist that the Central Europeans must be functioning democrats before they can join up. NATO can help them on that road, as it also helped stem authoritarian backsliding in Portugal, Spain, Greece and Turkey.'

Oddly, this rationale appears to have largely escaped notice by the Administration players most responsible for promulgating the partnership. When asked about the Central European argument that NATO membership is more important for internal stability than as a military shield against Russia, a senior Administration official responded, 'It's pretty compelling stuff when you think about it. I guess we've just been too fixated on Russia to have given enough thought to this aspect.'

Clinton's Russia-first emphasis is understandable but needs to be moderated. 'We resisted blackmail when Russia was strong,' says Henry Kissinger. 'Does it make sense to permit Moscow to blackmail us now with its domestic weakness?' The problem, says Council on Foreign Relations president Leslie Gelb, in an insight several Administration aides agree is 'right on', is that Clinton 'is determined to avoid being tagged with having lost Russia. Yet it should be obvious that democracy in Russia will be won or lost almost exclusively by the Russians themselves.' And if reform fails in Russia, says James Baker, an enlarged NATO would at least 'protect democracy' where it is showing signs of taking 'firm root — in Warsaw, Prague and Budapest.'

To be sure, the expansion of NATO is no trifling matter. Extending the free world's nuclear umbrella should never be undertaken idly. But leaving Central Europe in the cold would be an inexcusable folly. Refusing to help these democracies could eventually raise a question as real as the question of losing Russia is phony: Who lost Central Europe?

Michael Kramer, 'The Case for a Bigger NATO', *Time Australia*, 10 January 1994, p.24

99

Review and Discuss

- What does US Secretary of State Christopher see as the main purpose of the PFP proposal?
- Why are the Central and Eastern Europeans disappointed with the proposed 'evolutionary process' of their admission to the NATO alliance?
- According to the critics, what are the dangers of Clinton's Russia-first emphasis?

PART FOUR

A Strategy for War or Peace?

THE EVOLUTION OF NUCLEAR STRATEGY

CHAPTER TWELVE

THE NUCLEAR ARMS RACE BEGINS

T HE PHRASE 'nuclear arms race' is a familiar but deceptive term. In such a race there are no winners. The phrase was appropriate in the early 1940s when Americans and British scientists felt that they were competing against comparable research into atomic bombs in Germany. But by the time the multimillion dollar Manhattan Project had achieved the first successful atomic explosion in New Mexico in July 1945, Germany was beaten and the race had been rather one-sided. Nevertheless, Japan was still fighting on and the American government was prepared to use the new bomb to end the war. On 6 August 1945 Hiroshima, and on 9 August 1945 Nagasaki, were bombed. On 14 August 1945 Japan surrendered. President Truman's decision to use the bomb has since attracted much criticism. But the connection between the A-bomb's use and the war's end had an immediate impact on the reputation of the new weapons. In the West they were regarded as a valuable counter to the Soviet Union's considerable advantage in conventional forces, especially in Europe.

As we now know, the Soviets were well on their way to developing their own atomic bomb. Partly in response the Americans moved on to the thermo-nuclear (fusion) bomb (November 1952) and less than a year later the Russians followed suit (August 1953). In authorising the development of the 'super' or hydrogen bomb, Truman acted against the advice of some of his nation's top scientists. The General Advisory Committee of the Atomic Energy Commission (AEC) informed the President:

       We all hope that by one means or another the development of these weapons can be avoided. We are all reluctant to see the United States take the initiative in precipitating this development ... We base our recommendations on our belief that the extreme dangers to mankind inherent in the proposal

Devastation after the dropping of the atomic bomb on Nagasaki, Japan, August 1945; Hiroshima was also bombed (UPI). Why were atomic bombs dropped on Hiroshima and Nagasaki? What does the photograph reveal about the effects of an atomic bomb blast? What has been the role of nuclear weapons in military strategy since 1945?

Quoted by Herbert F. York, 'The Debate on the Hydrogen Bomb', *Scientific American*, October 1975, p.109

wholly outweigh any military advantage that could come from this development. Let it be clearly realized that this is a super weapon; it is in a totally different category from an atomic bomb... if super bombs will work at all, there is no inherent limit in the destructive power that may be attained with them. Therefore, a super bomb might become a weapon of genocide. We believe a superbomb should never be produced. **"**

British Prime Minister Winston Churchill was also concerned by the development of thermonuclear weapons.

Quoted in *Scientific American, Arms Control: Readings from Scientific American*, W.H. Freeman, San Francisco, 1973, p.351

66 There is an immense gulf between the atomic and hydrogen bombs. The atomic bomb with all its terrors, did not carry us outside the scope of human control or manageable events ... [but with the coming] of the hydrogen bomb, the entire foundation of human affairs was revolutionized, and mankind placed in a situation both measureless and leaden with doom. 99

Review and Discuss

- What dangers did the scientists and Churchill see in the development of thermonuclear weapons?

- Why do you think Truman pressed ahead with their development?

Although some prominent scientists, especially Robert J. Oppenheimer, argued that it was morally wrong for the United States to base its foreign policy on 'a weapon of genocide', other equally prominent scientists, including Edward Teller, argued that the Russians themselves would attempt to develop the fusion bomb as quickly as possible. The latter carried the day. Truman's decision in January 1950 to authorise the development of the 'super' had a succinct and revealing rationale: 'Can they do it?' he demanded, 'and if so, how can we not?'

THE IDEA OF NUCLEAR DETERRENCE

There were those in the US administration who were aware of the dangers of using nuclear weapons as a means of diplomatic leverage. George F. Kennan, then director of policy planning at the State Department, believed such weapons should be divorced from normal military calculations and reserved for what he called 'deterrent-retaliatory purposes' (i.e. to deter the Soviet Union from using its nuclear weapons on the United States). Kennan was here following the thinking of the American strategist Bernard Brodie, one of the first people to realise the military significance of nuclear weapons. In 1946, Brodie stated:

Bernard Brodie, *The Absolute Weapon*, Harcourt Brace, New York, 1946, p.76

66 The first and most vital step in any American security program for the age of atomic bombs is to take measures to guarantee to ourselves in case of attack the possibility of retaliation in kind. The writer in making this statement is not for the moment concerned about who will *win* the next war in which atomic bombs have been used. Thus far the chief purpose of our military establishment has been to win wars. From now on its chief purpose must be to avert them. It can have almost no other useful purpose. 99

The unavoidable conclusion flowing from Brodie's analysis was that military victory in total war was no longer possible. The main goal of military preparations in peacetime would simply be to ensure that a country's ability to retaliate with its own nuclear weapons should survive the enemy attack. This would be achieved by dispersing the weapons well away from cities — perhaps storing them underground.

By February 1946 Bernard Brodie had said all the important things that had to be said about the doctrine of nuclear deterrence. In terms of strategic reality Brodie's rules for nuclear deterrence began to become relevant late in 1949 after the first Soviet nuclear test. This was because the Soviet Union clearly felt it had to match US developments in nuclear weaponry. The Soviets poured resources into the nuclear arms race to match US technological innovations, as it demonstrated in the following table.

Ruth Leger Sivard, *World Military and Social Expenditures 1987–88*, World Priorities, Washington, 1987, p.14

Action ⇄ Reaction
In the Superpower Competition

	Nuclear Weapons			*Conventional Weapons*	
US 1945	atomic bomb	1949 USSR	USSR 1949	main battle tank	1952 US
US 1946	electronic computer	1951 USSR	US 1955	nuclear-powered submarine	1958 USSR
US 1948	intercontinental bomber	1955 USSR	US 1955	large-deck aircraft carrier	1975 USSR
US 1952	thermonuclear bomb	1953 USSR	USSR 1955	wire-guided anti-tank missile	1972 US
USSR 1957	intercontinental ballistic missile (ICBM)	1958 US	US 1959	photo reconnaissance satellite	1962 USSR
USSR 1957	man-made satellite	1958 US	US 1960	supersonic bomber	1975 USSR
USSR 1958	early-warning radar	1960 US	US 1960	computer-guided missile	1968 USSR
US 1960	submarine-launched ballistic missile (SLBM)	1968 USSR	US 1961	nuclear-powered aircraft carrier	1992 USSR
US 1966	multiple warhead (MRV)	1968 USSR	USSR 1961	surface-to-air missile	1963 US
USSR 1968	anti-ballistic missile (ABM)	1972 US	US 1962	long-range fighter bomber	1973 USSR
US 1970	multiple independently-targeted warhead (MIRV)	1975 USSR	US 1964	air-to-surface missile	1968 USSR
USSR 1971	sea-launched cruise missile	1982 US	USSR 1970	high-speed attack submarine	1976 US
US 1983	neutron bomb	199? USSR	US 1972	television-guided missile	1987 USSR
US 1985	new strategic bomber	1987 USSR	USSR 1972	heavy attack helicopter	1982 US
USSR 1987	single warhead, mobile ICBM	1992 US	US 1975	jet-propelled combat aircraft	1983 USSR
US 1990?	stealth bomber	199? USSR	US 1976	large amphibious assault ship	1978 USSR
			USSR 1978	multiple-launch rocket system	1983 US
			US 1987	binary (chemical) weapons	199? USSR

DULLES AND 'MASSIVE RETALIATION'

During the period of the Eisenhower administration the United States maintained at least a ten-to-one lead over the Soviet Union in nuclear weapons. Confident that American superiority would allow the US to threaten the Soviet Union with nuclear punishment for unacceptable Soviet acts, Secretary of State John Foster Dulles formally announced the policy of 'massive retaliation' in January 1954 (see p. 72). American defence policy would 'depend primarily upon a great capacity to retaliate, instantly, by means and at places of our choosing'. By April 1954, Dulles had modified his stance somewhat. 'In many cases any open assault by Communist forces could only result in starting a general war. But the Free World must have the means of responding effectively on a selective basis when it chooses.'

A thoughtful critic of the doctrine of massive retaliation was Henry Kissinger. He subjected the doctrine of total war and massive retaliation to searching analysis in his book *Nuclear Weapons and Foreign Policy* (1957). American defence policy had reached a desperate impasse resulting from over-reliance on total war. Kissinger argued that this impasse could only be broken by reliance on tactical nuclear weapons in limited war. He outlined possible 'rules' for the waging of limited nuclear war with tactical nuclear weapons, to which he believed the West could make the Soviet Union conform by threat of all-out nuclear war.

The views of Kissinger and others who advocated the notion of limited nuclear war were vigorously attacked by George F. Kennan in the 1957 Reith lectures for the BBC.

> 66 It appears to be their hope that by cultivation of the tactical weapon we can place ourselves in a position to defend NATO countries successfully without resorting to the long-range strategic one... that warfare can be thus restricted to whatever the tactical weapon implies; and that in this way the more apocalyptic effects of nuclear warfare may be avoided.
>
> It is this thesis which I cannot accept. That it would prove possible, in the event of an atomic war, to arrive at some tacit and workable understanding with the adversary as to the degree of destructiveness of the weapons that would be used and the sort of target to which they could be directed, seems to me a very slender and wishful hope indeed. 99

George F. Kennan, *Russia, the Atom and the West*, Oxford University Press, London, 1958, p.59

Review and Discuss

- What did Kissinger mean by 'limited nuclear war'?

- Why did Kennan reject the notion of limited nuclear war?

DEVELOPMENTS IN MISSILE TECHNOLOGY

The next technological breakthrough in the arms race was the long-range rocket. Both superpowers had been working on missile programmes since World War II, but in October 1957 the Soviets achieved a major technological success and propaganda boost when they launched Sputnik, the world's first artificial satellite. The Americans were not worried so much by the satellite as by the powerful rocket that launched it into space. The Russians drove the point home by successfully testing their first ICBMs in 1957. Sputnik and the ICBM tests 'jolted the collective American psyche' and created near-hysteria in the United States.

These developments in Soviet missile technology foreshadowed the future problem of measuring different nuclear arsenals. For Moscow it made strategic sense to produce rockets rather than bombers. The Soviet Union had no allies near its main opponent's territory and therefore no chance of friendly bases. Rockets gave it the swiftest and most efficient method of ending the American monopoly in nuclear delivery systems. In January 1960 the Kremlin concluded a major review of Soviet defence policy with the announcement that the newly formed Strategic Rocket Forces (SRF) were to be the lynchpin of the country's defence.

McNAMARA AND 'COUNTERFORCE'

These Soviet moves soon had a political effect in the United States. The new Kennedy administration began public discussion of the feasibility of limited nuclear war and the advantages of a 'counterforce strategy' in which the USA would put more emphasis on being able to destroy Soviet missiles in their launching pads than on hitting Soviet cities.

Early in 1962 the Kennedy administration changed the US targeting system so as to stress 'counterforce'. The changes were codified in the Single Integrated Operational Plan (SIOP) and were announced by Secretary of Defense Robert McNamara. In a speech in June 1962 NcNamara stated: 'The principal military objectives, in the event of a nuclear war stemming from a major attack on the Alliance, should be the destruction of the enemy's military forces, not of his civilian population.' He indicated that the ability to destroy an enemy society would still be available and that this would give 'the strongest imaginable incentive to refrain from striking our cities'.

In an interview in 1982 NcNamara talked about the circumstances of the nuclear arms build up during the 1960s.

> 66 Q. How did it [nuclear build-up] occur?
> A. Go back to 1960 when many in the U.S. believed there was a missile gap favouring the Soviets. With hindsight it became clear there wasn't any

missile gap. But Kennedy had been told there was. What actually happened was this: In the summer of 1960, there were two elements in the U.S. intelligence community disagreeing on the relative levels of the U.S. and Soviet strategic nuclear forces. One element greatly overstated the level of the Soviet nuclear force. When one looked over the data, it didn't justify this conclusion. And within two years of that time, the advantage in the U.S. warhead inventory was so great vis-à-vis the Soviets that the Air Force was saying that they felt we had a first strike capability and could, and should, continue to have one. If the Air Force thought that, imagine what the Soviets thought. And assuming they thought that, how would you expect them to react? The way they reacted was by substantially expanding their strategic nuclear weapons program... And the result is that during the last 25 years, and particularly during the last 15, there has been a huge build up, much more than people realise, in the nuclear strength of these two forces. **99**

Interview with Robert NcNamara, the *Guardian Weekly*, 15 August 1982

Review and Discuss

- In McNamara's view, how did the Soviets react to the US shift to counter-
- force strategy and nuclear arms build up?
- How justified was the Soviet reaction?

Critics of the new counterforce strategy focused on the threat it implied to the Soviet Union's land-based missiles and the fear that the Soviets would be bound to have of a sudden American pre-emptive strike. This was confirmed by the Soviet response to the change in US strategy, expressed by Marshal V.D. Sokolovsky:

66 A strategy which contemplates attaining victory through the destruction of the [Soviet] armed forces [by nuclear strikes] cannot stem from the idea of a 'retaliatory' blow; it stems from pre emptive action and the achievement of surprise. **99**

V.D. Sokolovsky, 'A Suicidal Strategy', *Red Star*, 19 July 1962

Public reaction in America was also largely negative. The new counterforce strategy was almost universally interpreted as making nuclear war more possible.

'MUTUALLY ASSURED DESTRUCTION'

The doctrine McNamara adopted to calm public opinion and contain the insatiable demands of the US military for new nuclear weapons was known as Assured Destruction. In early 1965 McNamara explained it to Congress in the following terms:

US Senate Armed Services Committee, Introduction, Note 1, *Military Procurement Authorization Fiscal Year 1966*, p.39

❝ A vital objective, to be met in full by our nuclear strategic forces, is the capability for Assured Destruction. It seems reasonable to assume the destruction of, say, one-quarter to one-third of its population and about two-thirds of its industrial capacity... would certainly represent intolerable punishment to any industrialized nation and this should serve as an effective deterrent. ❞

In 1969 it was recognised that the Soviet Union could inflict an 'unacceptable' level of damage on the United States and the word 'mutual' was added to the doctrine. (Mutual Assured Destruction [MAD] has remained the official declared US strategy until quite recently.)

However, in 1963 there was a split between the declared US strategy and the real war plan. Assured Destruction was there to deter an attack on the United States and to contain the appetites of the US military for new weapons. But if war actually came, it would probably be fought according to the rules and limitations laid down in the newly introduced SIOP. The reasons for this split are clearly put in the following statement:

❝ The gap between rhetoric and the actual war plans has been an enduring characteristic of the SIOP. Robert NcNamara... talked of Mutual Assured Destruction, invoking doomsday images of blowing the enemy population off the face of the earth; yet his war-plan in the mid-1960s actually called for hitting the enemy's military forces first, cities second. The deception was purposeful. Early proponents, like NcNamara, of more SIOP options to make deterrence more credible and more rational, even more 'humane' quickly realized that the more a politician talked about 'counterforce' strikes — hitting the enemy's missiles, not their cities — the more it appeared he lacked the will to blow up large chunks of the enemy's population. The Kremlin might take anything less than a total commitment to hold large populations hostage as a sign of weakness and might be tempted to start a war believing that it would not entail an all-out response. ❞

Peter Pringle & William Arkin, *SIOP: Nuclear War from the Inside*, Sphere Books, London, 1983, p.134

Review and Discuss

- Why was there a difference between the declared nuclear strategic policy of the US and the actual war plan?

Moscow, like Washington, persisted in its public declarations that nuclear war if 'imposed' on it by an 'aggressor' would be waged without limitations. Of course no one really knew what strategy the Soviets would actually follow if a nuclear war broke out. American strategists tended to assume that there was a similar split between declared strategy and the real war plan, a view reinforced in 1966 when a Russian general revealed that the Soviet targeting plan also had five categories of targets, similar to the 'options' in the American SIOP.

THE 'USABILITY' OF NUCLEAR WEAPONS: BERLIN AND CUBA

During the Berlin crisis of 1961, in which the West was at a hopeless disadvantage in conventional military forces at the point of confrontation, the option of a nuclear warning shot was considered by Kennedy's advisers and instantly rejected because of the risk of escalation. The Berlin crisis petered out when Khrushchev realised that American intelligence, using newly available reconnaissance satellites, had discovered that the Soviet nuclear forces were extremely inadequate.

This discovery put Khrushchev under considerable political pressure at home and internationally. In 1962 he took the great gamble of secretly deploying medium-range missiles on the territory of the new Soviet ally Cuba, in order to put the United States within range of a substantial Soviet missile force, and to close somewhat the strategic gap that was opening against him. The United States discovered the missiles before they became operational and imposed a blockade on Cuba. Khrushchev was forced to back down and withdraw the missiles (see p. 105).

The most significant fact about the Cuban missile crisis — from the point of view of nuclear strategy — was that a limited nuclear war was not considered. By October 1962 the new SIOP was in place with its various options for selective and limited nuclear attacks. In the face of real crisis, Kennedy reverted to the original deterrent formula. He stated that the USA would regard 'any nuclear missile launched from Cuba against any nation in the Western hemisphere as an attack by the Soviet Union on the United States *requiring a full retaliatory response upon the Soviet Union*' (emphasis added).

Reflecting on the Berlin and Cuban crises, Gwynne Dyer makes the following observation:

> 66 There is a measure of reassurance to be had from these events. The penalties for miscalculation — or even for success — in nuclear war are so terrifyingly huge that theories of controllability carry little weight when political leaders face real decisions in a crisis. They become extremely cautious and conservative in their actions; people do recognize the difference between simulation and reality. Thinking up theories for how to fight a nuclear war does not mean people will be tempted to try them out, at least in any situation short of an utterly apocalyptic crisis. 99

Gwynne Dyer, *War*, The Bodley Head, London, 1986, p.229

THE ACHIEVEMENT OF STRATEGIC PARITY

By the end of the 1960s the missile build-up backed by Brezhnev and his colleagues after the Cuban missile crisis had reached the point where the USA had to acknowledge that an American first strike would now be excessively costly in American lives. Kissinger put it succinctly in his memoirs:

> 66 For most of the post war period the Soviet Union had been virtually defence-less against an American first strike. Nor could it improve its position significantly by attacking since our counterblow would have posed unacceptable risks... [By 1969] the estimate of casualties in case of a Soviet second strike stood at over fifty million dead from immediate deaths (not to mention later deaths from radiation)... To pretend that such a prospect would not affect American readiness to resort to nuclear weapons would have been an evasion of responsibility. 99

Kissinger, *The White House Years*, pp.83–4

Kissinger's evaluation provided the foundations for the concept of strategic parity that was to underpin Soviet–US arms control talks in the early 1970s and led to SALT I and II. Parity meant that each side was recognised as having an assured chance of responding to a first strike by the enemy with a devastating counterattack of its own. Parity did not mean equality, however, in the sense that each side was recognised as having an *equal* chance of responding to a first strike. In the United States parity and equality became confused in the public debate. American politicians found it hard to accept the ambiguous concept of parity. In the 1968 presidential election campaign Nixon called for a return to unequivocal nuclear superiority over the Soviets. After his victory, however, Nixon blurred the issue, preferring the term 'sufficiency' which 'I think is a better term, actually, than either "superiority" or "parity"'.

One decision of the Nixon administration did lead to a major acceleration in the nuclear arms race. In 1968 the Johnson administration had flight-tested the first missiles with multiple independently targeted warheads (MIRVs). This technological development could double or triple the offensive power of the USA by putting several warheads on each missile. Had the incoming Nixon administration stopped the MIRV programme, it might have achieved a genuine slowing down of the arms race. Instead, it pushed on with MIRVs and, predictably, the Russians followed suit a few years later.

SCHLESINGER AND 'FLEXIBLE RESPONSE'

Early in 1972 the US Department of Defense set up the Foster Panel to review US nuclear strategy. The Foster Panel recommended 'a wide range of nuclear options which could be used... to control escalation' and its recommendations were incorporated into the US nuclear targeting strategy in January 1974. Secretary of Defense James Schlesinger publicly disclosed a change in targeting strategy that would give the US alternatives to 'initiating a suicidal strike against the cities of the other side'. The resulting revision of the US nuclear target plan, SIOP-5, explicitly took Soviet residential areas off the target list and made more elaborate provisions for attacking all elements of the Soviet leadership — party, Army, technocrats — in order to insure that 'all three of those groups... would individually and personally and organizationally and culturally know that their part of the world was not going to survive'.

Schlesinger explained to Congress in March 1974:

Quoted in Pringle & Arkin,
*SIOP: Nuclear War from
the Inside*, p.137

❝ If we were to maintain continued communications with the Soviet leaders during the war, and if we were to describe precisely and meticulously the limited nature of our actions, including the desire to avoid attacking their urban industrial bases … in spite of what one [said previously] that everything must go all out, when the existential circumstances arise, political leaders on both sides will be under powerful pressure to continue to be sensible … Those are the circumstances in which I believe that leaders will be rational and prudent. I hope I am not being too optimistic. ❞

Review and Discuss

• How would the Soviets have viewed Schlesinger's strategic thinking?

Schlesinger was not contemplating a counterforce first strike: 'I was more interested in selectivity than in counterforce per se. Going after selected silos might be a way of delivering a message.' Schlesinger clearly stated that national leaders on both sides could remain 'rational and prudent' even after nuclear warheads had exploded on their territory and that it could be strategically sensible to bargain by 'taking out' certain Soviet military industrial installations as a demonstration of US determination to prevail in a crisis. (Or perhaps Schlesinger did not really believe it, but merely wanted the Soviets to think that he did. Schlesinger was well aware of the role that prior declarations of strategic intentions might play in influencing the calculations of decision makers in an actual crisis. In the final analysis it was really a question of credibility.)

The need for credibility, however, impelled Schlesinger to approve the requests of the US military for new nuclear weapons — the Air Force's B-1 bomber and MX and cruise missiles and an 'improved accuracy program' for the Navy's Trident II missiles. These weapons all had an increased ability to strike Soviet counterforce targets.

For a brief moment at the beginning of the Carter administration in 1977, the idea of abandoning the whole massive edifice of nuclear war fighting technology and reverting to a strategy of minimum deterrence was raised at the highest level. Carter, himself a former submariner, asked why 200 missiles, all kept in submarines based at sea, would not be sufficient to deter any Soviet attack on the United States. That excellent question was not answered. Instead Carter was drawn in by the experts and by his own fascination with the technocratic elegance of the engineering and the sophistication of the US strategic nuclear theories. By the end of his term of office the various developments implicit in limited nuclear war theories were becoming all too real.

The Carter administration had gone ahead with the MX and cruise missile programme (but not the B-1 bomber — that was revived under Reagan) and also the Navy's Trident II missiles. Within two years Carter had prepared five

Presidential Directives on nuclear war plans — the most important being PD59 (July 1980) — using the Schlesinger 'flexible response' policy as a starting point and actually increasing the number and categories of SIOP options. The new plan — SIOP 5D — in addition to providing virtually limitless choices on whether to hit Soviet strategic forces or conventional military forces or economic targets, laid great stress on attacks on the leadership, Army or both. (It also contained options that would spare Moscow and the senior party leadership so they would survive as negotiating partners.) Secretary of Defense Harold Brown claimed that the Carter administration's changes were mainly a clarification and codification of existing US strategic doctrine.

BROWN AND 'COUNTERVAILING STRATEGY'

The purpose and direction of US strategic nuclear policy and the need to make that purpose and direction clear to the Soviets was spelled out on 20 August 1980 by Secretary of Defense Harold Brown:

> Deterrence remains, as it has been historically, our fundamental strategic objective. But deterrence must restrain a far wider range of threats than just massive attacks on US cities. We seek to deter any adversary from any course of action that could lead to general nuclear war. Our strategic forces also must deter nuclear attacks on smaller sets of targets in the U.S. or on U.S. military forces, and be a wall against nuclear coercion of, or attack on our friends and allies. And strategic forces, in conjunction with theatre nuclear forces, must contribute to deterrence of conventional aggression as well...
>
> By definition, successful deterrence means, among other things, shaping *Soviet* views of what a war would mean — of what risks and losses aggression would entail. We must have forces, contingency plans, and command and control capabilities that will convince the Soviet leadership that no war and no course of aggression by them that led to use of nuclear weapons — on any scale of attack and at any stage of conflict — could lead to victory, however they may define victory. Firmly convincing them of that fundamental truth is the surest restraint against their being tempted to aggression.
>
> Operationally, our countervailing strategy requires that our plans and capabilities be structured to put more stress on being able to employ strategic nuclear forces selectively, as well as by all-out retaliation in response to massive attacks on the United States. It is our policy... to ensure that if they chose some intermediate level of aggression, we could, by selective, large (but still less than maximum) nuclear attacks, exact an unacceptably high price in the things the Soviet leaders appear to value most — political and military control, military force both nuclear and conventional, and the industrial capability to sustain a war. In our planning we have not ignored the problem of ending the war, nor would we ignore it in the event of a war. And of course we have, and we will keep, a survivable and enduring

capability to attack the full range of targets, including the Soviet economic base, if that is the appropriate response to a Soviet strike...

This is not a first strike strategy. We are talking about what we could and (depending on the nature of the Soviet attack) would do *in response to* a Soviet attack. Nothing in the policy contemplates that nuclear war can be a deliberate instrument of achieving our national security goals, because it cannot be. But we cannot afford the risk that the Soviet leadership might entertain the illusion that nuclear war could be an option — or its threat a means of coercion — for *them*.

In declaring our ability and our intention to prevent Soviet victory, even in the most dangerous circumstances, we have no illusions about what a nuclear war would mean for mankind. It would be an unimaginable catastrophe.

We are also not unaware of the immense uncertainties involved in any use of nuclear weapons. We know that what might start as a supposedly controlled, limited strike could well — in my view would very likely — escalate to a full scale nuclear war. Further, we know that even limited nuclear exchanges would involve immense casualties and destruction. But we have always needed choices aside from massive retaliation in response to grave, but still limited provocation. The increase in Soviet strategic capability over the past decade, and our concern that the Soviets may not believe that nuclear war is unwinnable, dictate a U.S. need for more — and more selective — retaliatory options...

Harold Brown, 'The Flexibility of Our Plans: Strategic Nuclear Policy', Speech at Naval War College, Newport, Rhode Island, 20 August 1980, *Vital Speeches*, 1 October 1980

99

Review and Discuss

- Why did Secretary of Defense Brown place such emphasis on the 'flexibility' of the US nuclear strategy?

- Why did Brown attach such importance to the Soviet leadership's perceptions of American strategic nuclear policy?

REAGAN AND THE STRATEGIC DEFENSE INITIATIVE

The only new departure of the Reagan administration in the nuclear strategic domain was the Strategic Defense Initiative (SDI), soon dubbed Star Wars by the media. In a speech to the nation in March 1983 Reagan announced a new direction in strategic thinking:

66 Let me share with you a vision of the future which offers hope. It is, that we embark on a program to counter the awesome Soviet missile threat with measures that are defensive... What if free people could live secure in the knowledge that their security did not rest upon the threat of instant

Ronald Reagan, Speech to
the Nation, 23 March 1983,
Survival, XXV, May/June
1983, p.129

US retaliation to deter a Soviet attack; we could intercept and destroy strategic ballistic missiles before they reached our own soil or that of our allies? **99**

The desire for a policy based on strategic defence has existed since the introduction of nuclear weapons. Attempts at anti-ballistic missile (ABM) defence systems were mounted in the late 1960s and early 1970s in both the USSR and the USA. An ABM Treaty was part of SALT I. In effect, however, both sides concluded that no ABM system could ever be anywhere near 100 per cent effective. With Reagan's Star Wars programme the technological, financial, tactical and strategic questions were regarded as enormous and uncertain. Even Reagan's own Commission on Strategic Forces remained sceptical:

Brent Scowcroft,
*President's Commission on
Strategic Forces*, The
Pentagon, Washington,
1983, p.12

66 At this time, the Commission believes that no ABM technologies appear to combine practicality, survivability, low-cost and technical effectiveness sufficiently to justify proceeding beyond the stage of technology development. **99**

Nevertheless, the Star Wars advocates had two powerful reasons for pursuing the goal of space-based defences, despite the fact that they could never be impenetrable. First, the promise of an effective defence against nuclear attack was a useful political device to calm popular fears about a national strategy that envisaged fighting and prevailing in a nuclear war.

The second and more important reason for pursuing Star Wars research, in the view of its supporters, was rather more sinister: to the extent that space-based defences could eventually deal with a ragged retaliatory strike by an opponent devastated by a largely successful first strike, nuclear war fighting becomes more strategically credible and therefore more politically possible. This was precisely the view that the Soviets took of the Star Wars programme. In the words of Soviet leader Yuri Andropov:

Yuri Andropov, quoted in
McGeorge Bundy, George
F. Kennan, Robert S.
McNamara & Gerard
Smith, 'The President's
Choice: Star Wars or Arms
Control', *Foreign Affairs*,
63, 2, Winter 1984–85,
p.271

66 On the face of it, laymen may find it even attractive as the President speaks about what seem to be defensive measures... In fact, the strategic offensive forces of the United States will continue to be developed and upgraded at full tilt, and along a quite definite line at that, namely that of acquiring a first strike capability. Under these conditions the intention to secure itself the possibility of destroying with the help of anti-ballistic missile defences the corresponding strategic systems of the other side, that is of rendering it unable to deal a retaliatory strike, is a bid to disarm the Soviet Union in the face of the U.S. nuclear threat. **99**

Review and Discuss

- Why did the Soviets oppose the Star Wars programme? How legitimate were their fears?

Once again the key issue was one of perceptions — Soviet perceptions of the 'American threat'. Gwynne Dyer comments:

> To the extent that Star Wars is not mere political showbusiness, its ultimate strategic intent is to provide a partial defence not for American cities (which is unattainable), but for the intrinsically more defensible missile fields and other strategic installations from which the United States would try to wage and win a limited nuclear war. The more closely the United States approaches that goal, however, the more it will reinforce the existing predispositions of its technologically inferior Soviet rival to trump any American resort to limited nuclear war by going straight to a massive all-out nuclear strike that would saturate American defences and initiate the war of extermination.

Dyer, *War*, p.246

AMERICA, NATO AND THE INTERMEDIATE-RANGE NUCLEAR FORCES DEBATE

In the mid-1980s public attention was focused on the issue of intermediate-range nuclear forces (INF) in Europe. Such weapons were first deployed by the USA in the 1950s, to threaten Soviet territory from forward bases and aircraft carriers on the Soviet periphery. Naturally enough, coupled with the separate deployment of British and French nuclear missiles in the 1960s, they contributed to the Soviet feeling of encirclement. To counter the threat Moscow deployed land-based missiles in the western region of its territory.

The Russians made occasional reference to American forward-based systems in the arms negotiation talks of the early 1970s, but it seemed to be a low priority issue. The issue began to come alive, however, in 1977 when the Soviets decided to replace their ageing SS-4 and SS-5 missiles with the new SS-20, which is mobile, has three warheads and is more accurate than its predecessors.

By 1977, when strategic parity between the superpowers was generally accepted, America's Western European allies began to doubt the soundness of the US nuclear umbrella. NATO allies grew concerned that the US might not be willing to risk the destruction of an American target which might follow a nuclear exchange initiated in defence of Western Europe. To help uphold the link between the American and European pillars of NATO, the allies asked the USA to deploy new INF in Europe so that a regional Soviet threat to Europe could be deterred by regional US forces. As it turned out the United States had been working on a new medium-range, land-based missile (the Pershing II) since the early 1970s, with a view to its possible deployment in Europe. Soviet deployment of the SS-20 provided the necessary justification. In December 1979, NATO decided to deploy 108 advanced Pershing II missiles in West Germany plus 464 Tomahawk cruise missiles there and in four other countries of the alliance starting in 1983.

The decision caused strong protest in Moscow and considerable criticism in Western Europe. The SS-20 was indeed a powerful and menacing weapon, but as Raymond Garthoff, a former US ambassador, noted: 'A good case can be made for regarding the SS–20 as modernization.' McGeorge Bundy, national security adviser in the Kennedy–Johnson years, stated: '[It] does not give the Soviet Union any nuclear capability against Europe alone that it did not have in overflowing measure before.' To the Soviets, however, NATO's counter-weapon, the Pershing II, added a whole new strategic dimension. To quote McGeorge Bundy again: 'The Pershing II missile can reach the Soviet Union from West Germany in five minutes, thus producing a new possibility of a super-sudden first strike — even on Moscow itself. This is too fast.' Soviet commentators also claimed that the new weapons might tempt the United States into trying to launch a limited nuclear war on the USSR with missiles fired from Europe, in the hope that Moscow would retaliate on Europe alone.

SOVIET REJECTION OF 'LIMITED NUCLEAR WAR'

The Soviets have always insisted that they themselves do not believe in the concept of limited nuclear war. In July 1981 the Defence Minister, Dimitri Ustinov, wrote:

> 66 Could anyone in his right mind speak seriously of any limited nuclear war? It should be quite clear that the aggressor's actions will instantly and inevitably trigger a devastating counter strike by the other side. None but completely irresponsible people could maintain that a nuclear war may be made to follow rules adopted before hand with nuclear missiles exploding in a 'gentlemanly manner' over strictly designated targets and sparing the population. 99

D. Ustinov, *Pravda*, 25 July 1981, quoted in Steele, *Limits of Soviet Power*, p.43

In a similar vein, Brezhnev himself discounted the Western doctrine of limited nuclear war:

> 66 As a matter of fact, there can be in general no 'limited' nuclear war. If a nuclear war breaks out, whether it be in Europe or in any other place, it would inevitably and unavoidably assume a world wide character... So, those who possibly hope to set fire to the nuclear powder-keg, while themselves sitting to one side, should not entertain any illusions. 99

L.I. Brezhnev, 'Nuclear Weapons in Europe: A Soviet View', *Survival*, XXIV, January/February 1982, p.32

Review and Discuss

- Given Soviet awareness of the 'flexibility' built into US nuclear strategy, why was the declared Soviet strategy based on the view that nuclear war could not remain 'limited'?

Some Western analysts argue that Soviet writings on nuclear war and defence posture indicate a Soviet belief that they have the capability to survive and win a nuclear war. Harvard historian Richard Pipes argued this view in his 1977 article 'Why the Soviet Union Thinks it Could Fight and Win a Nuclear War' (see p. 139). Pipes' arguments and those of Western commentators with similar views have been scrutinised by Robert Arnett. Arnett, who has a thorough knowledge of Soviet military sources, summarises the issues thus:

> 66 What Soviet spokesmen have been saying about nuclear war does not support the claims of various Western analysts who argue that the Soviets believe they can win and survive a nuclear war... The Soviet usage of the dictum 'war is a continuation of politics' is a basic tenet of Marxist–Leninist theory explaining the causes of war and is not an expression of their views on survival or victory in a nuclear war. Soviet statements proclaiming that victory is possible in such a war... are necessary to keep up morale and are required by Marxist–Leninist ideology...
>
> Soviet spokesmen contend that nuclear war cannot serve as a practical instrument of policy and they continually talk about the dire consequences of such a war. Spokesmen at all levels, in different forums, generally agree that nuclear war would cause unprecedented damage. The Soviets seem to be acutely aware of the destructive capability of the U.S. arsenal... 99

Robert L. Arnett, 'Soviet Attitudes Towards Nuclear War: Do They Really Think They Can Win?', reprinted in John Baylis & Gerald Segal (eds), *Soviet Strategy*, Croom Helm, London, 1981, pp.66–7

Review and Discuss

- What explanation does Arnett offer for Soviet pronouncements that they will survive and prevail in a nuclear war?
- How does this relate to the arguments of Western analysts who claim that the Soviets believe they can win a nuclear war?

GORBACHEV AND 'REASONABLE SUFFICIENCY'

Gorbachev's coming to power led to a significant shift in Soviet strategic doctrine. The 27th Party Congress in February 1986 was presented with Gorbachev's 'new thinking': victory in nuclear war is not possible, therefore security must be gained by political, rather than military means. Gorbachev advocated multilateral co-operation and negotiation, and not unilateral military build up, as the means of attaining security. He introduced the concept of 'reasonable sufficiency' into Soviet military doctrine — a concept subjected to vigorous internal debate in 1987–88 by military and civilian analysts. Gorbachev argued that the Soviet Union should not aspire to military superiority over the West, nor even to strict parity in all weapons systems. Rather what was needed was sufficient military strength to accomplish the central objectives of deterring an attack against the Soviet Union and defending the homeland in the event of war.

In their analysis of the concept of sufficiency Soviet commentators began to explore a second notion: 'non-offensive defence'. The idea was that all nations, including the Soviet Union, should restructure their armed forces so that their own territory could be defended without posing a threat to their neighbours. Measures might include mutual troop withdrawals from border regions or replacing tanks with fixed artillery.

The significance of these two concepts for the restructuring and reduction of Soviet armed forces was profound because they were anchored in Gorbachev's assumption that world war could and would be averted by political means.

This shift in Soviet strategic thinking in 1987–88 has been extensively documented by Michael MccGwire in his *Perestroika and Soviet National Security* (1991). He argues that 'By the end of 1988 Soviet military doctrine, strategy and requirements had been set on a completely new track' and that 'these changes in Soviet defence and foreign policy were made possible by the assumption of "no world war".' He goes on:

> Soviet military behavior served for forty years in the West as a metaphor for the objectives of the world communist movement and as irrefutable evidence of the Soviet Union's efforts to dominate the world by military means. However, by the end of 1988 there had been a sea change in that behavior. The Soviet acceptance of intrusive verification of theatre as well as strategic forces, the readiness to destroy twice as many missiles as its opponents under the INF Treaty, the withdrawal from Afghanistan, the exchange of visits by the ministers of defense and heads of the joint staffs, and then the announcement of massive unilateral force cuts, these and other developments made it impossible for U.S. 'aggressive circles' and their allies in the Western military-industrial complex to continue using the Soviet military threat to justify anti-Soviet policies... While it had been essential to redefine the Marxist–Leninist theory of international relations in order to allow the reversal of policy toward the United States, on its own that would not have been enough. The West would have dismissed the new theory as propaganda and the reversal of policy as a tactical ploy. Concrete evidence of a sea change in Soviet military behavior was needed to persuade an understandably sceptical Western political-military establishment that a new era in East-West relations was beginning.
>
> And such a change in Soviet military behavior could only be justified if it were first assumed that world war could and would be averted by political means.

Michael MccGwire,
*Perestroika and Soviet
National Security*,
Brookings Institution,
Washington, 1991,
pp.343–4

Review and Discuss

- What assumption of Marxist-Leninist ideology governed Soviet military behaviour toward the West for over forty years?

- MccGwire refers to 'a sea change in Soviet military behavior' obvious by the end of 1988. What evidence does he present to support this view?

THE POST-COLD WAR ENVIRONMENT

The crumbling of the Soviet bloc in Eastern Europe in less than two years, followed by the collapse of the Soviet Union itself, is obviously a phenomenon of major importance as far as the international strategic environment is concerned.

It is clear that the combination of the loss of Eastern Europe as a glacis for the Soviets, the ongoing withdrawal of Soviet forces from these states, and the agreement on conventional forces reduction in Europe (see Chapter 13) renders practically impossible any conventional aggression with the potential reinforcement of massive nuclear and chemical surprise attacks as NATO feared. (In fact, it has been recently confirmed that that scenario was high on the Warsaw Pact's military agenda.)

Further, should Russia (or any other former post-Soviet state) retain a considerable nuclear arsenal despite INF and START, the combination of already agreed reductions, the technological and operational consequences of the continuing domestic crisis in the former USSR, and the dynamism of American technology will tilt the strategic balance increasingly towards the USA. In these changed conditions, it would be technically difficult for any post-Soviet leader to launch a surprise nuclear attack against Western Europe or the USA that would not be absolutely suicidal.

One final point about the new international environment. The abandonment of Marxist–Leninist ideology and most importantly its international component 'the worldwide class struggle', removes the principal factor that pushed the USSR from 1945 to 1987 into a declared strategy of permanent political and military expansion. From the West's point of view, it was the doctrine that made not completely implausible the possibility of the Soviets launching a major aggression, conventional or nuclear, against the capitalist West.

Review and Discuss

- What was the purpose of the 'Doomsday Project'?
- What kind of nuclear scenario did it envisage?
- Why did US strategists decide to shelve the project?

Doomsday Project set to bite the dust

By TIM WEINER

WASHINGTON, Monday: After spending 11 years and $US8 billion ($A11 billion) searching for ways to keep the Government running after a sustained nuclear attack on Washington, the Pentagon will shelve its project as a high-tech antique of the Cold War, military officials say.

The Doomsday Project, as it was known, sought to create an unbreakable chain of command for military and civilian leaders that would withstand a six-month-long nuclear war, which was regarded as a plausible length for a controlled conflict.

The nuclear tensions of that era having subsided, the project has less than six months to live. "On October 1, it's history," a Pentagon official said yesterday.

The project was an amalgam of more than 20 "black programs" — so highly classified that only a handful of military and civilian personnel knew of them.

Plans for surviving World War III date to early in the nuclear era. Among the many possible courses of such a war foreseen by planners was a continuing and controlled exchange of small numbers of weapons that would last for weeks or months, rather than an all-out Armageddon that would be over in hours or days.

Presidents since Harry Truman have been briefed on the Pentagon's plans, which relied on two huge underground shelters built in the 1950s, beneath mountains in Virginia and on the Pennsylvania–Maryland border.

In the 1980s, new nuclear war fighting strategies demanded ways to connect the President, the Secretary of Defence and top military leaders, who could give orders to fire nuclear weapons from anywhere in the nation.

Far more elaborate plans began with an order signed by President Ronald Reagan in January 1983 to create "continuity of government" during and after a long nuclear war.

The plan to keep the Government running after the White House and the Pentagon were destroyed included a network called the Presidential Survivability Support System.

Two hundred commandos were to secure surviving leaders in scores of secret bunkers. The fragmented leadership would be woven together with a communications system of space satellites and specially outfitted tractor-trailer trucks equipped with sophisticated transmitters.

Convoys of at least 16 leadlined trucks were to speed down the nation's highways eluding Soviet warheads after the Pentagon was destroyed.

Upon the trucks and throughout the nation, sophisticated radio and computer terminals shielded from the effects of nuclear explosions were to link surviving military and civilian officials after the capital was destroyed. Billions of dollars were spent on such equipment, much of which is now gathering dust in Army depots.

The *New York Times*, reprinted in the *Sydney Morning Herald*, 19 April 1994

DISARMAMENT AND ARMS CONTROL

CHAPTER THIRTEEN

THROUGHOUT the twentieth century disarmament, or at least the international control of armaments, has been a major aim in the foreign policies of most great powers. Since 1945 considerable efforts have been made to control military technology and achieve disarmament. In spite of these attempts, only minimal progress has been made.

It is important to recognise the difference between the terms 'disarmament' and 'arms control', which are often used interchangeably. 'Disarmament' means the reduction or elimination of weapons and is an aspiration with a long but not yet successful history. It should be noted that most plans for disarmament do not envisage a world totally without arms and from which the possibility of violence has been eliminated. In practice, the qualification first stated in the League of Nations Covenant — 'the maintenance of peace requires the reduction of armaments *to the lowest point consistent with national safety*' — has been accepted by most disarmament supporters.

'Arms control' is generally used to refer to co-operative agreements between states designed to regulate arms levels either by limiting their growth or by placing restrictions on how they might be used. Arms control is a relatively new idea and is less ambitious than disarmament, since it seeks not to eliminate weapons but to regulate their use or moderate the pace at which they are developed.

Since 1945 both approaches to the international control of nuclear arms have been tried. The quest for general and complete disarmament dominated international discussions throughout the 1950s and early 1960s. The arms control approach dominated negotiations from the early 1960s until 1978. Since 1978 there has been resort to both approaches.

THE QUEST FOR DISARMAMENT

In January 1946 the USA, USSR, Britain and France co-sponsored the first resolution to be adopted by the UN General Assembly. It pledged the member states to total nuclear disarmament, and to the use of nuclear energy for peaceful purposes alone. The resolution was unanimously adopted and for many months there was no whisper of opposition in any country to the policy of total nuclear disarmament. However, the task of devising a plan to implement Resolution I (1) was a long, weary, and in the end, unsuccessful one.

THE BARUCH PLAN

In early 1946 a committee headed by Dean Acheson and David Lilienthal prepared a plan for the international control of the development of atomic energy. The plan was presented to the United Nations Atomic Energy Commission (AEC) by US delegate Bernard Baruch in June 1946; it became known as the Baruch Plan. The plan proposed the creation of an International Atomic Development Authority

    " to which should be entrusted all phases for the development and use of atomic energy... including
>   1. Managerial control or ownership of all atomic energy activities potentially dangerous to world security.
>   2. Power to control, inspect, and license all other atomic activities.
>   3. The duty of fostering the beneficial use of atomic energy... *"*

In due course, the Baruch Plan was endorsed by the great majority of the UN General Assembly, but not the Soviet Union. The Soviets presented a counterproposal that differed fundamentally from the US plan. Deadlock resulted and for eight years a sterile debate on the Baruch Plan in the United Nation's AEC meant no progress towards disarmament.

In 1952, President Truman's delegate, Professor Ben Cohen, put forward to the newly created UN Disarmament Commission the Six Principles — a statement on the purpose of disarmament policy, and the conditions in which it could be put into effect. It was a forceful statement that indicated that the goal of disarmament was not to regulate but to prevent wars, by making war inherently *impossible*. States must be so disarmed that 'no state will be in condition of armed preparedness to start a war'. Cohen's Six Principles were endorsed by all the members of the General Assembly except the Soviet group and remained the foundation of disarmament statements during the following ten years.

In the years following 1952 the UN General Assembly continued to adopt resolutions pledging members to total nuclear disarmament and to the abolition of weapons of mass destruction. The West, however, stuck rigidly to the Baruch Plan. The Soviets stubbornly resisted it and without their co-operation no progress could be made.

THE ANGLO-FRENCH MEMORANDUM

In 1953 the General Assembly transferred the disarmament negotiations to a small sub-committee consisting of the USA, the USSR, Britain, France and Canada. Over the next eighteen months the British and French delegates (Selwyn Lloyd and Jules Moch) drew up a plan to break the deadlock over nuclear disarmament. In June 1954 they produced the Anglo–French Memorandum. This was a proposal for the drafting of a First Stage Treaty that would include reduction in ceilings on army size, and their (conventional) weapons; total nuclear disarmament and the abolition of all weapons of mass destruction, chemical, biological, and radiological; together with inspection so complete and effective that it would prevent violation of the treaty obligations in nuclear and conventional war-making plants.

In May 1955, after prolonged pressure by Western delegates in the sub-committee, Khrushchev finally agreed to accept the Anglo–French Memorandum as the basis for the negotiation of a First Stage Treaty of World Disarmament. But before negotiations could advance the US Pentagon found grave new difficulties with the proposals. In September 1955 the proposals of the Anglo–French Memorandum were formally withdrawn. (The sub-committee was disbanded in August 1957.)

THE 1959 JOINT RESOLUTION

In September 1959 Khrushchev attended the UN General Assembly in New York as First Delegate of the Soviet Union. In a long address he proposed a plan for the general and complete disarmament of all nations under strict and effective international control. President Eisenhower stated with no less conviction that disarmament was 'a continuing imperative', and within hours of Khrushchev's speech the US and Soviet delegations had drafted a resolution that declared that the members of the General Assembly

> ...striving to put an end completely and forever to the armaments race... and to use the resources thus released for the benefit of mankind... Considering that the question of general and complete disarmament is the most important one facing the world today, calls upon Governments to make every effort to achieve a constructive solution of this problem... [and expressed the hope that appropriate measures]... will be worked out in detail and agreed upon in the shortest possible time.

This joint Soviet–US Resolution of 1959 evoked such enthusiasm in the UN General Assembly that every single delegation insisted on acting as co-sponsors. A Committee of Ten Nations (five NATO, five Warsaw Pact) was set up with a mandate to draft a Treaty of World Disarmament. It met in Geneva in 1960 but made no progress. Nothing further happened until after Eisenhower's departure from the White House in January 1961.

THE McCLOY–ZORIN AGREEMENT

The new American President, John F. Kennedy, chose John McCloy, a distinguished Republican, as his disarmament negotiator and sent him to Moscow for talks with Khrushchev in September 1961. A 'joint statement of agreed principles as a basis for multilateral negotiations on disarmament' was issued by the Soviet Union and the United States on 20 September 1961 (the McCloy-Zorin Agreement). The Agreed Principles were supported in the UN General Assembly by President Kennedy:

> " Today, every inhabitant of this planet must contemplate the day when this planet may no longer be habitable. Every man, woman and child lives under a nuclear sword of Damocles hanging by the slenderest of threads, capable of being cut at any moment by accident or miscalculation or by madness. The weapons of war must be abolished before they abolish us.
>
> Men no longer debate whether armaments are a symptom or a cause of tension. The mere existence of modern weapons — ten million times more powerful than any that the world has ever seen, and only minutes away from any target on earth — is a source of horror, and discord and distrust. Men no longer maintain that disarmament must await the settlement of all disputes — for disarmament must be a part of any permanent settlement. And men may no longer pretend that the quest for disarmament is a sign of weakness — for in a spiraling arms race, a nation's security may well be shrinking even as its arms increase...It is therefore our intention to challenge the Soviet Union, not to an arms race but to a peace race — to advance together step by step, stage by stage, until general and complete disarmament is achieved. "

John F. Kennedy, Address to UN General Assembly, 25 September 1961, *Department of State Bulletin*, XLV, 16 October 1961, p.620

The McCloy–Zorin principles were unanimously adopted by the General Assembly and formed the basis of the attempt by a new Committee of Eighteen Nations (the ten NATO and WTO nations of the previous committee, plus eight non-aligned nations) to draw up a treaty of general and complete disarmament. The Eighteen Nation Disarmament Committee (ENDC) met in Geneva in March 1962. The American, Soviet and British Foreign Ministers — Dean Rusk, Andrei Gromyko and Sir Alec Douglas-Home — gathered in Geneva several days before the formal opening of the ENDC. In a series of informal talks the three discussed the Draft Treaty that Khrushchev had prepared and the outline scheme that Kennedy had presented to the UN General Assembly the previous September.

After eighteen days in Geneva Rusk, Gromyko and Douglas-Home left for home and left the work of the ENDC to junior ministers and officials. Douglas-Home had said that the delegates should take what was best from each and 'make a master plan of their own'. He had warned them 'not to find differences of principle where none existed'. The junior delegates seemed to ignore these wise words. After three years of fruitless negotiations the two draft treaties were shelved.

THE ARMS CONTROL APPROACH

Disarmament came gradually to be replaced by arms control. There was no sudden UN decision to abandon disarmament, but attempts at general and complete disarmament had made little progress and it was felt that the time had come to try a fresh approach. The peace movement of the later 1950s and early 1960s was clamouring for initiatives to end the arms race (see Chapter 14). If disarmament seemed too difficult to attain, some measure of arms control, formalised by treaty, would help satisfy public opinion.

Also, arms control measures were very flexible. They could be negotiated on an ad hoc basis, varying to fit local circumstances, and need not involve all nations. Naturally they appealed to governments that preferred to make public policy changes in small steps rather than in great leaps. The first arms control measure, negotiated in 1959 (Antarctic Treaty), had worked well. It demonstrated that arms control was feasible and worth pursuing.

Since the historical Antarctic Treaty of 1959 a series of arms control and communication and confidence-building measures have been signed. The major agreements are listed in the following table. Most of these are multilateral agreements arrived at under United Nations auspices. A small but significant number are bilateral agreements between the United States and the Soviet Union.

Three of the multilateral agreements are of major importance in the context of Soviet–American relations in a nuclear world.

1. *Partial Test Ban Treaty* (1963). This treaty — limiting nuclear tests to underground — was largely a response to rising public pressure over the dangers of radioactive fallout from the atmospheric tests that the USA, the USSR and the UK had conducted in the 1950s. Neither France nor China is a party to the Partial Test Ban Treaty. China has conducted atmospheric tests of nuclear weapons, but since 1974 France has conducted its nuclear explosions underground.

2. *Non-Proliferation Treaty* (1968). This is the most significant of the treaties that restrict the spread of nuclear weapons. Throughout the 1950s and 1960s there were fears that horizontal proliferation (i.e. more and more nations acquiring nuclear weapons) increased the danger of nuclear war. Under the NPT non-nuclear weapons nations agreed not to acquire weapons by any method while the USA, the USSR and the UK agreed not to supply them to such

Arms Control and Disarmament Agreements*

The end of the Cold War helped to give new life to the disarmament process. A record number of important official agreements were completed between 1990 and 1993. For the first time, international treaties were negotiated to: 1) reduce major conventional weapons and armed forces in Europe; 2) cut back stocks of nuclear weapons held by the superpowers (two treaties); and 3) eliminate world-wide all stocks of chemical weapons. Of the four treaties, however, only the first, reducing weapons in Europe, has entered into force and is on schedule. There is no control, as yet, on the arms trade, no treaty banning nuclear tests of fissile material for nuclear weapons, none requiring the destruction of nuclear weapons.

Nuclear Weapons

To prevent the spread of nuclear weapons—

Antarctic Treaty, 1959   **40 states[1]**
Bans any military uses of Antarctica and specifically prohibits nuclear tests and nuclear waste.

Outer Space Treaty, 1967   **93 states[1]**
Bans nuclear weapons in earth orbit and their stationing in outer space.

Latin American Nuclear-Free Zone Treaty, 1967   24 states[1]
Bans testing, possession, deployment of nuclear weapons and requires safeguards on facilities.

Non-Proliferation Treaty, 1968   **160 states[1]**
Bans transfer of weapons or weapons technology to non-nuclear weapons states. Requires safeguards on their facilities. Commits nuclear-weapon states to negotiations to halt the arms race. Commits non-nuclear states not to acquire nuclear weapons. Promotes peaceful uses of nuclear energy.

Seabed Treaty, 1971   **88 states[1]**
Bans nuclear weapons on the seabed beyond a 12-mile coastal limit.

South Pacific Nuclear-Free Zone Treaty, 1985   11 states[1]
Bans testing, manufacture, acquisition, stationing of nuclear weapons. Requests five nuclear weapons states to sign a protocol banning use or threat of nuclear weapons and nuclear testing.

To limit nuclear testing—

Limited Test Ban Treaty, 1963   **120 states[1]**
Bans nuclear weapons tests in the atmosphere, outer space, or underwater.

Threshold Test Ban Treaty, 1974   **US–Russia**
Bans underground tests having a yield above 150 kilotons (150,000 tons of TNT equivalent).

Peaceful Nuclear Explosions Treaty, 1976   **US–Russia**
Bans underground nuclear explosions for "peaceful purposes" having a yield above 150 kilotons; bans "group explosions" having a yield above 1,500 kilotons (1.5 megatons); entered into force in 1990.

To reduce the risk of nuclear war—

Hot Line and Modernization Agreements, 1963 US–USSR[2]
Establishes direct communication links between Moscow and Washington.

Accidents Measures Agreement, 1971   **US–USSR[2]**
Pledges US and USSR to improve safeguards against accidental or unauthorized use of nuclear weapons.

Prevention of Nuclear War Agreement, 1973   **US–USSR[2]**
Requires the two countries to consult if there is danger of nuclear war.

Nuclear Risk Reduction Centers, 1987   **US–USSR[2]**
Establishes high-speed communication centers in Washington and Moscow.

To limit nuclear weapons—

ABM Treaty (SALT I) and Protocol, 1972, 1974 US–USSR[2]
Limits antiballistic missile systems to one deployment site on each side. Bans nationwide anti-ballistic missile system, and development, testing, or deployment of sea-based, air-based, or space-based ABM system.

SALT I Interim Agreement, 1972   **US–USSR**
Froze the number of strategic ballistic missile launchers for five years; extended by parties until 1986 when President Reagan dropped US commitment.

SALT II, 1979   **US–USSR**
Limited number of strategic nuclear delivery vehicles and multiple-warhead launchers; was not ratified, but its limits were adhered to until 1986 when President Reagan dropped US commitment.

INF Treaty, 1987   **US–NIS[4]**
Eliminates US and USSR ground-launched missiles of ranges 300 to 3,500 miles. Requires dismantling within 3 years; extensive verification provisions.

START I and Protocol, 1991, 1992   **5 states[3]**
Reduces number of deployed US and former Soviet strategic nuclear warheads by approximately one-third; Lisbon Protocol makes Russia, Belarus, Ukraine, and Kazakhstan responsible for carrying out former USSR treaty obligations.

START II, 1993   **US–Russia[3]**
Reduces the number of deployed US and Russian strategic nuclear warheads to 3,000–3,500 each by year 2003; bans multiple-warhead land-based missiles.

Other Weapons

To prohibit use of chemical weapons—

Geneva Protocol, 1925   **132 states**
Bans the use in war of asphyxiating, poisonous, or other gases, and of bacteriological methods of warfare.

Chemical Weapons Convention, 1993   **147 states[3]**
Bans the use, production, development, and stockpiling of chemical weapons. Requires the destruction of all chemical weapons stockpiles within 10–15 years of the treaty's entry into force.

To destroy biological and chemical weapons—

Biological Weapons Convention, 1972   **126 states**
Bans the development, production, and stockpiling of biological and toxin weapons; requires the destruction of stocks; lacks verification mechanism.

Chemical Weapons Destruction Agreement, 1990 US–Russia
Obliges parties to destroy chemical weapons stocks to a maximum of 5,000 tons by the year 2002. Destruction schedule seriously delayed.

To limit conventional forces—

Conventional Armed Forces in Europe, 1990, 1992   30 states
Requires NATO and former Warsaw Pact states to reduce five categories of major conventional weapons. "Politically-binding" agreement puts ceilings on troop strength of army and air force units in Europe.

To register conventional arms—

UN Register of Conventional Arms, 1993   **71 states**
Voluntary agreement calls on states to provide data on major conventional weapons imported or exported during the previous year.

To prohibit techniques changing the environment—

Environmental Modification Convention, 1977   57 states
Bans military or other hostile use of techniques to change weather or climate patterns, ocean currents, ozone layer, or ecological balance.

To control use of inhumane weapons—

Inhumane Weapons Convention, 1981   **35 states**
Bans use of fragmentation bombs not detectable in the human body; bans use against civilians of mines and incendiary weapons; requires records on mines.

Dates shown are dates agreements were signed. 1. Number of parties as recorded by US Arms Control and Disarmament Agency. 2. No decision as yet about which state will succeed the USSR as party to this agreement. 3. Not yet entered into force. 4. NIS (Newly Independent States) includes all former Soviet republics, except Latvia, Lithuania, and Estonia.

Ruth Leger Sivard, *World Military and Social Expenditures 1993*, World Priorities, Washington, p.35

nations. The extensive nuclear proliferation predicted at the time has not materialised and without doubt the NPT has helped in that regard, but some nations refuse to be bound by the NPT. France and China did not sign and of course have become nuclear armed powers. Of more concern is the refusal of nations such as Argentina, Brazil, Israel, India, Pakistan and South Africa to be bound by the NPT. These tend to be the very nations about which there are most fears of acquiring nuclear weapons.

3. *CSCE Helsinki Agreement* (1975). At the Conference on Security and Cooperation in Europe, which took place at Helsinki, agreement was reached on what have become known as Confidence-Building Measures (CBMs). All thirty-five participating countries agreed to give prior notification of major military exercises involving more than 25 000 troops. US Ambassador Goodby described the Helsinki measures as having 'legitimised the concept of openness and cooperation among states, even on sensitive security issues, as a desirable way to improve relations and maintain peace'.

BILATERAL ARMS CONTROL AGREEMENTS

The United States and the Soviet Union have concluded a number of bilateral treaties, the most important of which are the two treaties arising out of the SALT discussions. A second category of agreements are designed to minimise the risk of accidental nuclear war. There also appears to be an indeterminate number of tacit understandings about the level and use of weapons that the two superpowers have agreed to.

1. *Hot-line Agreement* (1963). The Cuban missile crisis of October 1962 highlighted the importance of a clear, direct system of communications between Moscow and Washington. In June 1963 agreement was reached on three communications links (teletype, telegraph and radio-telegraph). The Hot-line Treaty was updated in September 1971 to incorporate new advances in communications technology (satellite link).

2. *Nuclear Accidents Agreement* (1971). During the 1960s there were increasing fears of a nuclear war starting accidentally through, for example, a computer malfunction or some military personnel deciding unilaterally to launch their weapons. The issue was discussed during the initial SALT negotiations and agreements reached on: a pledge by both sides to take measures each considers necessary to maintain and improve its safeguards against accidental or unauthorised use of nuclear weapons; arrangements for immediate notification should a risk of a nuclear exchange arise from such incidents, from detection of unidentified objects or other unexplained incidents; and advance notification of any planned missile launches beyond the territory of the launching country in the direction of the other country.

3. *Strategic Arms Limitations Treaty — SALT I* (1972). The SALT negotiations began in 1969 and successfully concluded their first stage in 1972 with two treaties. The SALT I Anti-Ballistic Missile (ABM) Treaty limited both parties

to the deployment of ABM systems at two sites. A 1974 Protocol to the ABM Treaty reduced the permitted number of sites to one each. Moscow has such a system deployed. The Americans subsequently decided not to go ahead with deployment of an ABM system to protect a cluster of ICBM silos in North Dakota. The second treaty was the SALT I Interim Agreement on Offensive Arms. This treaty essentially imposed a five-year quantitative freeze on the total number of ICBM and SLBM launchers (missile silos and submarine tubes) of each of the two superpowers. The parties were free to modernise their forces and choose their mix of missiles.

The SALT I Interim Agreement represented the first set of actual limits on strategic weapons ever achieved. Both sides recognised it as an important political achievement and as a first step toward achieving more meaningful limits on arms. However, as critics of the agreement pointed out, while SALT I imposed limits on ballistic missile launchers, it did not limit strategic bombers or their bombs, nor did it restrict the option to deploy a number of warheads on each ballistic missile (MIRVing).

4. *SALT II Treaty* (1979). The SALT II Agreement substantially revised the quantitative restrictions of SALT I and began as well to place certain qualitative constraints on the superpowers' strategic arsenals. At the time the SALT II Treaty was the most extensive and complicated arms control agreement ever negotiated. Essentially, SALT II placed an overall ceiling on the total missile launchers (2400 initially, to be reduced to 2250 by January 1981) each side was permitted to maintain. Within this overall ceiling several subceilings specified additional restrictions on particular types of weapons. The parties also agreed to several important bans: on the testing and deployment of new types of ICBMs, except for one new type of 'light' missile on each side (the Americans were busy on their MX missile); on heavy mobile ICBMs; and on rapid reload systems.

As noted in a previous chapter, SALT II was signed by Carter and Brezhnev

The struggle for peace: a Soviet cartoon of 1979 (Nicolai Kapusta, Radjanska Donetchyna, USSR). What is the object falling from the air? What is the device being used to catch it? (Note the shape.) From the date of the cartoon can you work out the event it is celebrating? Why was the celebration premature?

in Vienna in June 1979. Subject to ratification it was to remain in force until 31 December 1985. (The debate on its ratification in the US Congress and the reasons for its subsequent withdrawal by Carter have been discussed in Chapter 9.) Despite the lack of ratification the two superpowers stated that they would refrain from actions contrary to the SALT II provisions. Generally they remained within the numerical limits set by the treaty. In June 1985 President Reagan announced that the US will continue to refrain from under-cutting the expired SALT I agreement and the unratified SALT II agreement as long as the Soviet Union exercises equal restraint and actively pursues arms reductions agreements at Geneva'.

UN SPECIAL SESSIONS ON DISARMAMENT

During the 1970s disarmament remained on the UN's agenda but it became increasingly overshadowed by new crises such as energy, population, food, environmental pollution and international economic instability.

In 1978 the United Nations, using the rarely used mechanism of the Special Session of the General Assembly, focused world attention once again on the issue of disarmament. The 1978 Special Session was the first major disarmament gathering held since the 1932 World Disarmament Conference. It was attended by all 149 UN member states and was the largest disarmament gathering in world history. The Session's Final Document is widely regarded as the best detailed statement on disarmament ever endorsed by the world community. It summed up the dangers of the nuclear stockpiles to international security in the following terms:

> 66 Existing arsenals of nuclear weapons alone are more than sufficient to destroy all life on earth… The increase in weapons, especially nuclear weapons, far from helping to strengthen international security, on the contrary weak-ens it. The vast stockpiles and tremendous build up of arms and armed forces and the competition for qualitative refinements of weapons of all kinds to which scientific resources and technological advances are diverted, pose incalculable threats to peace. This situation both reflects and aggravates international tensions, sharpens conflicts in various regions of the world, hinders the process of détente, exacerbates the differences between opposing military alliances, jeopardises the security of all States, heightens the sense of insecurity among all States including the non-nuclear weapons States, and increases the threat of nuclear war. 99

'Final Document', General Assembly Special Session on Disarmament, the United Nations, 23 May–1 July 1978, reprinted in *Apocalypse Now?*, Spokesman, London, 1980

A second Special Session on disarmament of the UN General Assembly was held in 1982. The international political climate in mid-1982 was much worse than in mid-1978. The Soviet interventions in Afghanistan and Poland, US intervention in El Salvador and the conflicts in the Middle East and South Atlantic all poisoned the chances of international co-operation. The Special Session did reaffirm the 1978 Final Document, but little progress had been made since 1978.

THE IMPACT OF GORBACHEV

In December 1979, NATO responded to the Soviet Union's deployment of SS–20 missiles targeted on Western Europe with a 'two-track' decision on its own intermediate-range nuclear forces (INF). It agreed to negotiate with the USSR to avoid the deployment of cruise and Pershing II missiles, while at the same time going ahead with the necessary preparations for their deployment. NATO/WTO discussions on INF began in Geneva in November 1981, but ended in December 1983 when, in response to the initial deployment of cruise missiles in Western Europe, the Soviets walked out of the INF negotiations. No further talks took place until March 1985 when the two sides began a new range of negotiations in Geneva on the question of strategic arms, INFs and space weapons.

Undoubtedly a significant factor in the revival of the negotiating process was the energy and purpose of the new Soviet leader. In January 1986, Gorbachev presented a three-stage plan to eliminate nuclear weapons by the year 2000. Reagan's response was guarded since the 'umbrella' talks that began in March 1985 on START/INF and space weapons had been deadlocked on the Soviet demand that all future progress be linked to a limit on American plans for the Strategic Defense Initiative (SDI–Star Wars). The deadlock was highlighted when Reagan and Gorbachev met in Reykjavik in October 1986. Although the Soviets offered huge cuts in nuclear arsenals Reagan was not willing to restrict the SDI programme in return.

The INF treaty signed in Washington in December 1987 bore Gorbachev's personal stamp. He compromised on the Soviet insistence that British and French nuclear forces be included in any agreement. He compromised on Reagan's determination to have the 'zero option' — no intermediate nuclear missiles in Europe — even though that required far greater Soviet than NATO reductions. He also compromised on including shorter range nuclear systems where once again Soviet reductions would be greater. To the surprise of many, especially US military experts, Gorbachev reversed long-standing Soviet objections to 'intrusive' forms of verification and agreed to a complicated regimen of inspection to enforce the treaty.

Progress was made at the various Soviet–US summits between 1987 and 1990 on the START Agreement. The major components went back to the undertakings made at the Reykjavik Summit in 1986. Each side would agree to limit its strategic forces to 6000 warheads on 1600 delivery vehicles. There were to be subceilings. No more than 3300 warheads could be based on ICBMs. The overall effect of the various subceilings would be that the Soviets would increase the proportion of their strategic forces based on aircraft and submarines; more in tune with American ideas of strategic stability. (No agreement could be reached on SLBMs.) This treaty also provides for a rigorous mutual regimen of on-site inspection. The START Treaty signed in Moscow by Bush and Gorbachev in July 1991 represented roughly a thirty per cent reduction in the overall level of nuclear arsenals but, more importantly, a fifty per cent cut in the weapons Washington considered most dangerous — heavy land-based ICBMs.

Progress was also made in a third area of negotiation — on the reduction of conventional military forces in Europe. Talks in Vienna on Mutual and Balanced Force Reductions (MBFR), which had been bogged down for years, gave way to new, fruitful talks on Conventional Forces in Europe (CFE). Gorbachev authorised Soviet negotiators in Vienna to proceed with discussion of a 275 000 ceiling for Soviet and American troops in Central and Eastern Europe. Shortly after coming to office US President Bush proposed that the ceiling be reduced to 195 000 for each side. Gorbachev accepted the lower ceiling. This was a major concession, as the 195 000 ceiling would require a 370 000 cut in Soviet troops compared to a 100 000 cut in American troops.

Gorbachev radically altered and accelerated the course of arms control. In all three treaties that were concluded after he came to power — INF in 1987, CFE in 1990 and START in 1991 — he compromised on long-held Soviet claims and accepted many of the premises of the US negotiating position.

THE ARMS CONTROL AGENDA TRANSFORMED

Shortly before the disintegration of the Soviet Union and Gorbachev's fall from power, President Bush announced sweeping changes to the US tactical nuclear inventory (27 September 1991). One week later President Gorbachev matched the American initiative. Under the Bush–Gorbachev initiatives on theatre nuclear forces (TNF), all US and Soviet ground-based weapons would be destroyed and about half of all sea-based and air-based weapons.

Bush and Gorbachev also took important steps to limit strategic nuclear forces. All strategic bombers were taken off twenty-four hour alert and also all those ICBMs to be eliminated under START. The two leaders cancelled the mobile basing portions of their ICBM programmes. Bush repeated his call for a ban on land-based multiple independently-targeted warhead (MIRV) missiles. Gorbachev proposed a further reduction in Soviet strategic weapons and announced a one-year unilateral moratorium on nuclear testing.

When the USSR was finally dissolved and the Commonwealth of Independent States (CIS) was established at the end of 1991, a separate agreement on strategic forces was signed on 31 December 1991 in Minsk, which specified that all nuclear weapons would remain under a joint command based in Moscow. The decision to use strategic nuclear weapons would be made by the Russian President in agreement with the leaders of Belarus, Kazakhstan and Ukraine (the other three states where strategic nuclear weapons were based in the short term) and after consultation with the leaders of the other independent states.

It was clear that both the United States and Russia regarded the Russian Federation as the successor state to the Soviet Union as far as strategic nuclear forces were concerned. On this basis the strategic dialogue with the United States has been continued by President Boris Yeltsin.

On 28 January 1992 President Bush proposed that Russia, Belarus, Ukraine, Kazakhstan and the USA negotiate a ban on MIRVed ICBMs. As an inducement Bush offered to cut America's post-START inventory by approximately half. Further, he unilaterally cancelled three nuclear missile modernisation programmes.

One day later Russian President Yeltsin responded by detailing reductions that would in effect implement the cuts announced by Gorbachev the previous October. He also proposed to reduce Russian and US forces to 2000–2500 weapons on each side (thus implicitly accepting a ban on land-based MIRVed missiles). The details of various proposals were the subject of Russian–US ministerial discussion leading up to the Yeltsin–Bush Summit of June 1992. The American–Russian Charter signed by the two leaders in Washington declared 'the United States and Russia do not regard each other as adversaries and are developing relations of partnership'.

The charter envisages the two strategic nuclear powers co-operating to pre-serve global peace and to prevent the emergence of new hostile nuclear powers. Bush and Yeltsin reached agreement on further reductions in strategic nuclear forces. After some refinement this agreement was formalised in the START II Treaty signed by Presidents Bush and Yeltsin in Moscow on 3 January 1993. The treaty provides for further significant reduction in nuclear arsenals of the two powers.

> 66 At present, the United States and the former Soviet Union have deployed a total of 10 875 and 10 271 strategic nuclear warheads respectively. After the first START Treaty has been implemented these will have been reduced to at most 6000 on both sides. START 2 envisages a further reduction in two phases. During the first seven years after ratification of the treaty both sides will cut their strategic arsenals to between 3800 and 4250 warheads each. By 1 January 2003 both sides must reduce their strategic nuclear warheads to a total of 3500.
>
> Arguably the most important feature of the treaty is the elimination of landbased missiles with multiple warheads (so-called MIRVs)...
>
> Some Western commentators have played down the significance of START 2, given that a very substantial strategic arsenal will remain on both sides even after implementation... But it could be argued that the elimination of multiple warheads does constitute a qualitative restructuring of the arsenals that substantially enhances stability at a much reduced level and to a large extent takes the competitive element out of the maintenance of a nuclear deterrent force. 99

Christoph Bluth, 'American–Russian strategic relations: from confrontation to cooperation?', *The World Today*, vol.49, no.3, March 1993, p.49

Review and Discuss

- What does Bluth regard as the most significant feature of the START treaties?
- How does he answer those critics of START who point out that substantial nuclear arsenals will remain?

ARMS CONTROL: FROM NEGOTIATION TO IMPLEMENTATION

In the aftermath of the Cold War arms control negotiations have flourished. Agreements on nuclear, chemical and conventional weapons have been arrived at in quick succession. However, while reaching agreement on limiting or eliminating certain types of weapons has become easier, their implementation has become more difficult. The emergence of parliamentary independence and democratic debate in the states of the former Soviet Union has sometimes made ratification of arms control agreements uncertain. (The delay by Ukraine in ratifying START I is the most glaring example.) Even when agreements have been ratified, the new states are finding it difficult for economic and technical reasons actually to implement the arms reductions that have been agreed to.

Future efforts in arms control are likely to focus on the implementation of the gains achieved to date. In this respect ensuring the actual destruction of weapons to be reduced under the various agreements and the development of new and co-operative patterns of verification to increase mutual confidence will be high priorities.

The cost of weapons destruction for former Soviet republics is an issue that has been canvassed in US government circles. In November 1991 Congress agreed that America should shoulder some of the burden appropriating $400 million for this purpose. A further $400 million was allocated in October 1992.

Does the end of the Cold War mean the end of the need for arms control? The International Institute of Strategic Studies, in its *Strategic Survey 1992–1993*, gives a carefully qualified answer:

> " It has been said that with the end of the Cold War, the need for arms control has disappeared. There is some truth in this statement: the spectacle of tense summits and years of intense negotiations in Geneva and Vienna is clearly a thing of the past. Nor are the successes or failures of arms control any longer the barometer of the state of relations among major powers. But none of this had anything to do with arms control, which involves the mutual regulation of armaments in an effort to reduce the probability of their ever having to be used. That goal is clearly not a thing of the past, as the agreements of the last two years have shown and the large remaining agenda attests. Arms control as a circus has disappeared, and that is for the better: what remains is arms control as serious business and it would be best if everyone knuckled down to the task. "

International Institute of Strategic Studies, *Strategic Survey 1992–1993*, Brasseys for IISS, London, 1993, pp.218–19

THE POLITICS
OF PEACE

CHAPTER FOURTEEN

Among the first to realise that humankind faced the possibility of complete annihilation in a nuclear war was the world-famous German-born nuclear physicist, Albert Einstein. In 1945, at the age of sixty-six, Einstein realised the danger of the new weapons and devoted the last ten years of his life to an unceasing struggle to prevent a nuclear catastrophe. He came to the conclusion that the only hope for the survival of humankind was total disarmament and world government. Einstein was well aware of the Soviet Union's opposition to the idea of world government. The point was put to him explicitly in 1947 in a letter from four eminent Russian scientists, who argued that world government would ensure world supremacy of the capitalist monopolies and that Einstein's call for it prejudiced the cause of peace that he so warmly espoused. (In the early post-war years ideas about world government struck a sympathetic response in the Western world, but political events such as the Korean War and the growing hysteria in the United States about 'un-American' activities dampened enthusiasm and led to a change in feeling.)

THE RUSSELL–EINSTEIN MANIFESTO

Shortly before his death Einstein joined forces with British philosopher Bertrand Russell to issue an enormously influential manifesto calling attention to the appalling danger that nuclear weapons presented to civilisation. The manifesto was issued by Russell at a large press conference in London in July 1955.

> We are speaking on this occasion, not as members of this or that nation, continent or creed, but as human beings, members of the species Man, whose continued existence is in doubt. The world is full of conflicts; and, overshadowing all minor conflicts, the titanic struggle between Communism and Anti-Communism...
>
> We shall try to say no single word which should appeal to one group

44 YEARS OF THE *BULLETIN* CLOCK: A HISTORY OF THE COLD WAR

1947

Seven minutes to midnight

The clock first appears on the *Bulletin* cover as a symbol of nuclear danger.

1949

Three minutes to midnight

The Soviet Union explodes its first atomic bomb.

1953

Two minutes to midnight

The United States successfully tests a hydrogen bomb in late 1952.

1960

Seven minutes to midnight

The clock moves in response to the growing public understanding that nuclear weapons made war between major technical nations irrational. International scientific cooperation and efforts to aid poor nations are cited.

1963

Twelve minutes to midnight

The U.S. and Soviet signing of the Partial Test Ban Treaty "provides the first tangible confirmation of what has been the *Bulletin's* conviction in recent years — that a new cohesive force has entered the interplay of forces shaping the fate of mankind."

1968

Seven minutes to midnight

France and China acquire nuclear weapons; wars rage in the Middle East, the Indian subcontinent, and Vietnam; world military spending increases while development funds shrink.

1969

Ten minutes to midnight

The U.S. Senate ratifies the Nuclear Non-Proliferation Treaty.

1972

Twelve minutes to midnight

The United States and the Soviet Union sign the first Strategic Arms Limitation Treaty (SALT I) and the Anti-Ballistic Missile Treaty; progress toward SALT II is anticipated.

1974

Nine minutes to midnight

SALT talks reach an impasse; India develops a nuclear weapon. "We find policymakers on both sides increasingly ensnared, frustrated, and neutralized by domestic forces having a vested interest in the amassing of strategic forces."

1980

Seven minutes to midnight

The deadlock in U.S.–Soviet arms talks continues; nationalistic wars and terrorist actions increase; the rift between rich and poor nations widens.

1981

Four minutes to midnight

Both superpowers develop more weapons for fighting a nuclear war. Terrorist actions, repression of human rights, conflicts in Afghanistan, Poland, South Africa add to world tension.

1984

Three minutes to midnight

The arms race accelerates. "Arms control negotiations have been reduced to a species of propaganda... The blunt simplicities of force threaten to displace any other form of discourse between the superpowers."

1988

Six minutes to midnight

The United States and the Soviet Union sign a treaty to eliminate intermediate-range nuclear forces (INF); superpower relations improve; more nations actively oppose nuclear weapons.

1990

Ten minutes to midnight

(In Oct. 1989, the clock is redesigned to show the need for an expanded view of global security.) Democratic movements in Eastern Europe shatter the myth of monolithic communism; the Cold War ends.

1991

Seventeen minutes to midnight

The United States and the Soviet Union sign the long-stalled Strategic Arms Reduction Treaty (START) and announce further unilateral cuts in tactical and strategic nuclear weapons.

This clock (left) has appeared on the cover of the
Bulletin of the Atomic Scientists *since 1947. A*
symbol of the dangers of the nuclear age, it has
moved forward and back from its original position
of seven minutes to midnight. In December 1991
the clock was moved back from ten minutes to
midnight to seventeen minutes to midnight, where
it still stands (January–February 1994 issue). What
is the message of the 'doomsday clock'? How has it
acted as a barometer of the political climate in the
nuclear age? What background events have
influenced the editorial decision to move the clock
forward or back in each of the fifteen years
illustrated?

rather than another. All, equally, are in peril, and, if the peril is understood, there is hope that they may collectively avert it. We have to learn to think in a new way. We have to learn to ask ourselves, not what steps can be taken to give military victory to whatever group we prefer, for there are no longer such steps; the question we have to ask ourselves is: what steps can be taken to prevent a military contest of which the issue must be disastrous to all parties?... Many warnings [about the effects of H-bombs] have been uttered by eminent men of science and by authorities in military strategy... We have not yet found that the views of experts of this question depend in any degree upon their policies or prejudices. They depend only... upon the extent of the particular expert's knowledge. We have found that the men who know most are the most gloomy.

'The Russell–Einstein
Manifesto', in Joseph
Rotblat (ed.), *Scientists, the*
Arms Race and
Disarmament (UNESCO/
Pugwash Symposium),
Taylor & Francis, London,
1982, pp.301–3

Here, then, is the problem which we present to you, stark and dreadful and inescapable: shall we put an end to the human race; or shall mankind renounce war?

"

Russell and Einstein felt that the signatories of the statement should be so diverse in their politics that there could be no accusation of pro-communist bias. Russell and Einstein agreed on ten eminent signatories (among them six Nobel prize winners, including Max Born, Percy Bridgman and Linus Pauling). The statement was subsequently endorsed by thousands of scientists from many countries and became the credo of the Pugwash Conferences on Science and World Affairs.

THE PUGWASH MOVEMENT

The Pugwash movement took its name from the location of the first meeting, which was held in July 1957 in the small fishing village of Pugwash, Nova Scotia. It was made possible by the financial help of Cyrus Eaton, a Canadian-US industrialist who offered to cover all the expenses of the conference on condition that it was held in Pugwash, his birthplace. The first 'Pugwash Conference on Science and World Affairs' was a very small gathering with twenty-two participants from ten countries in the East and West (including the USA, the USSR, and United Kingdom, France and the People's Republic of China). It was so successful it was decided to convene further meetings. From this modest beginning the Pugwash movement has grown to encompass national organisations, usually sponsored by national academies of science, on every continent.

The purpose of the Pugwash conferences has been clearly explained by Joseph Rotblat, an original signatory of the Russell-Einstein Manifesto and a leading figure in the Pugwash movement since its inception.

> 66 The main purpose of the Pugwash Conferences is to bring together influential scientists and public figures, from all over the world, concerned with reducing the danger of nuclear war. Meeting in private as individuals, rather than as representatives of their governments, and with a minimum of publicity, Pugwash participants can exchange views and explore alternative approaches to arms control and measures to reduce tension with a degree of candor and flexibility seldom approached in official East–West and North–South contacts and negotiations. Yet because of the stature and influence of many of the Pugwash participants in their own countries, the results of Pugwash discussions often penetrate quickly to the official policy-making bodies. 99

Joseph Rotblat, 'The Pugwash Movement' in E. Laszlo & J.Y. Yoo (eds), *World Encyclopedia of Peace*, vol.2, Pergamon, Oxford, 1986, p.312

THE EFFECT OF PUGWASH

Through the growing network of Pugwash contacts, the results of meetings it sponsors have been passed on to government leaders, the United Nations and other international organisations, as well as the world scientific community. Pugwash conferences played crucial roles during the negotiations of the Partial Test Ban Treaty (1963), the Non-Proliferation Treaty (1968), the SALT I Anti-Ballistic Missile (ABM) Treaty (1972), and the Biological Warfare Convention (1972). Pugwash meetings have also helped clarify issues that have been central to the Strategic Arms Limitation Talks (SALT), the Conference on Security and Cooperation in Europe (CSCE) and the Mutual and Balanced Force Reductions (MBFR) talks.

For a number of years now Pugwash has been critical of a number of misconceptions underlying nuclear strategy, particularly the concept of limited nuclear war. The Pugwash scientists insist that it is a fallacy to believe that nuclear war can be limited in quality or quantity; that civil defence can provide a chance for the survival of the community; that a counterforce strategy can destroy the retaliatory capacity of the other side; and that parity in nuclear weapons is necessary for effective deterrence.

Joseph Rotblat offers the following assessment of the role of the Pugwash movement in the context of East–West relations.

> 66 It is impossible to assess quantitatively the effect of Pugwash on the nuclear arms race. But it is generally accepted that Pugwash was an important factor in abating the precariousness of the Cold War, and in helping to bring about a few successes towards nuclear disarmament. It serves as a useful

channel of communication between East and West, particularly at times when the official channels are closed because of ideological tensions or political crises. Pugwash has also stimulated scientists to be actively concerned with these problems and conscious of their social responsibility...

The name 'Pugwash' has become a symbol of successful international debate on controversial issues... Surely, at a time when a very high proportion of the scientific community is engaged in military research and development, when it is alleged that scientists are the instigators, and dictate the pace, of the nuclear arms race, it is of the utmost importance to realize that a group of scientists voluntarily give of their time, talent, and thought in the reverse direction, to stop the nuclear madness. **99**

Rotblat, 'The Pugwash Movement', in Laszlo & Yoo (eds), *World Encyclopedia of Peace*, pp.313–4

ORGANISING THE PEACE MOVEMENT IN EUROPE

One of the earliest manifestations of the organised peace movement in the immediate post-war years was also one of the most politically manipulated. This was the peace movement of 1948–1952. The strategic functions of the peace movement have been summarised by Marshall Shulman:

66 To reduce the danger of war during a period of maximum Soviet vulnerability; to neutralize the superior atomic capacity of the West by building up popular feeling against the use of the atomic bomb; to reduce the political advantages to the West of its atomic monopoly; and to weaken the West's aircraft delivery system by rendering the overseas airbases politically insecure. **99**

Marshall Shulman, *Stalin's Foreign Policy Reappraised*, Atheneum, New York, 1965, pp.80–1

The campaign originated in France early in 1948. Working through ostensibly non-communist front organisations, the Soviets began to exploit the movement for their own purposes. In April 1949 the World Congress of Partisans of Peace ended its meeting in Paris by setting up a permanent World Peace Council. By the end of 1949 the peace movement had become such a prominent and successful tactic that communist parties were urged by Moscow to make it the 'pivot' of their activities. The movement climaxed in 1950 with the famous Stockholm Peace Appeal, a ban-the-bomb petition that eventually gained millions of signatures.

The World Peace Council continued to exist until the demise of the USSR at the end of 1991. Its political position was well known: public enemy number one was 'American imperialism'. It did not condemn Soviet actions in Hungary (1956), Czechoslovakia (1968) or Afghanistan (1979).

THE CAMPAIGN FOR NUCLEAR DISARMAMENT IN BRITAIN

Perhaps the best known peace movement has been the Campaign for Nuclear Disarmament (CND). Two factors were important in its formation. The first stimulus was Britain's first H-bomb test on Christmas Island in the Pacific in 1957. The second and more fundamental reason was the failure in late 1957 of the Labour Party to pass — as widely expected — a resolution in favour of unilateral abandonment of nuclear weapons by Britain.

The CND's inaugural meeting was held in London on 17 February 1958. Speakers included the philosopher Lord Russell, novelist/essayist J.B. Priestley and the historian A.J.P. Taylor. The new movement took a strong line:

> The purpose of the campaign is to press for a new British initiative to reduce the nuclear peril and to stop the armaments race.
>
> We shall seek to persuade the British people that Britain must:
>
> (a) Renounce unconditionally the use or production of nuclear weapons and refuse to allow their use by others in her defence;
>
> (b) Use her utmost endeavour to bring about negotiations at all levels for agreements to end the armaments race and to lead to a general disarmament convention;
>
> (c) Invite the co-operation of other nations, particularly non-nuclear powers, in her renunciation of nuclear weapons.

Frank Longford, The Search for Peace, Harrap, London, 1985, p.122

The CND's first phase of mass support and political significance lasted from the inaugural meeting in February 1958 until the end of 1963. During this period it organised mass rallies and marches at a national level. The main

Members of the Campaign for Nuclear Disarmament demonstrating outside the US embassy in London in the early 1960s (Keystone). What is the CND and what does its symbol mean? What is the message on the demonstrators' placards? What aspect of US strategic policy are the demonstrators objecting to? What impact has the anti-nuclear movement had on the conduct of US policy?

demonstration of CND strength became the annual four-day Aldermaston March at Easter. (Aldermaston was the site of the Atomic Weapons Research Establishment.)

After 1963 CND began to decline for a number of reasons. The worldwide protests against nuclear testing appeared to have some success when the United States, the Soviet Union and Britain signed the Partial Test Ban Treaty in 1963 and a number of other arms control agreements followed. A second factor was the difficulty for any movement to sustain mass support and momentum over a long period of time. The later 1960s and 1970s were a lean period for the CND. Public support was low and the press no longer took the CND seriously as a national body.

Its resurgence after 1979 was an interesting phenomenon. The Conservative government that came to power in Britain in 1979 publicly stressed the need for an independent British nuclear force and committed itself to acquiring Trident missiles. The government also emphasised civil defence, highlighting the gap between existing measures and the known results of a nuclear attack. This provided a favourable campaign issue for CND. Its revival was also assisted by the issues that were causing concern in Western Europe at the same time: new fear of nuclear war in response to new missiles (SS–20, cruise and Pershing II) and the development of first-strike technology, the collapse of détente and, after 1980, the policies and rhetoric of the Reagan administration. (The peace campaigns at various nuclear bases — such as Greenham Common and Molesworth in Britain — were independent of the CND and do not appear to have been linked with any peace organisation.)

The CND is part of an international movement but at an organisational level it is less involved internationally than it was in the early 1960s. One reason for its limited international involvement in the recent revival of the peace movement has been the existence of the European Nuclear Disarmament (END) movement.

THE END CAMPAIGN

END was launched in a declaration in April 1980 inspired primarily by the Marxist historian E.P. Thompson. END was, so far as Britain was concerned, a unilateralist grouping closely allied with the CND and with some overlap of members and national leaders. However, there were two distinctive aspects of END's campaigning. First, Thompson developed an extended critique of deterrence theory, alliance blocs and what he called the mentality of exterminism. END's programme went beyond nuclear disarmament and called for a reconstruction of the states system. Second, Thompson argued that the goals of END could only be achieved by popular movements against governments co-ordinated internationally. Thus END put great store on the international nature of the peace movement, with specific emphasis on the campaign against cruise and Pershing missiles.

END's immediate goal was the establishment of a nuclear-free zone stretching from Portugal to Poland, thus developing a peace movement in Eastern Europe. Critics of END pointed out the difficulty of locating and nurturing unofficial peace movements in the East. Nevertheless END developed links with opposition bodies in Eastern Europe, for example Charter 77 in Czechoslovakia, and with independent peace movements that emerged from the Protestant Church in the German Democratic Republic, among students for a time in Hungary, and on a very small scale inside the Soviet Union — the Moscow Group for Establishing Trust.

In his later writings Thompson quoted frequently from some of the 'independent voices in the Communist bloc'. One such quotation, from a book titled *Anti-politics* (1984) by the Hungarian novelist George Konrád, encapsulates the END movement's political approach:

> 66 European identities are emerging at a critical pace in both East and West. The mass movement against new missile deployment in Western Europe is more than just a protest against a concrete military measure... it is a cry for autonomy, for self determination. We cannot allow the Soviet and American political elites to make the decisions that affect our lives. In both East and West, the European political vanguard has declared that our societies have the right to decide their own destinies...
>
> Although both super powers regard it as the gravest offence for someone to 'drive a wedge' between them and their European allies, it seems to me that we Europeans can best safeguard the lives and security of Russians and Americans by extricating ourselves from their noisy quarrels... The time has come to put compromise between the Soviet Union and the other European states, between the Russian people and the other peoples of Europe, between communists and non-communists. 99

Dan Smith & E.P. Thompson (eds), *Prospects for a Habitable Planet*, Penguin, Harmondsworth, 1987, pp.33–4

END worked hard to distance itself from organisations with communist links, partly because of END's stand against the nuclear weapons and alliance systems of both Eastern and Western blocs and also to avoid accusations that END was communist-inspired and a tool of the Soviet Union — an allegation that Western European governments made against national peace movements when they began to gain strength.

THE PEACE MOVEMENT ON THE CONTINENT

After the 1979 NATO decision to modernise its INF with cruise and Pershing II missiles, the continental nations designated for their deployment — Italy, Belgium, the Netherlands and West Germany — were each the scene of peace movement initiatives. The Italian, Belgian and Dutch peace movements in the early 1980s were relatively small. The West German movement attracted more attention because it became large enough to pose a serious challenge to a well-established government position.

West German public unease about nuclear weapons goes back to the debate in the late 1950s about the nuclear armament of the *Bundeswehr* (Federal Armed Forces). Large numbers of the general public, as well as numerous scientists, artists and intellectuals, took part in rallies and demonstrations, but this protest movement collapsed with the withdrawal of the Social Democrats' (SPD) support. In the 1960s and until the late 1970s anxiety about nuclear weapons was latent. In 1977–78, however, official and public consensus on security began to break down over the issue of the Enhanced Radiation Weapon (neutron bomb). The revival of the peace movement in West Germany can be traced to this event.

A variety of groups carried the banner of the peace movement in the Federal Republic. The largest group, about a quarter of the total, was the so-called KOFAZ faction of the German Communist Party (DKP). The KOFAZ faction blamed the United States for the arms race and the risk of nuclear war, and unconditionally supported the negotiation and disarmament proposals of the Soviet Peace Power. Because of its numbers and sophisticated organisation, the faction exerted a disproportionate influence on the peace movement.

Another significant group was the so-called Green Party, which combined ecological concerns with peace initiatives. The Green Party won some seats in Parliament in the March 1983 elections, though its share of seats did not threaten traditional coalition politics.

Apart from occasional anti-NATO outbursts, mainly from the KOFAZ faction, the German peace movement as a whole was pro-NATO, but opposed to NATO's current military doctrine. The peace movement called for an alternative NATO strategy that did not rely on the threat to use nuclear weapons in Europe.

The activities and ideas of the West German peace movement were watched closely by Moscow and Washington. As NATO's frontline state, West Germany was the Western alliance's most important member, and at the same time its most vulnerable politically and militarily. NATO's military strategy and political cohesion depended on Germany remaining in the alliance and on the maintenance of the political and military status quo in Europe. As it turned out, the German peace movement was no threat to the country's continuing allegiance to NATO.

THE PEACE MOVEMENT IN THE UNITED STATES

In the early post-war years, a number of prominent intellectuals and some organised groups of peace activists expressed opposition to the nuclear underpinning of American national security policy. Lewis Mumford, an historian of American and European civilisation, questioned the basis of his country's nuclear strategy in a letter to the *New York Times* in March 1954:

> 66 The power of the hydrogen bomb has, it is plain, given pause even to the leaders of our Government. Their very hesitation to give away the facts

in itself gives away the facts. Under what mandate, then, do they continue to hold as secret the results we may expect from the use of such weapons of extermination — not merely on our own cities and people but on all living organisms, not merely on our own present lives but on the lives of countless generations to come?

Are our leaders afraid that when the truth is known our devotion to the perfection of scientific weapons of mass destruction and extermination will turn out to be a profoundly irrational one: repulsive to morality, dangerous to national security, inimical to life?

Do they suspect that the American people are still sane enough to halt the blind automatism that continues, in the face of Soviet Russia's equal scientific powers to produce these fatal weapons?

Do they fear that their fellow countrymen may well doubt the usefulness of instruments which, under the guise of deterring an aggressor or insuring a cheap victory, might incidentally destroy the whole fabric of civilization and threaten the very existence of the human race?...

Our very need for secrecy in an abortive effort to monopolize technical and scientific knowledge has produced pathological symptoms in the whole body politic: fear, suspicion, non-cooperation, hostility to critical judgement, above all delusions of power based on fantasies of unlimited extermination, as the only possible answer to the political threats of Soviet Russia...

Are there not enough Americans still possessed of their sanity to call a stop to these irrational decisions which are automatically bringing us close to total catastrophe?

There are many alternative courses to the policy to which we have committed ourselves, practically without debate. The worst of all these alternatives, submission to communist totalitarianism, would still be far wiser than the final destruction of civilization.

As for the best of these alternatives, a policy of working firmly towards justice and cooperation, and free intercourse with all other peoples, in the faith that love begets love as surely as hatred begets hatred — would, in all probability be the one instrument capable of piercing the strong political armour of our present enemies.

Lewis Mumford, Letter to the Editor, *New York Times*, 28 March 1954

99

Review and Discuss

- What suggestions did Mumford put forward to explain the United States government's secrecy over the development of the H-bomb?

- What did he see as the social consequences of secrecy?
- What were Mumford's views of the alternatives to American policy of the time?

Another academic who became increasingly critical of the direction of American security policy was the sociologist C. Wright Mills. In his best known book, *The Power Elite* (1956), Mills claimed that post-war America was ruled by an oligarchy of political, military and business chiefs whose hidden monopoly of big decisions pre-empted the democratic process. In the late 1950s he wrote a number of articles, and a book entitled *The Causes of World War III* (1958) in which he stated: 'Surely war and peace are now the most important issues men anywhere can reason about.' The title of the first chapter, 'War becomes total — and absurd', indicated the theme of the book.

THE RADICAL PACIFISTS

The most active peace workers in the early post-war years were the American pacifists, who worked through established peace organisations such as the Fellowship of Reconciliation and the War Resisters League, as well as the newer American Friends Services Committee and the American Liberties Union. The best known and most eloquent of their spokespeople, the Reverend A.J. Muste, had sought since the 1930s to reorient American pacifism into a radical direct action group. For decades he met with only limited success. Then, dramatically after 1956, non-violent resistance began to catch the imagination of peace activists.

On 6 August 1957, the anniversary of the Hiroshima bombing, a small group engaged in an act of calculated civil disobedience by publicly entering the site of Atomic Energy Commission (AEC) bomb project in Nevada. Similar acts of resistance to the military occurred and their proponents organised themselves into the Committee for Non-Violent Action (CNVA), formed in 1957 by Muste and other radical pacifists.

SCIENTISTS, STUDENTS AND WOMEN TAKE ACTION

Scientists also took a higher public profile on the nuclear weapons issue. In April 1957 Nobel Prize winner Albert Schweitzer broadcast an appeal to fifty nations to stop the testing of nuclear weapons. In June 1957 Linus Pauling, another Nobel Laureate, released a petition signed by 11 000 scientists (almost 3000 of them American) calling for 'immediate action... to effect an international agreement to stop the testing of all nuclear weapons'. Less than a year later Pauling published *No More War* (1958), a trenchant analysis of the dangers of nuclear war and a first-hand account of the scientists' movement against it.

In late June 1957 a meeting in New York of twenty-seven prominent Americans established the National Committee for a Sane Nuclear Policy (SANE). On 15 November 1957 SANE launched its first advertisement in the *New York Times*. 'The challenge of the age,' it contended, was not to acquire new and more powerful weapons but 'to develop the concept of higher loyalty — loyalty by man to the human community'. The advertisement created considerable interest and by mid-1958 SANE had 130 chapters representing 25 000

Americans. In September 1958 a national conference broadened SANE's aim from achieving a test ban to securing general disarmament.

SANE and CNVA challenged America's internal Cold War consensus and encouraged other citizen actions. In April 1959 a coalition of pacifist and socialist students in the Midwest organised the Student Peace Union, which by 1960 claimed 5000 members. At Harvard, Columbia, Berkeley and other campuses across the United States students formed activist groups to promote disarmament and civil liberties.

In 1961 Women Strike for Peace came together when a group of Washington area women took themselves and their children into the streets to protest against continued atmospheric nuclear testing. In 1962 the atomic scientist Leo Szilard established the Council for a Livable World as a means of lobbying for nuclear arms control and a stronger United Nations.

The revived peace movement was attacked in Congress and in the press as communist inspired. Its prospects for advancement rose and fell according to the temperature chart of international tensions and popular faith in prevailing national leadership. After gaining momentum during the prolonged Berlin crisis, the movement lost ground after Kennedy's 'successful' handling of the Cuban missile crisis in October 1962. Then in June 1963 Kennedy's appeal for détente in his American University address combined with the Partial Test Ban Treaty led to a shift in popular sentiment in support of administration policies. The scene seemed set for further initiations towards Soviet–American détente and nuclear arms reduction.

THE IMPACT OF VIETNAM

What the peace movement got instead was the Vietnam War. Historian Charles De Benedetti has said that the American peace movement was a 'movement of many movements… [which] expanded and contracted according to domestic perceptions of the morality and (especially) the cost of the war'. He summed up the impact of the Vietnam War on the peace movement:

> For the most part, the peace movement found the Vietnam War a source of unending internal arguments and an extraordinary distraction from the prior need for disarmament and a reduction in cold war tensions. Speaking for different constituencies, activists quarrelled vehemently over matters of social radicalism, non violent tactics, and even the preferred outcome of the war. They also suffered great public obloquy. Public opinion polls indicated high levels of resentment toward the antiwar movement, while dissidents found themselves subjected frequently to harassment and intimidation, sometimes to physical attack, and often to surveillance and disruption by police and military authorities. Not surprisingly, therefore, the country's principal peace organizations experienced little real growth during the war, in spite of proliferating antiwar sentiment… The failure of American peace activists to expand the size of their organizations in grassroots America at a time of tremendous challenge to warmaking authority was dispiriting in itself. But it also bred a fuller contempt among peace activists toward the peaceable promises of American democracy.

Charles De Benedetti, 'Pacifism and Peace Movements', in Jack P. Greene (ed.), *Encyclopedia of American Political History*, vol.2, Charles Scribners, New York, 1984, pp.905–6

Review and Discuss

- What were some of the difficulties facing peace activists during the Vietnam years?

- What longer-term legacy does De Benedetti suggest was an outcome of the Vietnam War?

In the mid-1970s peace activists were able to turn away from their Vietnam concerns. Yet those concerns had coloured their experience. Post-Vietnam peace activists were sensitive to United States intervention in the Third World, as well as showing growing concern over the runaway international arms race. Politically the movement progressed toward the left. With most American institutions at least tacitly supporting the Cold War and the arms race, serious peace activists increasingly came to question the inner workings of American electoral politics and corporate capitalism. Hopes for transformation of the existing order were optimistic at the best of times. In November 1980 Ronald Reagan was elected President.

CHALLENGES IN THE 1980s

Most commentators regarded the Reagan administration as the most bellicose in Cold War history. Certainly it triggered an upsurge in peace activism. Driven by the worsening Cold War and encouraged by a blossoming Western European peace movement, the American peace movement began to attract new supporters from its traditional constituencies (church people, the liberal intelligentsia, organised women and younger dissidents). In De Benedetti's judgement

The peace movement: a Canadian cartoon (courtesy Roy Carless, sighted in David Rosen [ed.] Megatoons: Cartoonists Against Nuclear War, Eden Press, Montreal). What does the missile in the cartoon represent? What does the dog represent? Who are the three people clinging to the missile? Why are they concerned about the dog's actions?

the movement benefited from the participation of younger professional people and from some selected labour unions, but it remained organisationally centred in the pacifist and liberal groups that had anchored it for half a century.

The peace movement has tended to receive little media attention in the USA. Nevertheless, on occasions the movement has mobilised impressive numbers of people and mounted dramatic displays that the media could not ignore. The most remarkable effort took place in New York City on 12 June 1982 when about three-quarters of a million people swamped Manhattan to protest against nuclear arms build up and affirm popular support for a special United Nations session on disarmament.

Although unilateral disarmament continues to be an aim of an important section of the peace movement, public opinion polls have shown this to be a non-starter with the overwhelming number of American people. The same opinion polls, however, have shown support for two other proposals for which the peace movement has been campaigning. These were:

(1) 'no first use' of nuclear weapons; and
(2) the idea of a 'nuclear freeze'.

The no-first-use proposal was strongly supported in the Spring 1982 issue of the prestigious journal *Foreign Affairs* by four distinguished Americans — McGeorge Bundy, George F. Kennan, Robert McNamara and Gerard Smith:

> 66 It is time to recognise that no one has ever succeeded in advancing any persuasive reason to believe that any use of nuclear weapons, even on the smallest scale, could reliably be expected to remain limited... Any use of nuclear weapons in Europe, by the Alliance or against it, carries with it a high and inescapable risk of escalation into the general nuclear war which would bring ruin to all and victory to none... Given the appalling consequences of even the most limited use of nuclear weapons and the total impossibility for both sides of any guarantee against unlimited escalation, there must be the gravest doubt about the wisdom of a policy which asserts the effectiveness of any first use of nuclear weapons by either side. 99

McGeorge Bundy, George F. Kennan, Robert McNamara & Gerard Smith, 'Nuclear Weapons and the Atlantic Alliance', *Foreign Affairs*, Spring 1982, p.757

In their article the authors were careful to stress that 'it is obvious that any such policy would require a strengthened confidence in the adequacy of the conventional forces of the Alliance'. The article, however, generated considerable controversy, with the critics concentrating their attentions on the need to deter Soviet superiority in conventional military forces.

In the next issue of *Foreign Affairs*, an American general stated:

> 66 The no first use proposal fails to account for the conventional force imbalance. If in a political crisis the Soviets believed they could launch a successful conventional attack against NATO without fear of a possible nuclear response, their incentive to do so — and thus the probability of armed conflict — would be greatly increased. 99

General David C. Jones, *Foreign Affairs*, Summer 1982, p.1173

In the same issue Bundy, Kennan, McNamara, and Smith replied to the various criticisms of the no-first-use proposal and reaffirmed their position:

> 66 The threat [to use nuclear weapons first] is steadily declining in credibility while its political costs within the Alliance are growing. A continued reliance

Foreign Affairs, Summer 1982, p.1179

on threats that would be disastrous to execute strikes as morally insupportable and empty of logic. We think that adequately deterrent conventional strength is more credible, more unifying, more civilised, and attainable. **99**

As supporters of the Reagan administration were quick to point out 'no first use' became a slogan for many in the peace movement who chose not to think about the alternative, conventional force provisions and considerable expense associated with such a policy. The debate on no first use began to divide the peace movement. There were those who grasped the manifold complications of alternative proposals and were prepared to work toward their solution and there were those who refused to acknowledge they existed.

The second widely supported proposal was the nuclear freeze resolution. Proposed by Senators Edward Kennedy and Mark Hatfield, this called for a 'mutual and verifiable freeze on testing, production, and further deployment of nuclear warheads, missiles and other delivery systems'. Some polls indicated that more than seventy per cent of Americans favoured a bilateral and negotiable freeze on nuclear weapons. In May 1982 a CBS/*New York Times* survey showed this support for the nuclear freeze idea. But when all questions used in the survey are examined a different picture emerges. More than seventy per cent said verification was essential for such an agreement; eighty per cent said they would oppose it if either side could cheat without detection; and almost seventy per cent said they would oppose a freeze if it resulted in greater Soviet strength. As one commentator on the peace movement remarked:

James Finn, 'The Peace Movement in the United States', Werner Kaltefleiter & Robert L. Pfaltzgraff (eds), *The Peace Movements in Europe and the United States*, Croom Helm, London, 1985, p.166

66 What is being supported is an attitude, a sentiment, not a policy that has found its program. If a freeze seems to promise greater safety and stability, people will support it. If it endangers or reduces security, they will question or reject it. As the proposed resolution moves towards the necessary issues of verifiability, trust in Soviet agreements, and the present balance of nuclear and conventional forces, the present supporters of freeze will find themselves taking different paths. The apparent consensus will begin to unravel. **99**

THE PEACE MOVEMENT'S CRITICS

Critics of the peace movement pointed out that there were some peace activists who ignored or sympathetically misread Soviet behaviour. There is undoubtedly an element of truth in this judgement. But the question needs to be asked: why did they read Soviet behaviour in this way? Some activists did this out of a developed analysis that has anti-Western, anti-capitalist overtones. Others did it because they disagreed with their critics about Soviet military and political intentions.

A further point that must be conceded to the critics of the peace movement is that at times there has been Soviet involvement in, and manipulation of, its activities. The extent and effect of such Soviet intervention since 1945 is difficult to assess since such activities are for the most part carefully disguised. It is also true that there has been widespread smearing of the motives and political affiliations of many peace activists by hard liners on national security matters.

The following extract from a recent analysis of the 'facts and fallacies' of the nuclear freeze campaign is one example:

> ❝ The congeniality of views between some involved in the U.S. nuclear freeze movement and the Soviet Union is not a coincidence. Soviet exploitations of the 'peace' issue can be traced to the 1950s and the Stockholm Peace Appeal, the earliest in a series of campaigns to play upon Western fears of nuclear war. The principal outlet for Soviet activity in this area has been the World Peace Council, a global organisation enjoying the support of the Moscow based U.S.A. Institute which provides speakers, fluent in English, for participation in a wide range of pro-freeze activities... The U.S. nuclear freeze campaign is regarded by the Soviet Union as an important tool contributing to change in the global correlation of forces by driving a political military wedge between the United States and its principal allies. ❞

Jacquelyn K. Davies, 'The U.S. Nuclear Freeze Campaign', in Kalterfleiter & Pfaltzgraff (eds), *Peace Movements in Europe and the United States*, p.175

No doubt many American expert analysts liked to think this way. But not all. George F. Kennan had this to say in late 1982:

> ❝ There has... grown up in this country in these past years an anti nuclear movement of extraordinary popular strength and intensity of feeling... It is the reflection of a deep uneasiness among our people about the direction in which our present governmental course is leading us. It is now being attacked by its opponents as being communist inspired; and its adherents are being dubbed as the conscious or unconscious tools of Moscow. Some of this, I suppose, was inevitable; but I must say that I can think of nothing more contemptible than this effort to pin a communist label on a movement that is actually overwhelmingly motivated by nothing other than a deep concern for the security of this country and this civilization in the face of a volume of weaponry quite capable of putting an end to both. ❞

George F. Kennan, 'The Arms Race and the Antinuclear Movement', *The Nuclear Delusion*, Hamish Hamilton, London, 1984, pp.235–6

Review and Discuss

- How do Davies and Kennan differ in their assessment of the role of the peace movement? Why do you think they differ?

In the second half of the 1980s Soviet foreign policy under Mikhail Gorbachev created an opening for historic achievements in arms control (the INF, CFE and START Treaties between the USA and the USSR). With the underlying tensions between the superpowers ebbing, anti-nuclear activists moved on to new issues, especially environmental ones such as global warming.

This trend is clear in Ruth Leger Sivard's *World Military and Social Expenditures*, published annually in Washington since 1974. The 1991 edition devotes fifteen of its sixty-four pages to environmental issues.

In the 1990s peace activists have become much more aware of the need to research political climate and opportunity structure in order to facilitate the impact of the peace movement on the making of foreign policy. Two social scientists (both peace activists) who have recently undertaken such an analysis argue that the peace movement should expend more energy on efforts to democratise the process of foreign policy-making if it hopes to be more effective.

66 The institutional structure for the formulation of foreign policy seriously constrains democratic participation in that process and limits the potential for peace movement influence. Given this constraint, if the peace movement is to influence policy and prevent U.S. military action, changes in the institutional structure are necessary. We contend that the movement should change its strategic emphases from opposing presidential initiatives and pushing legislation to expanding the opportunities for citizen input into foreign policy making. The demise of the Soviet Union has created a political opening in which peace and populist groups might further democratize the American political system, especially its foreign policy institutions. 99

Ron Pagnucco & Jackie Smith, 'The Peace Movements and the Formulation of U.S. Foreign Policy', *Peace and Change*, vol.18, no.2, April 1993, p.176

WHY DID THE COLD WAR END?

I N NOVEMBER 1989 Zbigniew Brzezinski, former National Security Adviser in the Carter administration, published an article titled "Is the Cold War Over?" in the Moscow monthly *International Affairs*. He subtly pointed out that debate over the 'end of the Cold War' could itself be regarded as part of the conduct of the Cold War. Brzezinski went on to suggest that what was needed was a clear definition and articulation of the West's concept of the termination of the Cold War. Such a definition should be 'symbolically compelling and politically substantive'. He put forward the following proposal:

> In explicitly defining the meaning of the end of the Cold War, the West should not be shy in focusing on the symbolic and philosophical. The fundamental issue has been, and still is, freedom of choice versus coercive ideological orthodoxy. Let us not forget that human rights have been the central stake in the Cold War, and the West's identification with human rights has been our greatest moral strength. The Cold War will thus have a terminal date when the Berlin wall is firmly scheduled for dismantling... and when some — even if not immediately all — of the East European states firmly schedule free elections.
>
> Peoples on both sides of the East–West divide would understand such a definition of the Cold War's end... Such a definition would also facilitate the eventual progressive departure of major portions of American and Soviet forces from central Europe, whose prolonged presence there has been a major manifestation of the Cold War. The West should therefore not be shy in proclaiming the important connection between the philosophical and military symptoms of the Cold War.

Zbigniew Brzezinski, 'Is the Cold War Over?', *International Affairs* (Moscow), no.11, November 1989, p.36

Review and Discuss

- What two criteria does Brzezinski insist must be met before a 'terminal date' can be set for the end of the Cold War?
- What further development would follow if the criteria were met?
- Have political developments since the publication of the article meant that the author's criteria have been met?

'WHO WON THE COLD WAR?'

November 1989 turned out, in fact, to be the very month in which the Berlin Wall was dismantled — an act that was certainly 'symbolic' and 'substantive' in relation to the end of the Cold War. As we have seen in an earlier chapter, the destruction of the Berlin Wall set the stage for the reunification of Germany and the end of the Soviet Empire in Eastern Europe.

The magnitude of these developments has ushered in a wide-ranging debate over the reasons for the end of the Cold War. Such a debate is likely to be as controversial and politically important as that over the origins of the Cold War. The political significance of the debate lies in whether the particular US foreign policy orientation towards the Soviet Union that dominated the 1980s was vindicated.

In analysing the Cold War's conclusion it is essential to distinguish between the domestic origins of the crisis in Soviet communism and the external forces that influenced the nature and timing of the Soviet response. Without doubt the ultimate cause of the Cold War's outcome is to be located in the failure of the Soviet system itself. External forces did hasten and intensify the crisis, but the Soviet response under Gorbachev — domestic liberalisation and foreign policy accommodation — took Western experts by surprise. After all, the traditional Soviet response would have been renewed repression at home and aggression abroad.

Although the end of the Cold War caught almost everyone (especially hard-liners) by surprise, there has been an amazingly quick response from former Reagan administration officials and experts, who are claiming that Reagan's confrontational policies were the decisive trigger for the turn-around in Soviet foreign policy and the demise of communism. Two critics of this 'Reagan victory school' described these simplistic views in the following terms:

> **"** This new conventional wisdom, the 'Reagan victory school', holds that President Ronald Reagan's military and ideological assertiveness during the 1980s played the lead role in the collapse of Soviet communism and the 'taming' of its foreign policy. In that view the Reagan administration's ideological counter-offensive and military buildup delivered the knock-out punch to a system that was internally bankrupt and on the ropes.
>
> ...As former Pentagon officials like Caspar Weinberger and Richard Perle... and other proponents of the Reagan victory school have argued, a combination of military and ideological pressures gave the Soviets little choice but to abandon expansionism abroad and repression at home. In that view, the Reagan military buildup foreclosed Soviet military options while pushing the Soviet economy to the breaking point. Reagan partisans stress that his dramatic 'Star Wars' initiative put the Soviets on notice that the next phase of the arms race would be waged in areas where the West held a decisive technological edge. **"**

D. Deudney & G.J. Ikenberry, 'Who Won the Cold War?', *Foreign Policy*, no.87, Summer 1992, pp.124f.

By way of contrast Deudney and Ikenberry see the role of Reagan's and his administration's military assertiveness in far more ambiguous terms when situated in the context of the wider Western response to the Soviet challenge.

Deudney & Ikenberry,
'Who Won the Cold
War?', *Foreign Policy*,
p.125

    For every 'hardening' there was a 'softening': Reagan's rhetoric of the 'Evil Empire' was matched by his vigorous anti-nuclearism; the military buildup in the West was matched by the resurgence of a large popular peace movement; and the Reagan Doctrine's toughening of containment was matched by major deviations from containment in East–West economic relations.

Each of these three themes — Reagan's anti-nuclearism, the resurgence of the peace movement and the growing East–West economic ties — is analysed in some detail to show that in important ways key aspects of Western behaviour towards the USSR were becoming increasingly benign and co-operative.

By far the most important of these, according to the authors, was Reagan's own deep antipathy towards nuclear weapons and his view that their abolition was both a desirable and realistic goal. Reagan's anti-nuclearism is discussed in some detail and here Deudney and Ikenberry draw on the perceptive analysis of Michael MccGwire as presented in his *Perestroika and Soviet National Security* (1991). MccGwire argues persuasively that Reagan's anti-nuclearism, especially as revealed at the Geneva (November 1985) and Reykjavik (October 1986) Summits, decisively influenced Gorbachev's views at a formative time in the development of the Soviet leader's thinking about security issues. MccGwire argues that these summit meetings convinced Gorbachev that it was possible to work with the West to halt the nuclear arms race.

For Deudney and Ikenberry Reagan's anti-nuclearism had a decisive influence on Soviet–US relations in the Gorbachev years. 'Reagan's anti-nuclearism was more important than his administration's military buildup in catalyzing the end of the Cold War.'

Not so, respond the Reagan supporters. Patrick Glynn, a conservative scholar who worked for the US Arms Control and Disarmament Administration (ACDA) holds the following view:

    To judge from informal conversations I have had with citizens of Eastern Europe and the former Soviet Union over the past two years, the conviction that Ronald Reagan won the Cold War by being tough on the communists is nigh-universal in those areas.

Glynn goes on to portray in starkly contrasting terms the policies of the Reagan and Carter administrations towards the Soviet Union. It is clear where his preference lies:

    It was only after three to four years of unremittingly tough policies under Reagan — both public and private statements of Soviet officials at the time characterized them as such — that the desired sea-change in Soviet leadership opinion took place. That, we now know, was Reagan's simple plan — to negotiate, but to do so from a position of strength. He reestablished a position of strength through a massive arms buildup, through deliberately tough talk (culminating in the 'evil empire' line), through uncompromising (and widely criticized) positions on arms control, through active harassment of Soviet imperial efforts in the Third World (including Grenada), through a tightening of technological export controls, and through (for the Soviets) the frightening prospect of the Strategic Defense Initiative (SDI)...

The Jimmy Carter–Cyrus Vance approach of rewarding the Soviet buildup with one-sided arms control treaties, opening Moscow's access to Western capital markets and technologies, and condoning Soviet imperial expansion was perfectly designed to preserve the Brezhnev-style approach, delivering the Soviets from any need to reevaluate (as they did under Gorbachev) or change their policies. Had the basic Carter–Vance approach been continued… the Cold War and the life of the Soviet Union would almost certainly have been prolonged. **99**

Patrick Glynn, Letter to the Editor, *Foreign Policy*, no.90, Spring 1993, pp.171–3

In their reply to Glynn, Deudney and Ikenberry emphasise the need to take a long view in seeking to explain the end of the Cold War:

66 It is vital not to overconcentrate on the events of the late 1970s and 1980s in ending the Cold War. The ultimate reason for its end was the internal crisis of the Soviet system — a crisis that external pressure, at most, intensified. Moreover, the West's interaction with the Soviet Union during that conflict was a mixture of a relatively consistent willingness to counterbalance and a relative willingness to accommodate. Glynn's conventional wisdom… plays down the deeper forces and long-term consistencies, and ignores the importance of Western moderation and accommodation in taming the great Soviet bear. **99**

Deudney & Ikenberry, 'Who Won The Cold War?', *Foreign Policy*, pp.175–6

This conclusion — that it was primarily the internal crisis of the Soviet system which was responsible for the end of the Cold War — is also the view of Raymond L. Garthoff, a retired US diplomat and one of America's sharpest analysts. For Garthoff 'the American role in ending the Cold War was necessary but not primary'.

66 The West did not, as is widely believed, win the Cold War through geopolitical containment and military deterrence. Nor was the Cold War won by the Reagan military buildup and the Reagan Doctrine, as some have suggested. Instead, 'victory' for the West came when a new generation of Soviet leaders realized how badly their system at home and their policies abroad had failed. What containment did was to successfully stalemate Moscow's attempts to advance Soviet hegemony. Over four decades it performed the historic function of holding Soviet power in check until the internal seeds of destruction within the Soviet Union and its empire could mature. At that point, however, it was Gorbachev who brought the Cold War to an end…

In the final analysis, only a Soviet leader could have ended the Cold War, and Gorbachev set out deliberately to do so. Although earlier Soviet leaders had understood the impermissibility of war in the nuclear age, Gorbachev was the first to recognise that reciprocal political accommodation, rather than military power for deterrence or 'counterdeterrence', was the defining core of the Soviet Union's relationship with the rest of the world. The conclusions that Gorbachev drew from this recognition, and the subsequent Soviet actions, finally permitted the Iron Curtain to be dismantled and ended the global confrontation of the Cold War. **99**

Raymond L. Garthoff, 'Why Did the Cold War Arise, and Why Did it End?', in Michael J. Hogan (ed.), *The End of the Cold War: Its Meaning and Implications*, Cambridge University Press, 1992, pp.129, 131

Review and Discuss

- What does the phrase 'Reagan victory school' suggest about why the Cold War came to an end?
- Why are Deudney and Ikenberry critical of the 'Reagan victory school'?
- Why might Glynn's 'conventional wis-dom' be favoured by the US foreign policy establishment?
- Who played the more important role in bringing the Cold War to an end — Reagan or Gorbachev?

WHAT DOES THE END OF THE COLD WAR MEAN?

The ideological commitments that fuelled the Cold War led to American involvement in the affairs of other nations. Some of this was undoubtedly constructive — the Marshall Plan is a classic example. But other US involvements, overt and covert, were less constructive and sometimes subversive of real liberalism and democracy. By simplistically dividing the globe into a communist Evil Empire controlled by Moscow and a Free World led by Washington, US policy-makers promoted numerous anti-democratic regimes, so long as they claimed to be anti-communist, into membership of the Free World. Washington used Cold War rhetoric to justify assassination plots, deals with drug barons, and to portray corrupt anti-communist rebels as Freedom Fighters.

Having said that, the Soviets were playing the same game. Although Soviet assistance too was sometimes constructive (the building of the Aswan Dam for example), it was frequently directed in the expectation of some geopolitical advantage to the USSR in the Cold War. Moscow often supported dictatorial regimes cynically claimed to be called Marxist or Socialist by their leaders (e.g. in Somalia and Ethiopia). Both the Soviets and the Americans distrusted the neutral and non-aligned nations. They much preferred it when countries around the world were either their allies or the satellites and surrogates of the other side.

But the end of the Cold War means major changes to the political influence of the old adversaries.

66 The demise of the Cold War system inevitably means a sharp reduction of the influence of the two major adversaries. While this is obvious in the case of the former Soviet Union, it is no less true of the United States. To a far greater degree than has generally been realized, American political influence has rested significantly on the Cold War. It was concern over the reality of Soviet power and the uncertainty of Soviet ambitions that induced the Europeans and the Japanese to put their security in American hands to play a historically passive role in world affairs. So long as fear

IMAGINE! COMMUNISM JUST SELF-DESTRUCTING LIKE THAT!

The social effects of Cold War competition: an American cartoon of November 1989 (Tony Auth, the Philadelphia Inquirer). What thoughts are uppermost in the mind of the person on the ladder? What conditions are depicted as common features of life 'behind the lines'?

of Soviet power was real, the most prudent, as well as the most economic, course for these countries was to rely on American leadership. For this they paid a certain price, both economic and political, of deference to the United States, whether in the form of trade concessions, financing of the U.S. treasury's deficits, purchases of U.S. made military equipment, or allowing Washington alone to negotiate with Moscow...

The retreat of the Soviet Union from the contest, indeed the disappearance of that state itself, has dramatically altered the balance within the former Cold War coalition led by the United States. Today, the United States — in part because of exaggerated Cold War preoccupations, in part because of irresponsible fiscal and economic policies of its own making — has lost both its economic and its political freedom of action. Washington cannot finance its unquenchable deficits without the willingness of the Europeans and the Japanese to buy treasury bonds; it cannot undertake large-scale military interventions without their financial contributions, as the Gulf war of early 1991 demonstrated. The United States fought the Cold War, but today it is the Western Europeans who are financing, organizing, and influencing the political future of what was once the Soviet Cold War empire. **99**

Ronald Steel, 'The End and the Beginning', in Michael J. Hogan (ed.), The End of the Cold War: Its Meaning and Implications, pp.111–12

Review and Discuss

- Why did the Europeans and the Japanese 'put their security in American hands'?
- Where does the growing European and Japanese economic strength now leave the USA?

CONCLUSION

The Cold War has been an important episode in the history of international relations, but history inexorably moves forward. It is possible to suggest some of the emerging features of the post-Cold War world. Russia, and more gradually the United States, will become less central. We will see a return to multipolarity in a system of greater and lesser powers. Military power will be of continuing importance but it seems likely to decline in relation to other factors, especially economic ones. As economic power becomes more significant in international relations there will be an increase in the relative weight of Japan and the European Community (especially with a unified Germany) and a decrease in the relative weight of the USA and the former Soviet Union.

It seems clear that there will be a return to the more traditional pattern of shifting mixes of co-operation and competition among all nations, whether former Cold War allies or former adversaries. Co-operation may be difficult to maintain in at least two spheres. 'The end of the Cold War may mark the start of a new era of global economic competition between the United States, Japan, and the European Community.' More ominous is the rise in ethnic conflict. Local and regional conflicts that were largely subsumed into the global confrontation of the Cold War are now assuming their places in the world order. This is already occurring in Yugoslavia and the former Soviet empire itself.

The power of Russia and America to influence the course of events in these post-Cold War situations must now be seriously questioned. Whether the foreign policy elites of these two nations recognise the changed situations is another matter.

The pace of history quickens: an American cartoon of November 1989 (Tony Auth, the Philadelphia Inquirer). Who is in control and what equipment is he operating? What conclusions are suggested about events happening in Eastern Europe?

66 Unavoidably, the end of the Cold War means a dramatic decline in the ability of the United States to determine the course of events. This has not yet become fully apparent to foreign policy elites. Some, in the wake of the U.S.-initiated and mostly U.S.-fought Gulf war, and of the collapse of the Soviet Union, refer to the United States as the only superpower. To be a 'superpower' in a world where the instruments of power are either restricted by economic dependency or directed against a foe that has largely ceased to exist, however, is to render the term meaningless. It took two to fight the Cold War, two to ensure abdication by the lesser players, two to give American leaders a sense of mission and freedom of action, two to justify the suppression of American domestic social and economic needs to the exigencies of a Great Power struggle.

Two have been reduced to one, and the contest has shifted to other arenas. It is no longer between the United States and the Soviet Union, no longer over the pretensions of ideology, no longer waged by military interventions or by the accumulation of nuclear weaponry. With the end of the Cold War, the United States will be forced to adjust to a competition where its familiar instruments are inapplicable and where its allies and dependencies are increasingly rivals. It is not merely the end of the Cold War, but a dramatic reshifting of the world power balance. For the American economy, distorted by a half-century of reliance on military spending, for American political elites, who had come to believe that they were 'born to lead', and for an American public, deprived of an enemy to justify its sacrifices, the experience will be a wrenching and possibly threatening one. 99

Steel, 'The End and the Beginning', in Hogan (ed.), *The End of the Cold War: Its Meaning and Implications*, p.112

QUESTIONS FOR RESEARCH AND DISCUSSION

- Explain what is meant by the term 'Cold War'. What were the main causes of the Cold War? How did it develop between 1945 and 1953?
- 'The Cold War was based on suspicion and misunderstanding.' To what extent do you agree with this statement? Give examples from both sides in support of your argument.
- 'Security concerns have been more important than Communist ideology in the history of Soviet foreign policy.' Discuss.
- Has the post-war confrontation between the Soviet Union and the United States been one of ideological conflict or the exercise of power politics? Give reasons for your answer.
- Write articles — one for the *New York Times*, one for *Pravda* — describing events in Europe from early 1945 to 1948. Each article should try to defend its own country's action.
- Why and how did the problem of Germany affect relations between the two superpowers between 1945 and 1961?
- What do you understand by the term 'containment'? What developments led the United States to adopt the doctrine of containment? What were the strengths and weaknesses of the containment doctrine from the US point of view?
- Why did war break out in Korea in 1950? Which of the two superpowers gained or lost most from being involved in the Korean War?
- What are the strengths and weaknesses of the traditional/orthodox and revisionist interpretations of Cold War origins? How have post-revisionist accounts gone beyond these interpretations?
- Why was there a 'thaw' in the Cold War after 1953? What form did the thaw take? (Consider Soviet–American relations up to the time of Nixon's visit to Moscow in 1972.)
- What do you understand by the 'domino theory'? How significant has it been in influencing the conduct of US foreign policy? Comment on both positive and negative aspects of the influence.
- How and why did America become involved in the Vietnam War? What problems did the Americans face in fighting the war? How successful were they?
- How well or otherwise do you think President Kennedy handled America's

response to events in Cuba from 1960 to 1962? Give reasons for your answer.

- What do you understand by the term 'détente'? Why did the Soviet Union and the United States adopt a policy of détente in the 1970s? Why did détente break down?

- Why did Soviet–American relations enter a new Cold War phase in the late 1970s and early 1980s?

- Why did the Russians invade Afghanistan in 1979? How did Soviet intervention in Afghanistan affect Soviet–American relations in the 1980s?

- What was Cold War II? Who was to blame? When and why did tension ease?

- Why were there uprisings in several Soviet satellite countries, notably Hungary, Czechoslovakia, and Poland, and why did Russia crush them?

- Describe and account for the political liberalisation in Eastern Europe at the end of the 1980s.

- 'At the beginning of 1989 the Communists had been in complete... control of Eastern Europe. At the end of the year they were gone.' How and why did this happen?

- What are the claims of the Reagan victory school? How adequate are they as an explanation of the end of the Cold War?

- 'The world owes much to Gorbachev.' Summarise and evaluate Gorbachev's contribution to the improvement in international relations in the late 1980s.

- How did the Gulf War demonstrate the changed nature of Soviet–American relations resulting from the end of the Cold War?

- Why were the Central and Eastern European states keen to seek admission to NATO after the end of the Cold War?

How did NATO react to the request? Why?

- 'The US cannot begin to solve the problems of the Soviet successor states; at the same time, it cannot afford to ignore them.' What were the dilemmas facing Western policy-makers on the break up of the USSR? How did they try to handle them?

- 'The successor to a doctrine of containment must be a strategy of enlargement.' What did the Clinton administration mean by a policy of 'enlargement'? How was it implemented?

- How and why has the Cold War been used by the leaders of both sides as a device to keep their own side united and to justify military expenditure?

- How far and in what ways has the military exerted influence on defence and foreign policy in the USA and USSR?

- What do you understand by the term 'deterrence'? How has the concept of deterrence influenced the development of the Soviet–American nuclear relationship since the early 1960s?

- To what extent has the nuclear arms build up been a deterrent to war? What dangerous aspects of the arms build up have been emphasised by its critics?

- What have been the main attempts at arms control since the early 1960s? To what extent have they succeeded in limiting the nuclear arms race?

- What have been the main obstacles to the achievement of arms control by the Soviet Union and the United States since the early 1960s?

- What have been the main aims and achievements of Soviet and American arms control negotiation since 1985?

- 'With the end of the Cold War the need for arms control has disappeared.' Do you agree with this judgement? Explain your answer.

- What arguments have been put forward in the debate over multilateral versus unilateral approaches to nuclear disarmament? Why did the USA and USSR find it difficult to reach agreement on nuclear disarmament in the 1970s and 1980s?
- Explain how new weapons technology can upset the nuclear 'balance of terror'. Why is outer space becoming increasingly important in the arms race?
- Why was Star Wars (SDI) so important to Reagan? Why did the Soviets oppose it so strongly? How was the issue eventually resolved?
- What have been the main aims and achievements of the peace movements as shown by their actions since 1945?
- How have the challenges facing the peace movement changed with the end of the Cold War? How has the peace movement responded to the challenges?
- Explain why the UN has been only occasionally successful in maintaining peace in the world since 1945. Why has the UN been more successful in recent years?
- Write a 750-word biography of the person whom you think has contributed most to international peace since 1945.
- What are the dangers of regarding Soviet–American rivalry as the major axis of world affairs? In what ways has the wider significance of Soviet/CIS–American rivalry diminished since the early years of the Cold War?
- What sources can you use to keep up to date on developments in Soviet/CIS–American relations? How can you ensure a balanced coverage?
- What are the main obstacles to writing a balanced account of Soviet/CIS–American relations since 1945? How far do you think they can be overcome?

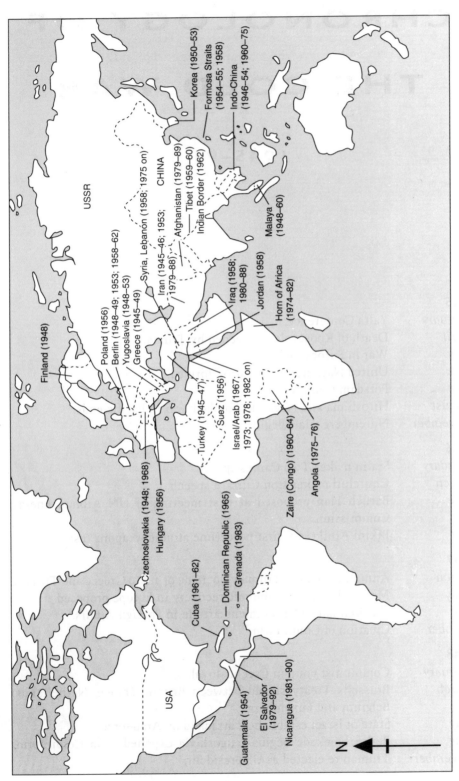

Principal flashpoints of the Cold War

CHRONOLOGY OF THE COLD WAR

1945–91

1945

February	Yalta Conference.
April	Death of Roosevelt; succeeded by Truman.
May	War in Europe ends.
June	United Nations Organisation formed.
July	Potsdam Conference.
August	Hiroshima and Nagasaki bombed; war in Pacific ends.
November	Nuremberg trials begin.

1946

February	Stalin makes Two Camps speech.
March	Churchill makes Iron Curtain speech.
June	Baruch Plan proposed at first meeting of UN Atomic Energy Commission.
July	Bikini Atoll tests, first peacetime atomic weapons tests.

1947

March	Announcement of Truman Doctrine of aid to Greece and Turkey.
June	Marshall Plan for economic recovery in Europe proposed.
July	G.F. Kennan's 'Containment' article in *Foreign Affairs*.
October	Creation of Cominform.

1948

February	Communist coup in Czechoslovakia.
March	Brussells Treaty signed between Britain, France, Netherlands, Belgium and Luxemburg.
May	State of Israel established; attacked by Arab forces.
June	Berlin blockade begins. Yugoslavia expelled from Cominform.
November	Truman re-elected as US president.

1949

January	COMECON established.
April	Armistice between Israel and Arabs. North Atlantic Treaty signed by twelve nations; NATO established.
May	Berlin blockade ends.
September	USSR explodes its first atomic bomb. Federal Republic of Germany established.
October	German Democratic Republic established.
December	Chinese nationalists withdraw to Formosa; communists take control of mainland.

1950

January	USA decides to build hydrogen bomb.
April	US National Security Council produces NSC–68.
June	North Korea invades South Korea.
September	US divisions land at Inchon.
November	Chinese launch counteroffensive against UN forces across Yalu River.
December	UN troops fall back to 38th parallel.

1951

February	UN condemns communist China as aggressor in Korea.
April	Truman dismisses MacArthur for insubordination.
July	Truce talks start in Korea.
September	ANZUS Treaty signed. USA and Japan sign mutual security pact.
October	Greece and Turkey join NATO.

1952

March	USSR proposes neutralised Germany.
May	European Defence Community proposed. Korean truce talks deadlocked.
October	Nineteenth CPSU Congress in Moscow.
November	Eisenhower elected US President. First US thermonuclear bomb exploded at Eniwotek (western Pacific Ocean).

1953

March	Death of Stalin; succeeded by Malenkov (Premier) and Khrushchev (First Secretary).
June	East German rising suppressed by Soviet troops.
July	Korean armistice signed at Panmunjon.
August	USSR explodes thermonuclear bomb.

1954

January	US Secretary of State Dulles announces 'massive retaliation' policy.
March	French garrison at Dien Bien Phu attacked.
May	Dien Bien Phu falls; first Geneva Conference starts.
July	Geneva Conference agrees to partition Vietnam at 17th parallel.

August	France refuses to join European Defence Community.
September	SEATO established by Manilla Pact.
October	West Germany admitted to NATO and permitted to rearm.

1955

February	Malenkov succeeded by Bulganin.
May	Warsaw Pact signed. Austrian State Treaty ends four-power occupation of Austria.
July	Geneva Summit; Eisenhower announces Open Skies proposal.
September	Nasser announces arms deal with Soviet bloc.
November	Baghdad Pact formed.

1956

February	Khrushchev denounces Stalin in a speech to 20th Congress CPSU; promotes 'peaceful coexistence' policy.
April	Cominform dissolved.
June	Polish workers' revolt suppressed by Soviet troops.
July	Nasser announces nationalisation of Suez Canal.
October	Soviet suppression of Hungarian uprising. Israel invades Sinai.
November	Eisenhower re-elected as US President. British and French paratroops land in Suez Canal zone.
December	Britain and France withdraw from Suez Canal; Israel from Sinai.

1957

March	Treaty of Rome establishes EEC.
June	Khrushchev routs 'anti-Party group', now undisputed leader.
October	USSR launches Sputnik satellite.

1958

January	USSR proposes summit conference; offer rejected by USA.
June	De Gaulle returns to power in France.
July	Revolution in Iraq; US troops land in Lebanon.
August	Quemoy and Matsu blockaded.
November	USSR demands German peace treaty and demilitarised West Berlin.

1959

January	Batista overthrown in Cuba; Fidel Castro takes power.
May	Death of Dulles.
June–July	Nixon in USSR; argues with Khrushchev on merits of democracy.
September	Khrushchev visits USA; meets Eisenhower at Camp David.
December	First *Polaris* submarine commissioned by USA.

1960

May	U–2 spy plane shot down over USSR; Paris Summit breaks down.
July	Soviet technicians withdrawn from China.
October	US embargoes trade with Cuba.
November	Kennedy elected US President. Moscow conference of world communist parties; Sino–Soviet split confirmed.

December	US offers a multilateral nuclear force to Europe; civil war in Laos.

1961

January	USA breaks off relations with Cuba.
April	Abortive Bay of Pigs invasion.
May	Cease-fire in Laos.
June	Khrushchev and Kennedy meet at Vienna Summit.
July	Second Berlin crisis.
August	Berlin Wall built.
October	Tension over Berlin eases as Khrushchev backs down. Stalin's body removed from the Lenin mausoleum.

1962

January	Organisation of American States expels Cuba.
July	Geneva neutrality agreement on Laos signed by fourteen nations.
August–October	Cuban build up of missiles, technicians and troops from USSR.
October	Cuban missile crisis; USA responds with blockade; USSR agrees to withdraw its missiles.
December	Nassau Summit between Kennedy and Macmillan (British Prime Minister).

1963

January	France formally rejects multilateral nuclear force; France blocks Britain's membership of EEC.
June	Agreement to establish 'hot line' between Washington and Moscow.
August	Partial Test Ban Treaty signed in Moscow between USA, UK, USSR.
November	President Kennedy assassinated in Dallas; succeeded by Johnson. Coup against Diem in South Vietnam.

1964

January–June	Heavy fighting in South Vietnam against communist Vietcong insurgents.
August	US Congress passes Tonkin Gulf Resolution. US air strikes against North Vietnam.
October	Khrushchev deposed; replaced by Brezhnev — Kosygin leadership.
November	Johnson re-elected US President.

1965

January	Death of Churchill.
February	US commits troops to Vietnam; retaliatory bombing of the North.
April	US intervention in Dominican Republic.
August	Fighting breaks out between India and Pakistan over Kashmir.

1966

January	Indo-Pakistan ceasefire.
March	France withdraws from the military command structure of NATO.
September	NATO moves its headquarters from France to Brussels.

1967

January	Treaty prohibiting military use of space signed by sixty-two countries.
June	Six-Day War between Israel and Arab states. Johnson and Kosygin meet in Glassboro, N.J.
August	ASEAN established.
December	NATO adopts doctrine of 'flexible response'.

1968

January	Tet offensive in Vietnam.
July	Brezhnev announces Brezhnev Doctrine.
August	Warsaw Pact forces invade Czechoslovakia.
September	Albania leaves Warsaw Pact.
November	Nixon elected US President.

1969

March	Soviet and Chinese troops clash on Manchurian border; death of Eisenhower.
June	Nixon announces 'Vietnamisation' plan.
November	Nuclear Non-Proliferation Treaty signed by over 100 countries, but *not* France, China, Israel, India, Pakistan or South Africa. USA renounces biological warfare and first use of chemical weapons. G.F. Kennan urges US withdrawal from Vietnam.
December	Soviet–German talks in Moscow.

1970

January	France agrees to British membership of EEC.
April	SALT talks open in Vienna.
May	US and South Vietnamese troops enter Cambodia.
August	USSR and West Germany sign Non-Aggression Treaty.
October	US Senate approves the building of anti-ballistic missiles.

1971

February	Treaty to denuclearise the seabed signed by seventy-four countries, but *not* France or China.
May	Mansfield Amendment on withdrawal of US troops from Europe defeated in Congress.
June	*New York Times* publishes Pentagon Papers.
July	Nixon accepts invitation to visit China.
September	Death of Khrushchev. US–Soviet Nuclear Accidents Agreement.
October	UN admits China to membership, expelling Taiwan.

1972

February	Nixon visits China.
May	Nixon visits USSR for summit with Brezhnev; SALT I signed including Treaty on the Limitation of Antiballistic Missiles and the Interim Agreement on the Limitation of Strategic Offensive Weapons.
June	Second round of SALT agreements signed, including Agreement on the Prevention of Nuclear War.
October	Egypt asks for withdrawal of Soviet advisers.
November	Nixon re-elected US President.
December	East and West Germany sign Basic Treaty; recognise each other's sovereignty; death of Truman.

1973

January	Britain joins EEC; death of Johnson. Vietnam ceasefire agreement signed.
March	North Vietnam releases last of US prisoners of war.
June	Washington summit between Nixon and Brezhnev.
July	CSCE opens in Helsinki.
October	Fourth Arab–Israeli War (Yom Kippur War). MBFR talks open in Vienna.

1974

April	Twenty-fifth anniversary of NATO.
June	Moscow summit between Nixon and Brezhnev.
August	Nixon resigns over Watergate; Ford becomes US President.
November	Vladivostok Summit between Ford and Brezhnev.

1975

April	Fall of Saigon (Vietnam) to North Vietnamese forces. Fall of Phnom Penh (Cambodia) to Khmer Rouge.
June	Suez Canal reopens.
August	Helsinki Final Act signed by thirty-five countries at CSCE.
October	Cuban troops arrive in Angola.

1976

February	SEATO disbands.
September	Death of Mao Zedong.
November	Carter elected US President.

1977

June	USA announces plans to deploy cruise missiles.
September	USA and USSR agree to abide by SALT I after its expiry.
December	USSR deploys SS–20s in Europe.

1978

January	New hot line agreement between USA and USSR.
March	Carter warns USSR against involvement in domestic affairs of other countries.

May	UN Special Session on Disarmament.
September	Sadat (Egypt) and Begin (Israel) meet with Carter at Camp David.

1979

January	USA and China open diplomatic relations. Vietnam invades Cambodia. Shah flees Iran.
February	China invades Vietnam; withdraws within a month.
March	Egyptian–Israeli peace treaty signed.
June	Carter and Brezhnev sign SALT II agreement in Vienna.
July	Sandinista rebels take Managua; Somoza regime overthrown in Nicaragua.
October	Shah of Iran comes to USA for medical treatment.
November	US embassy in Tehran seized; diplomats taken hostage.
December	NATO announces intention to deploy cruise and Pershing missiles ('two track' policy). Soviet forces invade Afghanistan.

1980

January	US Senate suspends SALT II debate.
May	Death of Yugoslavian President Tito.
August	Massive strikes in Poland led by Walesa; Gdansk Agreements recognise trade union Solidarity.
September	Iraq attacks Iran.
November	Reagan elected US President.

1981

January	US hostages released by Iran.
November	INF talks open in Geneva.
December	Martial law imposed in Poland.

1982

April	Argentina seizes Falkland Islands.
June	Israeli forces invade Lebanon. British forces retake Falkland Islands. START talks open in Geneva.
August	US marines land in Lebanon.
November	Death of Brezhnev; succeeded by Andropov.
December	Poland lifts martial law.

1983

March	Reagan outlines SDI.
April	US embassy in Beirut bombed, killing more than fifty people.
September	USSR shoots down Korean Airlines flight 007 over its airspace.
October	US marine barracks destroyed by car bomb in Lebanon; over 240 marines killed. US troops invade Grenada.
November	First cruise missiles arrive in Europe. Soviet negotiators walk out of INF talks in Geneva.
December	Soviet negotiators walk out of START talks in Geneva.

1984

February   Death of Andropov; succeeded by Chernenko. US troops withdraw from Lebanon.

July   USA and USSR modernise hot line.

November   Reagan re-elected US President.

1985

March   Death of Chernenko; succeeded by Gorbachev. US–Soviet arms control talks officially resume in Geneva.

April   Warsaw Pact Treaty renewed for thirty years.

September   In UN General Assembly Soviet Foreign Minister Shevardnadze criticises US SDI.

October   US says SDI research does not violate the 1972 ABM Treaty.

November   Reagan and Gorbachev Summit in Geneva.

1986

January   Spain and Portugal join EEC.

April   Major accident at Chernobyl nuclear plant near Kiev, USSR.

October   Reagan and Gorbachev Summit in Reykjavic; discuss proposal for a fifty per cent cut in strategic missiles. US Congress approves aid to the Contras in Nicaragua.

November   Death of Molotov.

December   Soviet dissident Sakharov released from internal exile.

1987

February   US Senator Sam Nunn says SDI testing violates ABM Treaty.

June   Reagan urges Gorbachev to tear down Berlin Wall.

December   Reagan and Gorbachev Summit in Washington; INF Treaty signed, eliminating 2611 intermediate-range nuclear missiles. Palestinian Intifada against Israel begins.

1988

February   Gorbachev announces Soviet intention to withdraw from Afghanistan.

May   US Senate and Supreme Soviet ratify INF Treaty. Reagan and Gorbachev Summit in Moscow; sign INF Treaty.

August   Ceasefire in Iran–Iraq war.

September   First INF missiles removed from Molesworth (UK) and Ramstein (West Germany).

October   Gorbachev replaces Gromyko as USSR President.

November   Bush elected US President.

1989

February   USSR completes military withdrawal from Afghanistan. Hungarian CP endorses idea of multiparty system. MBFR talks in Vienna formally concluded after sixteen years.

March	CFE talks open in Vienna. Elections for new Soviet Congress of People's Deputies; Yeltsin wins Moscow seat with eighty-nine per cent of vote.
April	Withdrawal of Soviet troops from Hungary begins.
May	Estonia, Latvia and Lithuania declare common position on sovereignty. Pentagon officials reveal 1269 missiles destroyed by USA and USSR in first year of INF Treaty.
June	Chinese government orders suppression of prodemocracy demonstration in Tiananmen Square. Solidarity wins a decisive majority in Poland's free parliamentary elections. START negotiations resume in Geneva.
July	Death of Gromyko. Bush meets with Solidarity leader Walesa in Gdansk.
September	Hungary opens its borders with Austria for East German refugees.
October	Hungarian CP formally disbands. Massive demonstrations in Leipzig against East German regime; Honecker forced to resign as head of state. Shevardnadze criticises Soviet invasion of Afghanistan; also admits radar station at Krasnoyarsk violates 1972 ABM Treaty. Warsaw Pact foreign ministers formally abandon Brezhnev Doctrine; pledge non-interference in each other's affairs.
November	Massive prodemocracy demonstration in East Berlin. East Germany announces opening of all its borders, including Berlin Wall; dismantling of Berlin Wall begins. Mass demonstrations in Prague and Bratislava; Czech CP leadership resigns; end of CP monopoly of power. Chancellor Kohl announces plan for German reunification.
December	Gorbachev meets Pope John Paul II; first meeting between Pope and a Soviet leader. Bush and Gorbachev Summit in Malta. East German Parliament abolishes special status of CP. Lithuanian Parliament abolishes special status of CP. Latvian Parliament abolishes special status of CP. Death of Sakharov. Brandenburg Gate reopened in Berlin. Anti-government demonstrations in Romania; Ceaucescu toppled from power and executed. Havel elected as Czechoslovakia's new President.

1990

January	Bulgarian national assembly abolishes special status of CP.
February	Ottawa Conference; foreign ministers of USA, USSR, Britain, France, West Germany, East Germany agree on formal talks on German reunification ('two-plus-four' formula). USSR and Czechoslovakia agree to phased withdrawal of Soviet troops from Czechoslovakia.
March	Lithuanian Parliament declares independence; Gorbachev denounces the move. Soviet Congress of People's Deputies abolishes special status of CP. Estonian Parliament votes for gradual secession from USSR.

May	Latvian Parliament declares independence; Gorbachev denounces the move. USSR begins dismantling disputed Krasnoyarsk radar station. Yeltsin elected parliamentary leader of Russian Republic.
June	Bush and Gorbachev Summit in Washington; agree to cut strategic weapons by thirty per cent, chemical weapons by eighty per cent.
July	NATO Summit in London declares formal end to Cold War; invites Gorbachev to address future summits. Yeltsin resigns from CP; mayors of Moscow and Leningrad also resign from CP. Gorbachev and Kohl agree that unified Germany will belong to NATO.
August	Iraq invades Kuwait; USA and USSR issue joint condemnation of invasion. US chemical weapons removed from West Germany.
September	Two-plus-four Treaty on German reunification signed in Moscow.
October	East and West Germany formally unite as Federal Republic of Germany with Berlin as capital. Gorbachev wins Nobel peace prize for his role in ending Cold War.
November	Gorbachev and Kohl sign twenty-year friendship treaty in Bonn. Germany and Poland sign treaty guaranteeing permanency of existing border. CSCE Summit in Paris; includes signing of CFE Treaty and Paris Charter, ending economic and military division of Europe. UN passes Security Resolution 678 authorising use of force in Persian Gulf.
December	Resignation of Shevardnadze; warns that reactionary forces threaten USSR.

1991

January	Soviet elite troops seize buildings in Vilnius (Lithuania) and Riga (Latvia); Yeltsin and Bush condemn the action.
February	Leaders of Warsaw Pact countries sign agreement dissolving alliance. UN forces expel Iraq from Kuwait in Operation Desert Storm.
April	Georgia declares independence from USSR.
May	Last US and Soviet INF missiles destroyed under terms of 1987 treaty.
June	Yeltsin elected to newly created presidency of Russia. Last Soviet soldiers leave Hungary and Czechoslovakia. COMECON formally disbands.
July	Gorbachev attends G-7 Summit in London. Bush and Gorbachev summit in Moscow; sign START I Treaty.
August	Hard-liners stage coup against Gorbachev; Yeltsin opposes coup, which collapses; Gorbachev resigns as head of CP. Estonia, Latvia, Lithuania, Ukraine and Byelorussia declare independence.
September	Baltic republics apply for membership of UN; USA and EEC recognise independence of Baltic states. Leningrad changes name

back to St Petersburg. Gorbachev announces USSR will withdraw 11 000 military personnel from Cuba.

October   USSR establishes diplomatic ties with three Baltic states.

November Open Skies talks in Geneva; USSR agrees to allow over-flights of territory to ensure arms control compliance. Shevardnadze reappointed foreign minister.

December Ukrainians vote for independence; Kravchuk elected president. Russia, Ukraine and Byelorussia declare that USSR ceases to exist and establish CIS; eleven republics sign CIS Treaty in Alma-Ata. Russia, Kazakhstan, Byelorussia and Ukraine agree to uphold all arms control agreements entered into by USSR. Gorbachev resigns as USSR President; Russian flag replaces red Soviet flag over Kremlin.

GLOSSARY

Anti-ballistic missile (ABM) A defensive missile designed to destroy an incoming enemy missile. ABM defences were developed in the USA and USSR in the 1960s. A treaty to limit ABM deployments was signed in 1972.

Bipartisanship A situation in which both major political parties agree on a policy. There was a high level of bipartisanship between the Democrats and Republicans in the USA on foreign policy during the Cold War.

Brezhnev Doctrine A doctrine put forward to justify Soviet intervention in Czechoslovakia in August 1968. It stated that Soviet intervention in a socialist country was warranted if that country was in danger of departing from socialism. Gorbachev renounced this doctrine in October 1989.

Brinkmanship A confrontationist approach to foreign policy in which a state is prepared to go to the brink of war in pursuit of its objectives. The policy was associated with US Secretary of State John Foster Dulles in the 1950s.

Conventional forces in Europe (CFE) An abbreviation from 'Negotiations on Conventional Armed Forces in Europe'. These negotiations began in Vienna in March 1989 and dealt mainly with the conventional forces of NATO and the Warsaw Pact in Europe as a whole. Thus they were broader in scope than the previous MBFR talks. The CFE Treaty was signed in Paris in November 1990.

Comecon Council for Mutual Economic Assistance An organisation set up by the USSR in January 1949 to co-ordinate the economic development of Eastern Europe and the USSR.

Containment The doctrine put forward by George F. Kennan and adopted by the USA in March 1947 as the basis for its policy towards the USSR during the Cold War. It involved providing assistance to any government threatened by 'Communist expansionism'. *See also* **Truman Doctrine**

Cruise missile A guided missile that flies to its target close to the earth's surface. Cruise missiles can be launched from aircraft, ships, submarines, or land sites.

Confidence and security building measures (CSBM)   Measures taken to demonstrate a country's lack of hostile *intent*, as distinct from measures that actually reduce military *capabilities*. A conference on CSBM and Disarmament in Europe was held in Stockholm between 1984 and 1986. The Stockholm Document, signed September 1986, provided for the notification and observation of military activities. A second Conference on CSBM began in Vienna in March 1989.

Conference on Security and Cooperation in Europe (CSCE) A conference of all the European countries, the USA and Canada. It first met in 1973. The Helsinki Accords of 1975 formally recognised the post-World War II territorial boundaries of Europe. The Charter of Paris of 1990 ended the economic and military division of the continent.

Détente   A relaxation of tensions in the relationship between two countries/ alliances. When applied to US–Soviet relations, it refers to the period from the late 1960s to the late 1970s and the period following Gorbachev's coming to power in 1985.

First strike   An initial nuclear attack by one country designed to knock out an adversary's strategic nuclear arsenal.

Glasnost   A Russian term meaning 'openness'. It was used by Mikhail Gorbachev to suggest the way in which all aspects of Soviet life needed to be open to public scrutiny. *See also* **Perestroika**.

Intercontinental ballistic missile (ICBM)   A land-based missile capable of travelling over 5500 kilometres to deliver one or more nuclear warheads.

Intermediate-range nuclear forces (INF)   Nuclear missiles with a range of between 200 and 5500 kilometres. INF negotiations between the USA and USSR began in late 1981 but were suspended between 1983 and 1985. In 1987 an INF Treaty providing for the total elimination of land-based INF was signed in Washington.

Iron Curtain   The boundary between the Soviet bloc countries of Eastern Europe and the West European countries. The phrase was first used by British Prime Minister Winston Churchill in March 1946.

McCarthyism   A political movement in the USA in the late 1940s and early 1950s led by Senator Joe McCarthy of Wisconsin. McCarthy claimed that the Truman administration was under communist influence and more generally that liberals were communist sympathisers.

Marshall Plan   A programme of US economic assistance to Western Europe. Named after US Secretary of State George C. Marshall it was adopted in June 1947 to strengthen the Western economies, thereby reducing the domestic appeal of communism.

Multilateralism   In the context of arms control negotiation, this is the view that nuclear arms reduction should be on the basis of steps agreed to by both sides.

Multiple independently targetable re-entry vehicle (MIRV)   A technological development in the late 1960s and early 1970s that enabled a single missile to carry more than one nuclear warhead. Once separated from the missile each MIRV could be directed against a different target.

Mutual and balanced force reductions (MBFR) These talks took place in Vienna between 1973 and 1989 and were aimed at reducing conventional force levels in Central Europe. *See also* **Conventional forces in Europe**.

Mutual[ly] assured destruction (MAD) An approach to nuclear deterrence that focuses on the ability of the USA to launch a nuclear attack even after a Soviet first strike. Since mutual destruction is assured, the belief is that a first strike would thereby be deterred.

North Atlantic Treaty Organisation (NATO) The major defence organisation of the Western alliance. It was established in April 1949 with the USA, Canada, Britain, France, Belgium, the Netherlands, Luxemburg, Italy, Denmark, Norway, Iceland and Portugal as members. Greece, Turkey and West Germany joined in the 1950s and Spain in 1982. *See also* **Warsaw Pact**.

Neutron bomb Called an 'enhanced radiation' weapon, this battlefield nuclear bomb is designed primarily to kill people and to inflict less damage on buildings and landscape than other nuclear weapons.

Peaceful coexistence A Soviet doctrine, put forward by Nikita Khrushchev, which suggests that peaceful relations between socialist and capitalist countries are possible. War could be avoided, but peaceful competition would continue in the ideological, political and economic spheres.

Perestroika A Russian term meaning 'restructuring'. Mikhail Gorbachev used the term to indicate the way in which Soviet institutions needed to be reformed if the USSR was to meet its various economic, political and social objectives. *See also* **Glasnost**.

Revisionism In the context of explaining the Cold War this refers to an interpretation that emphasises American expansionism as the source of the conflict. The actions of the USSR are seen to be primarily defensive.

Second strike capability The ability to launch a retaliatory nuclear attack sufficient to inflict intolerable damage after being hit by an adversary's first strike.

Strategic arms Long-range nuclear weapons capable of hitting an adversary's territory. ICBMs, SLBMs, and strategic bombers are so called.

Strategic Arms Limitation Talks/Treaty (SALT) The SALT bilateral negotiations between the USA and USSR ran from 1969 to 1979 and were focused primarily on limiting ICBMs on both sides. The role of bombers and cruise missiles were contentious issues in the talks. The USA and USSR signed an Interim Agreement in 1972 (SALT I) and a more far-reaching treaty in 1979 (SALT II).

Strategic Arms Reduction Talks/Treaty (START) START (the successor talks to SALT) began in 1982, were suspended in 1983 and resumed again in 1985. Their focus was the strategic arms of the two sides, which were to be significantly reduced under the agreements finally arrived at (START I, July 1991; START II, January 1993).

Strategic Defence Initiative (SDI)   (popularly known as Star Wars) A programme launched by President Reagan in 1983 that was a much more ambitious attempt to develop defences against ballistic missiles than the earlier ABM plans, drawing on a much wider range of technologies.

Strategic parity   The situation in which there is an approximate equality in nuclear arms between the USA and USSR. Such a situation has been the case since about the late 1960s.

Strategic superiority   A situation in which the nuclear weapons possessed by one side put it at an advantage in relation to its adversary. The USA was in such a position of superiority in relation to the USSR until the late 1960s.

Submarine-launched ballistic missile (SLBM)   A ballistic missile carried in and launched from a submarine. American SLBMs have included the *Polaris*, *Poseidon* and *Trident*.

Tactical nuclear weapons   Short-range nuclear weapons that could be launched by artillery, missiles or aircraft during battle. Both NATO and the USSR deployed thousands ready for use in a European war.

Theatre nuclear forces (TNF)   Intermediate-range nuclear weapons systems, notably NATO's Pershing IIs targeted on the USSR, and the Soviet SS-20s and Backfire bombers targeted on Western Europe. The 1987 INF Treaty eliminated these weapons.

Triad   A term used to describe the three central elements of US and Soviet nuclear forces: ICBMs, SLBMs, and strategic bombers, each of which presents different defensive problems to an adversary.

Truman Doctrine   A policy of economic and military aid to Greece and Turkey launched by President Truman in March 1947 to counter 'Communist expansionism'. *See also* **Containment**.

Two camps doctrine   A doctrine put forward by Joseph Stalin in September 1947 as the basis for the USSR's Cold War policy. The USSR was cast in the role of the leader of the 'anti-imperialist and democratic camp' in opposition to the US-led 'imperialist and anti-democratic camp'.

Unilateralism   In the context of nuclear arms control this is the view that the West should undertake measures of disarmament, even though the Soviet bloc might not have agreed to do likewise.

Warsaw Pact   A military organisation linking the USSR and countries of Eastern Europe. It was set up in May 1955 as a counter to NATO. Also referred to as the Warsaw Treaty Organisation (WTO).

LIST OF ABBREVIATIONS

ABM	Anti-ballistic missile
ACDA	(US) Arms Control and Disarmament Administration
AEC	Atomic Energy Commission
ASEAN	Association of South East Asian Nations
CSBMS	Confidence and security building measures
CCP	Chinese Communist Party
CFE	Conventional forces in Europe
CFM	Council of Foreign Ministers
CIA	(US) Central Intelligence Agency
CIS	Commonwealth of Independent States
Comecon	Council for Mutual Economic Assistance
Cominform	Communists Information Bureau
Comintern	Communist International
CND	Campaign for Nuclear Disarmament
CNVA	Committee for Non-Violent Action
CPSU	Communist Party of the Soviet Union
CSCE	Conference on Security and Cooperation in Europe
DKP	German Communist Party
EEC	European Economic Community
END	European Nuclear Disarmament
ENDC	Eighteen Nation Disarmament Committee
GATT	General Agreement on Tariffs and Trade
ICBM	Intercontinental ballistic missile
INF	Intermediate-range nuclear forces
KGB	Russian Secret Service
MAD	Mutually assured destruction
MBFR	Mutual and Balanced Force Reduction
MIRV	Multiple independently-targetable re-entry vehicle
NACC	North American Cooperation Council

NAFTA	North American Free Trade Area
NATO	North Atlantic Treaty Organisation
NPT	Non-Proliferation Treaty
NSC–68	National Security Council Memorandum 68
PFP	Partnership for Peace
PLO	Palestine Liberation Organisation
SALT	Strategic Arms Limitations Talks/Treaty
SLBM	Submarine-launched ballistic missile
SDI	Strategic Defense Initiative
SEATO	South East Asian Treaty Organisation
SIOP	Single Integrated Operational Plan
SRF	Strategic Rocket Forces
START	Strategic Arms Reduction Talks/Treaty
TNF	Theatre Nuclear Forces
UAR	United Arab Republic (of Egypt, Syria and Yemen)
UN	United Nations
WEU	Western European Union
WTO	Warsaw Treaty Organisation

FURTHER READING

KEEPING ABREAST OF RUSSIAN–AMERICAN RELATIONS

The student of Russian–American relations needs to keep up with current developments — events and interpretations. The reading of quality metropolitan daily newspapers is indispensable, while news magazines such as *Time*, *Newsweek*, the *Economist* and the *Guardian Weekly* provide immediate but thoughtful coverage.

The major relevant journals offer more considered judgement. On the American side, *Foreign Policy* and *Foreign Affairs* should be consulted, especially the annual survey of 'America and the World' in *Foreign Affairs*. For the United States government point of view see *Department of State Bulletin*. Journals analysing Soviet developments include *Problems of Communism* and *Slavic Review* (both American), *Soviet Studies* (British) and the October issue each year of *Current History*, which is devoted to the Soviet Union/Russia. For the Soviet point of view, *Current Digest of Soviet Press* and *International Affairs* (Moscow, monthly) are essential.

A number of annual publications monitor international security issues. The International Institute of Strategic Studies (IISS) in London puts out two volumes: *Military Balance* and *Strategic Survey*. The Stockholm International Peace Research Institute (SIPRI) publishes *World Armaments and Disarmament*. Another valuable item in this category is Ruth Leger Sivard's *World Military and Social Expenditures* (World Priorities, Inc.). The *Bulletin of the Atomic Scientists* is very useful for nuclear, strategic and disarmament issues. The monthly the *World Today*, published by the Royal Institute of International Affairs, should also be consulted.

GENERAL WORKS — COLD WAR; RUSSIAN-AMERICAN RELATIONS

Beschloss, Michael R. & Talbott, Strobe. *At the Highest Levels: The Inside Story of the End of the Cold War.* Little, Brown, Boston, 1993.

Gaddis, John Lewis. *The Long Peace: Inquiries Into the History of the Cold War.* Oxford University Press, New York, 1987.

—— *Russia, The Soviet Union and the United States: An Interpretative History.* 2nd edn. Wiley, New York, 1990.

Halle, Louis J. *The Cold War as History.* Harper & Row, New York, 1967.

Halliday, Fred. *The Making of the Second Cold War.* 2nd edn. Verso, London, 1986.

Hogan, Michael J. (ed.). *The End of the Cold War: Its Meaning and Implications.* Cambridge University Press, 1992.

Kennan, George F. *The Nuclear Delusion: Soviet-American Relations in the Atomic Age.* Hamish Hamilton, London, 1984.

LaFeber, Walter. *America, Russia, and the Cold War 1945-1992.* 7th edn. Knopf, New York, 1993.

Sivachev, N.V. & Yakovlev, N.N. *Russia and the United States: U.S.-Soviet Relations from the Soviet Point of View,* University of Chicago Press, 1979.

RUSSIA/SOVIET UNION — FOREIGN POLICY

Arbatov, Georgi. *Cold War or Détente? The Soviet Viewpoint.* Zed, London, 1983.

Mastny, Vojtech. *Russia's Road to the Cold War: Diplomacy, Warfare, and the Politics of Communism 1941-1945.* Columbia University Press, New York, 1979.

MccGwire, Michael. *Perestroika and Soviet National Security.* Brookings Institution, Washington, 1991.

Miller, Robert F. *Soviet Foreign Policy Today.* Allen and Unwin, Sydney, 1991.

Nogee, Joseph L. & Donaldson, Robert H. *Soviet Foreign Policy since World War II.* 3rd edn. Pergamon, New York, 1988.

Ponomaryov, B., Gromyko, A. & Khostov, V. (eds). *History of Soviet Foreign Policy 1945-1970.* Progress Publishers, Moscow, 1974.

Steele, Jonathan. *The Limits of Soviet Power: The Kremlin's Foreign Policy — Brezhnev to Chernenko.* Rev. edn. Penguin, Harmondsworth, 1985.

UNITED STATES — FOREIGN POLICY

Ambrose, Stephen E. *Rise to Globalism: American Foreign Policy since 1938.* 7th edn. Penguin, Harmondsworth, 1993.

Gaddis, John Lewis. *The United States and the Origins of the Cold War 1941–1947.* Columbia University Press, New York, 1972.

Gaddis, John Lewis. *Strategies of Containment: A Critical Appraisal of Postwar American National Security Policy.* Oxford University Press, New York, 1982.

Spanier, John. *American Foreign Policy since World War II.* 12th edn. Holt, Rinehart & Winston, New York, 1990.

Williams, William A. *The Tragedy of American Diplomacy.* 2nd edn. Delta, New York, 1972 (orig. 1959).

Yakovlev, Nikolai. *Washington Silhouettes: A Political Round-Up.* Progress Publishers, Moscow, 1985.

THE NUCLEAR DIMENSION

Bobbitt, Philip *et al* (eds). *US Nuclear Strategy: A Reader.* Macmillan, London, 1989.

Calder, Nigel. *Nuclear Nightmares: An Investigation into Possible Wars.* British Broadcasting Commission, London, 1979.

Carter, April. *Peace Movements: International Protest and World Politics Since 1945.* Longman, London, 1992.

Freedman, Lawrence. *Atlas of Global Strategy: War and Peace in the Nuclear Age.* Macmillan, London, 1985.

Holloway, David. *The Soviet Union and the Arms Race.* Yale University Press, New Haven, 1984.

Mandelbaum, Michael. *The Nuclear Question: The United States and Nuclear Weapons 1946–1976.* Cambridge University Press, New York, 1979.

Myrdal, Alva. *The Game of Disarmament: How the United States and Russia Run the Arms Race.* Pantheon, New York, 1982.

Talbott, Strobe. *The Master of the Game: Paul Nitze and the Nuclear Peace.* Vintage, New York, 1989.

Zuckerman, Solly. *Nuclear Illusion and Reality.* Collins, London, 1982.

ACKNOWLEDGEMENTS

The author and publisher would like to thank the following copyright holders for permission to reproduce photographic and illustrative material.

APL/Bettmann, pp. 101, 167; APL/UPI, pp. 71, 177; Auth, Tony, copyright *Philadelphia Inquirer*. Reprinted with permission of Universal Press Syndicate. All rights reserved, pp. 154, 157, 231, 232; *The Bulletin of the Atomic Scientists* copyright © 1991 reproduced with permission of the Educational Foundation for Nuclear Science, 6042 South Kimbark Ave, Chicago, IL., 60637, USA, p. 210; Carless, Roy, p. 221; Chicago Tribune Company, pp. 100, 142; *Detroit News*, a Gannett newspaper, copyright 1962, p. 110; Gibbard, Les/the *Guardian*, p. 131; Herblock Cartoons/the *Washington Post*, pp. 59, 88; Interfoto MTI, Hungary, p. 138; Kapusta, Nicolai, *Radjanska Donetchyna*, USSR, p. 203; Kelly, Walt, p. 45; Moir, A., *Sydney Morning Herald*, p. 170; Oliphant, Pat, © Los Angeles Times Syndicate. Reprinted with permission of Universal Press Syndicate. All rights reserved, pp. 125, 146; The Photo Library, pp. 5, 214; Popperfoto, pp. 21, 69, 122; *Punch*, pp. 84, 118; Reuters, p. 161; Sovfoto, p. 99; Wide World, pp. 37, 82, 94, 104, 126, 137; Zaobao, Heng-Lianhe, Singapore/Cartoonists and Writers Syndicate, p. 169.

Every effort has been made to trace and acknowledge copyright holders. Where the attempt has been unsuccessful, the publisher would be pleased to hear from the party concerned.

INDEX